The Practice of Lojong

Books by Traleg Kyabgon

The Essence of Buddhism: An Introduction to Its Philosophy and Practice
Mind at Ease: Self-Liberation through Mahamudra Meditation
The Practice of Lojong: Cultivating Compassion through Training the Mind

THE PRACTICE OF
LOJONG

Cultivating Compassion through Training the Mind

Traleg Kyabgon

Foreword by Ken Wilber

Shambhala
Boston & London
2007

Shambhala Publications, Inc.
Horticultural Hall
300 Massachusetts Avenue
Boston, Massachusetts 02115
www.shambhala.com

9 8 7 6 5 4 3 2 1

First Edition
Printed in the United States of America

⊛ This edition is printed on acid-free paper that meets the American
National Standards Institute z39.48 Standard.

Distributed in the United States by Random House, Inc. and in
Canada by Random House of Canada Ltd

Interior design and composition: Greta D. Sibley & Associates

Library of Congress Cataloging-in-Publication Data
Kyabgon, Traleg, 1955–
The practice of lojong: cultivating compassion through training the
mind / Traleg Kyabgon; foreword by Ken Wilber.
p. cm.
Includes bibliographical references.
ISBN-13: 978-1-59030-378-8 (alk. paper)
1. Blo-sbyon. 2. Spiritual life—Buddhism. 3. Spiritual life—Bka'-
gdams-pa (Sect) I. Title.
BQ7805.K93 2007
294.3'444—dc22
2006035650

*This book is dedicated to the memory
of my sister, Yudruk Dronma Khashotsang
(1957–2006), who passed away this year.
May the Kadampa masters Atisha, Dromtonpa,
Chekawa, and so on look upon her and
all unliberated sentient beings with the
eyes of wisdom and compassion.*

Contents

Foreword

It is my honor to introduce *The Practice of Lojong* by one of today's most respected and renowned Tibetan Buddhist masters, Traleg Kyabgon Rinpoche. It is Rinpoche's belief, which I heartily second, that not only are the secrets of *lojong* an antidote to much of today's emotional pain and suffering, they contain the very practices that can fully awaken the mind and liberate awareness. And not just in a passing, self-help kind of fashion, a "Gosh, I feel better" kind of way, but by striking right at the heart of suffering itself while simultaneously pointing to the enlightened or fully liberated mind.

Grand Promise or Honest Assertion?

The word *lojong* is Tibetan for "mind training." The practice is revered throughout Tibet as containing the very essence of the great Mahayana Buddhist teachings, helpfully organized into seven easily understood groups. Further, these teachings are distilled and presented in their absolutely essential core: practice these, and you practice all. They are said to be able, in and of themselves, to lead one to enlightenment, which the Tibetans also call "the Great Liberation," because it is a liberation from suffering and an awakening to ultimate reality itself. Lojong contains practices that are said to do exactly that because they are grounded in and evoke *bodhichitta*, the mind and heart of enlightenment.

What is this enlightened mind and awakened heart? There are many ways of describing it, but the best way is to experience it directly, for oneself, and that is what this book is all about: the practice and direct experience of awakened mind and heart.

Although this awakened mind-and-heart is literally indescribable—and what direct experience isn't?—a few things may be said about it. In his introduction, Rinpoche himself emphasizes that, among other things, awakened awareness is the view from the mountaintop. Without that perspective, we will always be looking up from the valley rather than understanding the full vista. He goes on to point out that the *lo-* of lojong "emphasizes the mind's cognitive nature, its ability to discriminate, distinguish, and so forth. *Lo*-jong is about training the mind . . . in a very fundamental way. That is why [Chögyam] Trungpa Rinpoche translates *lo-jong* as 'basic intelligence.'"

What is this basic intelligence? And what kind of "cognitive nature" is being emphasized here? Given the anti-intellectual and anti-cognitive bias in our culture at large, it might be surprising to hear the word *cognitive* used in any but a derogatory fashion. But notice that the *gni-* of *cognitive* is similar to the *kno-* of *knowledge*, which is related to the word *gnosis*. In Sanskrit, the equivalent terms are *prajna* and *jnana*. And it is jnana—or gnosis—that is said to be the enlightened knowledge, the enlightened mind and heart, that is awakened by lojong practice. Gnosis is none other than the view from the mountaintop, the nondual view that is capable of delivering us from suffering and awakening the enlightened mind.

The teachings of lojong, in other words, are an unsurpassed manual for the awakening of gnosis.

It gets more interesting. Gnosis in action, according to Buddhism, is *compassion*. And it is the twofold practice of nondual awareness and compassion that characterizes and evokes bodhichitta, or the enlightened mind and heart. The point is that lojong contains extraordinarily profound and effective practices for awakening both gnosis and compassion. And the result of that, by any other name, is enlightenment—an enlightenment that flies on the wings of nondual awareness and compassion in action.

Welcome, then, to one of the most highly revered manuals of the Great Liberation. Your guide to this precious treasure is Traleg Rinpoche, who, I believe, is one of the most deeply insightful and profound teachers, not only of the Tibetan tradition but of any tradition, East or West. He combines an undeniable grasp of Mahayana and Vajrayana Buddhism with a thorough familiarity with us barbarians in the West and our many strange ways.

I say that facetiously, of course; but still, the difficulties of translating a teaching from one culture to another are notorious, yet time and again I have been struck by Rinpoche's easy fluency with Western culture and especially its overall intellectual canon, something that, frankly, is missing in most foreign teachers. In fact, I know of no other teacher who better grasps both the Tibetan and the Western traditions than Traleg Rinpoche, and thus the combination of the depth of his own enlightenment and his capacity to transmit it are matched by few Tibetan teachers. This makes Rinpoche an ideal Vajrayana teacher for Westerners, and I heartily recommend that, if this book speaks to you, please check out his other works. (Although there are many, two of my favorites are *Mind at Ease* and *The Essence of Buddhism.*)

This is a manual for the awakening of gnosis, a manual of the Great Liberation. I hope this sounds intriguing to you, because it just as well might have been titled "a manual for the delivery of your own mind—by delivering you from your own mind." It is only with gnosis, or jnana, that we are delivered—delivered by the view from the mountaintop, a view so high that it is far beyond even your own soul, your own ego, your own separate self. For it is the separate-self sense, the self-contraction, the egoistic coil in consciousness, that fractures and tears this present moment into a subject versus an object, a self-in-here versus a world-out-there, and this self-in-here then suffers the slings and arrows of outrageous fortune, a world of victimhood and sorrow, terror and torture, and self-delusion. Yet the cure for all of those is the simple awareness of presence in this here and now, an awareness that exchanges self for other and sees beyond both, this view from the mountaintop and its compassion in action that together make room for an enlightened world—an awakened mind and heart—whose radiance outshines the self-contraction and the tortures of the ego, releasing awareness—releasing you—into your own true nature, which is none other than bodhichitta itself.

This is a manual for just that training, a manual for awakening your own true heart and mind. May it mean as much to you as to the countless numbers of other souls it has previously awakened.

—Ken Wilber

Preface

As with my two previous publications, I have tried to keep this book accessible to people who may be completely new to Buddhism while at the same time presenting something useful and relevant to long-term students of lojong. I hope this book will encourage readers to remind themselves of the importance of changing their attitude toward life and others. This is not just about cognitive changes, but about sensory and affective changes as well. Fundamentally, we do not have the power to stop other people from doing certain things, but we do have the power to resist becoming too adversely affected by the wrongs done to us by others, whether real or imagined.

Acknowledgments

Once again I would like to thank Sam Bercholz for encouraging me to write this book, and Emily Bower for her continued support and editorial skill. I also want to thank Dee Collings again for her help with the book, as well as Rudy Wurlitzer for his helpful editorial comments. Last, but not least, I would like to thank Ken Wilber for going over the manuscript and making some very poignant suggestions, which were incorporated into the main text, and for writing the foreword. This book is dedicated to the memory of my sister, Yudruk Dronma. Writing it has been a tremendous personal help to me in dealing with her death.

The Practice of Lojong

Introduction

Anyone even vaguely familiar with Buddhism will understand that it places greater emphasis on the mind as the principal means for salvation than it does on an external deity. While this general assumption is certainly correct, the Buddhist canon, as preserved in several Asian languages, contributes a vast literature on the purification, discipline, and transformation of the mind. The *lojong* teachings have been extracted from the most essential and fundamental aspects of these teachings and practices.

The teachings of the Buddha are contained in a body of texts called the Kangyur (Tib. *bKa' 'gyur*) in Tibetan. *Ka* means "the spoken word of the Buddha," and *gyur* means "translation." The Kangyur consists of 103 volumes (some traditions count it as 101), containing the Indian Buddhist canon, or "three baskets" (Skt. *Tripitaka;* Tib. *de snod gsum*), comprising three different types of teachings: the *sutra-pitaka* (basket of Buddha's discourses), the *vinaya-pitaka* (basket of monastic rules and regulations), and the *abhidharma-pitaka* (basket of psychology and metaphysics).[1] The Kangyur also contains the more esoteric Buddhist teachings, called tantras. While these tantras were not taught directly by the Buddha, they are nonetheless attributed to him indirectly, and are therefore part of the accepted literature of Indian Buddhism.

Tibetan Buddhists do not rely on the Kangyur alone. There is also a collection of commentaries known as the Tengyur (Tib. *bsTan 'gyur*). *Ten* is short for *tenchoe*, which means "commentarial material," while *gyur* again means "translation." The Tengyur contains roughly 213 volumes and consists mainly of Indian commentaries translated from Sanskrit, although there are also texts from China and other Asian countries. Sometimes Buddha said one thing in one context and something completely different in another, or gave a different answer to the same question at different times, so the commentaries are meant to help us classify the different discourses and interpret their contextual meaning. The commentaries are an extensive body of literature in their own right and encompass both exoteric and esoteric teachings as well as treatises on logic, metaphysics, epistemology, composition, grammar, and literature.

Not many people have the time to go through the prodigious amount of literature contained in the Kangyur and Tengyur. We have to rely instead on the great masters who were able to devote themselves to this monumental task and extract the essential points for subsequent generations. These distillations of the teachings are known as the "pith instructions" (Skt. *upadesha;* Tib. *man ngag sde*) and can be clearly distinguished from the strictly logical or metaphysical approaches of Buddhist doctrine. They are "the essence of the essence" (Tib. *snying poe snying po*) of the Buddhist teachings, because they go to the heart of what we need to cultivate in our everyday lives. They can be practiced directly, without having to absorb the subtleties of Buddhist philosophy and logic, and will have an immediate effect on our spiritual development.

According to the Buddhist tradition, these pith instructions must be transmitted by someone who has genuinely engaged with them in total sincerity, without tiring or being distracted from assimilating their subtle meanings, even though the corpus of lojong material may seem at first glance to be very simple and straightforward. We cannot simply practice by perusing a book or two about lojong or about any other of the Buddhist methods. The concept of lineage is therefore of vital importance in the lojong tradition, as it is in all other Buddhist contexts, for this guarantees both the authenticity and the authority that has been imbued in the practices themselves. The notion of pith instructions is really based upon this harmonious blend of transmission, lineage, and spiritual instructions.

The lojong teachings therefore represent this genre of upadesha, or corpus of meditation instructions—a set of teachings that are clearly distinguishable from the exegetical or expository corpus. In the Tibetan Buddhist context, individual practitioners need to be instructed through one of these two methods, but preferably both. It is through upadesha that we become great meditators, and through attention to the teachings that we receive a comprehensive scholastic training in Buddhist metaphysics, epistemology, and logic.

We owe the lojong teachings to the great kindness of the early masters of the Kadampa tradition. *Ka*, again, means "the canonical literature spoken by the Buddha," while *dam* is an abbreviation of *dam ngag*, which means "upadesha instructions." As such, extracting the essence of the essence of Buddha's own words and using that as upadesha is the meaning of the term *Kadam*. The principal Kadampa master was Atisha Dipamkara Shrijnana (982–1054), who was invited to Tibet to restore some semblance of order in the midst of the cacophony of partial Indic and native interpretations of Buddhist practices and teachings that mushroomed in the aftermath of the assassination of Langdharma, Tibet's last dynastic ruler. Langdharma's death ushered in a long period of political unrest and social disarray. Some historians claim that Atisha in fact wanted to teach some of the unorthodox tantric methods of the time as well as propagate the *doha* teachings, or realized songs of the Indian mahasiddhas, but his Tibetan hosts actively discouraged him, insisting that he strictly adhere to the sober Mahayana teachings of the bodhisattva path. Atisha's *Lamp for the Path to Enlightenment* (*Bodhipathapradipa*) and Shantideva's *The Way of the Bodhisattva* (*Bodhicharyavatara*) became the exemplary paradigmatic texts for all future followers of the Kadampa tradition.[2]

While the Kadampa tradition and teachings are undoubtedly rooted in original Indian Mahayana Buddhism, they nevertheless have a distinctly native Tibetan flavor, as reflected in the teaching style of the great lojong masters. One good example is Potawa Rinchen Sel, who employed local stories and examples taken from the everyday life of eleventh-century Tibet to make the teachings accessible to a large popular audience.

Atisha is credited as the initiator of what might be described as the Kadampa lojong movement. He received the lojong teachings from Serlingpa (tenth century) and passed them on to Dromtonpa Gyalwey Jungney (1005–64), who put them into a rudimentary and systematic format, which was, in turn, transmitted to the so-called three Kadampa brothers: Potowa Rinchen Sel (1031–1105), Chengawa Tsultrim Bar (1038–1103), and Puchung-wa Shonu Gyaltsen (1031–1106). The lojong teachings were traditionally passed from teacher to student in secret, rather than through public discourse. The Kadampa luminaries Langri

Thangpa (1054–1123), Sharawa Yonten Trak (1070–1141), and Chekawa Yeshe Dorje (1101–75) further propagated these teachings, especially in the central Tibetan areas of U and Tsang. Chekawa was to have an enduring influence on the future lineage of lojong practice, as the growing numbers of Kadampa practitioners found his seven points of mind training both profound and practical. This influence appears to have continued in the West, with a growing number of people following his formulations of lojong practice. It is his text, the *Seven Points of Mind Training*, that we are following here. Two important training centers of Kadampa lojong practice were established at Retring and Narthang, the latter having become famous for its Kangyur edition bearing the same name.

The Kagyu tradition has been greatly affected by the Kadampa teachings, as have the other three major lineages of Tibetan Buddhism. Preeminent among lineage holders was Je Gampopa Sonam Rinchen (1079–1153), whose training in Kadampa monasteries enabled him to skillfully blend the stream of Mahamudra that he had received through Milarepa with the monastic discipline of the Kadampa.

Closer to our own time, Jamgön Kongtrül Lodro Thaye (1813–99) wrote a commentary on the seven points of mind training, which, while very short itself, included a huge collection of Indo-Tibetan lojong material, in his *Dam ngag dzo*, or *Treasury of Meditation Instructions*. The real inspiration for the lojong teachings came from Mahayana sources, especially from Shantideva and Atisha, each of whom contributed to the concept of generating *bodhichitta* through "exchanging self for others" (*paratmaparivartana*) and "equalizing self with other" (*paratmasamata*).

In my humble opinion, these teachings present a profound antidote to the rampant victim mentality that has become so prevalent in our times. Blaming others without taking any responsibility for our own actions has almost become a socially acceptable behavior. As all the great Mahayana masters, particularly the Kadampa ones, have emphasized, blaming others for our unhappiness only exacerbates our own misery. Such compulsive blaming is a form of entrapment that is not only self-perpetuating but that robs us of our power and free will. As I explain throughout this book, the practice of lojong is a kind of strength training for the mind, a practice that will make us feel less like a victim and more like the author or architect of our own life. By identifying ourselves as the victim, we give power to others, but when we refuse that role, we take the power back.

Lojong is not an old-fashioned or inappropriate way of looking at life's difficulties; on the contrary, the insights it provides have become more acutely relevant, mostly due to the rapid increase of "victims." A person who feels like a victim sometimes wants others to inhibit or repress their behavior. The point is, however, that we are not omnipotent and therefore cannot prevent suffering by stopping others from behaving in ways that displease us and we cannot introduce all kinds of laws that prescribe how people should behave. The personal belief that we have been victimized not only does not empower us, it generates apathy, resentment, and anger. These regressive attitudes are based on the assumption that we should never experience any discomfort, especially at the hands of someone else. However, this way of viewing the world, if not broken or interrupted, can lead to a vicious cycle, that in turn generates even more problems.

This agonizing cycle occurs because we basically have a distorted expectation of the world: We want samsara to be nirvana—but samsara is not nirvana. When we find out that samsara really is samsara, we become angry. For example, if we become personally involved with somebody and they leave us, our response may be anger. As the Buddha taught, we are doing everything wrong in terms of how we handle life's problems. We first have to accept samsara if we are to make any real progress. If we expect samsara to be nirvana, we will never be able to embark on the spiritual path.

The word *lojong* literally means "training the mind"—*lo* meaning "mind" and *jong* meaning "to train." Tibetan Buddhism has many different words for "mind," each of which distinguishes a different aspect and function of consciousness. The most common words are *sem, namshey,* and *lo. Sem* literally means "that which is intent upon an object," or the aspect of intentionality, for when we are conscious, we must be conscious of something, whether it is an external or an internal object. *Namshey* simply means "consciousness." This is the simple state of being conscious as opposed to the developed state of consciousness in a fully evolved, rational human being. All living creatures have *namshey;* it is the state of being that distinguishes sentient things from inanimate objects. *Lo* emphasizes the mind's cognitive nature, its ability to discriminate, distinguish, and so forth, while *jong* emphasizes the need to train that mind to fully realize its nature. *Lo*-jong is about training the mind to be intelligent in a very fundamental way. That is why Trungpa Rinpoche translates *lojong* as "basic intelligence."

Buddhism does not accept cognition as a purely intellectual activity, but instead as something that also has an emotional aspect. We should think of "intelligence" as the mind's capacity to feel and experience emotions as much as its ability to think more clearly. In other words, the purpose of lojong is to learn to make intelligent use of our emotional nature as well as to think in a correct and beneficial fashion. From a purely Mahayana perspective, this intelligence comes about through switching our perspective, thereby learning to see things in a different way. The unintelligent way of seeing things has its basis in egoistic obsession, which leads to a completely unhealthy emotional repertoire. We are definitely not using our intelligence if our egoistic tendencies have the upper hand. It is when we try to move away from that egocentric perspective that we are thinking intelligently. The seven points of mind training make us more intelligent by reorienting the way we think, what we think about, and how we utilize our emotions. From the Mahayana perspective, we can gradually move from an unintelligent to an intelligent approach.

The seven points of mind training, and bodhisattva training in general, are about recognizing where we are on a scale whose ideal is "perfection," and then gradually improving upon this. These lojong points are based on an intelligent interpretation of our experiences and the way we use our thoughts and emotions, for it is always up to us whether we use them for our and others' betterment or for our peril. Perfection can be attained, but we have to aim toward it through mind training. This implies that we will have to take our time and adopt a graduated approach. It is not a question of being either totally selfish, egoistic, and self-absorbed or being completely selfless, altruistic, and concerned about others. The point is to slowly and thoroughly turn our imperfections into perfections so that we will be able to travel the path of the *Aryas,* or elevated beings.

Whatever perfections we are supposed to attain from practices such as the seven points of mind training can only be attained through the recognition of our imperfections. If we did not have egoistic obsessions, there would be no mind training, because there would be no need for perfection. That is why the Mahayana teachings say that instead of being ashamed of our imperfections and regarding them as something terrible, we should see them as "manure in the *bodhi*-field." *Bodhi* means "enlightenment," while *manure* refers to all the things we constantly have to grapple with as well as the afflictions we have to suffer.

All worldly activities are utilized in the lojong practices by using our intelligence. To put it another way, it is important not to deprive our emotions of nourishment by suppressing them, either through meditative training or by excessive intellectualization and rationalization. Intelligence occurs when we clearly distinguish negative emotions from positive ones, and obsessive thinking from those thoughts that are helpful to us and others.

We develop that kind of intelligence through training in nonegoistic ways of understanding our world and evaluating ourselves. Self-evaluation is not rejected in Buddhism, as some Western Buddhists seem to think. Self-evaluation born out of intelligence is regarded as useful, while self-evaluation born from egoistic obsession is not.

The lojong approach boils down to a fundamental question: why do we suffer? Why do we have so many negative emotions and delusory mental states? From the Buddhist point of view, the cause of these problems is our egoistic perception, a deluded condition that inevitably leads to the distorted thinking and disturbed emotions that keep us from a clear approach to anything, including ourselves.

The value of mind training does not lie in learning how to adopt a different point of view that will utilize our willpower without using our intelligence. We may bring about changes in our lives that way, but if we fail to use an intelligence that transcends egoism, those changes will be superficial. Real change doesn't originate from a worldly or intellectual decision that says, "I will stop doing this and begin to do that," or "I will try to see things in this or that way." It comes from a transcendental view or knowledge (Skt. *prajna*; Tib. *sherab*) that allows us to sustain a panoramic perspective of our predicament. Only then will we be able to experience lasting relief from the vicious cycles that entrap us.

Lojong really means training the mind to see things from a mountaintop rather than from the valley below. Through practicing lojong meditations we will be able to attain enough distance to make us understand the kind of mess we have gotten ourselves into and the torments these confusions inevitably bring. According to the Kadampa masters, our real problem is that we always blame other people for our misery and never tire of the abuse we suffer from subjecting ourselves to our own self-obsessed egoistic minds. Lojong practices will give us the opportunity not to blame others and, for a moment, to look at ourselves and vow not to continue with this kind of predictable foolishness.

One way to stop this behavior is to say, "I shall look into myself and see what sort of self-destructive acts I engage in and then try to stop them." However, Mahayana practices such as lojong do not recommend that approach, advising us instead to strike at the heart of the matter. Their rationale is that if we try to confront our emotions, behaviors, and beliefs directly, the result will only be superficial, because we are dealing with symptoms rather than with the causes of our problems. The Mahayana teachings point out that if we want to eradicate a noxious plant, we have to cut it out at the root; amputating the branches will never destroy the plant completely. In a similar fashion, dissecting our minds in order to identify the malignant and isolating aspects of ourselves that we might manage and improve upon will never be enough to return our lives to some semblance of normalcy. By striking directly at our self-obsessions instead of worrying about them, we will be able to adopt the transcendental perspective of lojong. That is the only way to deliver a deathblow to the whole mechanism of self-centeredness, an act that will cure our other problems naturally, without needing to address them directly.

This approach to our shortcomings is another important facet of the Mahayana known as skillful means (Skt. *upaya;* Tib. *thabs*). When our minds are fully engaged in a positive attitude through the practice of lojong, our old negative habits will gradually dissipate without our having to do anything directly. That is the lojong way of effecting a transformation that will truly give us relief from our torment. By recognizing that we put ourselves through more unnecessary turmoil and suffering than anybody else could ever possibly inflict on us, we will respond to whatever other people subject us to in a more relaxed and effective fashion.

The basic premise of this whole argument rests on the simple presumption that our sphere of influence regarding how others treat us is very limited. We are not omnipotent and have no control over how external circumstances and situations unfold. All kinds of occurrences can and do happen. Natural calamities, such as earthquakes and floods, can bring devastations and misery to our lives. While we have no control over external events, we can have complete control over ourselves. We can gain some kind of self-mastery, not in the obsessive sense of a martial art but in the sense of rising above our inner conflicts.

Our ability to deal with adverse circumstances and situations will also change as a result, because one of the central practices of lojong involves turning adverse circumstances and situations to our own advantage. If we can develop self-mastery, even external adversity can be used for our spiritual growth. If we are only getting more mired in our delusional thoughts, then not only will we be unable to utilize what can go wrong externally, but we will have no way of dealing with our internal sufferings, which will only result in an exponentially greater impact. The suffering generated from within is always far worse than the suffering we experience at the hands of other people or external situations.

Many great Mahayana teachers have said that while we can use all kinds of avoidance techniques to escape dealing with others, we cannot escape ourselves. They say that our inner demons are our own shadows—they come up while we are sleeping as dreams and nightmares, and they give shape, form, and color to everything we see, hear, smell, taste, and touch in our waking hours. These subtle inner thoughts have a huge impact on how we respond to others, how we conduct ourselves, and how we evaluate ourselves. By understanding that the real source of our pain and suffering comes from within rather than without, we develop the kind of intelligence the lojong practices are emphasizing. That is not to say that other people or events cannot cause problems for us, but there are many different ways of handling them.

In the end, it is only through mind training that we can expect to find relief from our suffering. The ultimate reason we do any of the practices of wisdom and compassion is that they are a way of enriching our life, a way of ending our suffering. Compassion is not only the answer to other people's suffering, it is also the answer to our own. Without it, we cannot adopt the transcendental perspective; we will always be looking up from the valley rather than understanding the vista from the mountaintop. Without that view, we can never free ourselves from egoistic obsessions, and if we cannot do that, our suffering will continue.

When we generate compassion toward others as part of lojong practice, we are showing compassion for ourselves as well. Our wish to free others from suffering has to go hand in hand with the wish to free ourselves from suffering. To think that we can put an end to our own suffering without thinking about others is the biggest misconception we can have. It is also a misconception we have inculcated in ourselves from time immemorial. As the Kadampa masters say, we actually need others in order to develop ourselves as human beings. It is not true that we only develop when we feel loved, cared for, appreciated, respected, and admired; we also grow when we are despised, belittled, held back, and denigrated. If we use our own intelligence—the Mahayana type of intelligence—we will find a way to grow through those situations.

POINT ONE

The Preliminaries

The preliminaries (Tib. *ngöndro*) are the basis upon which we build our practice. Their contemplation lends a sense of urgency to our spiritual endeavors and serves as an antidote (Skt. *pratihara;* Tib. *gnyen po*) to the negative tendencies that frustrate our goals. They remind us of what is really important in life and inspire us to use our time constructively instead of squandering it on meaningless and superficial activities. Time passes very quickly, and unless we recognize the urgency of our situation by thoroughly and unflinchingly reflecting on these preliminary reminders, we will dissipate our opportunities and forfeit the things that are of real benefit to us.

If our spiritual practice doesn't have a strong foundation, we will never have what it takes to persevere. Myriad distractions, such as worrying about defaulting on our mortgage or paying our insurance, or scheming about how to get the boss's job, will diminish our intelligence and obscure our spiritual aspirations. Lazy and complacent, we will crawl out of bed and drift without purpose through the motions of our day. According to the lojong texts, the antidote to this worldly malaise is to contemplate the preliminaries at the beginning of each practice session, an act that will not only sharpen our intelligence but will renew our enthusiasm for the spiritual path.

It is common to assume that our bodies are our most important part, since they are clearly larger than our heads, yet if we think about it, our heads are more valuable because that's the apparent location of our sense faculties and intelligence. Just as the head is more important than the body, the preliminaries are more important than the main practice, because they generate the direction and motivation to pursue the spiritual path. One of the most important preliminaries, the one that takes precedence over all the others, is the quality of interested humility. *Mögu* is the Tibetan word that encompasses both "interest" (*mös pa*) and "humility" (*gus pa*). *Mögu* is often translated as "devotion" in Western texts, but while this is not entirely wrong, it does not convey the full meaning of the Tibetan term. For example, while the Kagyu Lineage Prayer says, "Devotion is the head of meditation," if it were to say "Interested humility is the head of meditation," we would recognize the full meaning of the term. We specifically equate interested humility with the "head" of our meditation, because it is an unerring guide and protection on the spiritual path.

If we wish to make any real progress on the spiritual path, we must become worthy vessels for the precious nectar of the Dharma. A practice that is sustained by interested humility will have more depth, breadth, and longevity than one punctuated by sporadic and undisciplined bursts of enthusiasm. Without curiosity and humility nothing can be retained or absorbed, because our minds are already too full of judgments and prejudices. As Patrul Rinpoche says in *The Words of My Perfect Teacher*:

> Not to listen is to be like a pot turned upside down. Not to be able to retain what you hear is to be like a pot with

a hole in it. To mix negative emotions with what you hear is to be like a pot with poison in it.[1]

The following story provides another illustration: A conceited man went in search of a Zen master. When he eventually found one that was sufficiently revered, he pompously requested a teaching. But first the Zen master insisted on serving him a cup of tea. The master kept pouring the tea even after it had spilled over the rim of the cup and onto the table, until the man cried out, "Stop! The cup is too full!" The master replied, "So are you."

Our egoistic projections bring all kinds of humiliations upon ourselves, often causing us to act in irrational, destructive, and deceitful ways. Despite these embarrassments, we should never associate humility with groveling at someone's feet or other distorted forms of behavior. Humility is characterized by inquisitiveness and the desire to learn. If we are overconfident or arrogant when we undertake a journey, we will encounter many more difficulties than someone who is open enough to listen and to put into practice what the great adepts of the Buddhist tradition prescribe. As Aryadeva (third century), a disciple of Nagarjuna and the author of several important Madhyamaka texts, says in his famous *400 Stanzas* (*Catusataka*):

An unprejudiced, intelligent and interested
Listener is called a vessel.[2]

Despite the numerous worldly successes we may have attained, we still have to be continually convinced that life without spiritual practice will leave us emaciated and impoverished. Only by becoming humble and receptive will we discover the energy, enthusiasm, and courage to help us explore new spiritual dimensions.

Taking Refuge

Before we contemplate the four preliminaries, we take refuge in
the Triple Gem (Skt. *tri-ratna;* Tib. *dkon chok gsum*), or the Buddha,
Dharma, and Sangha. These Three Jewels are the foundation
stone of all Buddhist practice, for they are the source of all good
qualities and they plant the seeds of liberation within us. Without
them, attempting to practice mind training is equivalent to em-
barking on the spiritual path in the dark. Taking refuge in the
Triple Gem is an act of faith, for we can't determine the truth of
lojong through analysis alone. Although Buddhism advocates test-
ing what we have learned through logic and personal experience,
intellectual rigor is not particularly reliable at the beginning of
the path. There must be room for faith as well. As Jamgön Kongtrül
explains:

> Generally speaking, if you have no faith you will not
> develop "white" qualities. Hence, faith must precede all
> religious practice. Although there are many kinds of faith,
> deep confidence and sincere respect for the Precious Ones
> are included in them all.[3]

It's very important to feel that our practice is correct and that
it will work. We know the Buddhist path to be true, because Buddha Shakyamuni applied these techniques and liberated himself
from samsaric bondage. Knowing this, we can have confidence
in his attainments and take refuge in the Buddha. Siddhartha of
the Shakya clan, as he was called before he became universally
known as Gautama Buddha, succeeded by employing certain spiritual techniques, which have been clearly laid out and enshrined
in his teachings. Knowing this, we can have confidence in his

teachings and take refuge in the Dharma. Buddhism is a living tradition that has been continuously practiced by communities of followers. Knowing this, we can have confidence in the support system and take refuge in the Sangha.

1 • *First, train in the preliminaries*

Our lives are short and we only have limited time to bring about any real and lasting change. If we fail to separate the essential from the nonessential, we will lose ourselves in everyday preoccupations and petty pursuits, and when the time comes to die, it will be too late to change. While we have time, instead of harping on our dissatisfactions, we should reflect on the favorable conditions for practice and resolve to make the most of our opportunities by inscribing the following thought permanently in our minds:

"I have wasted enough time. Why waste any more? From now on, I'll do something constructive and beneficial with my life, instead of squandering it in meaningless activities."

Precious Human Body

We begin by recognizing that our human body is the basis for enlightenment, because it provides a genuine opportunity for spiritual practice. Normally we take our human body for granted, allowing the negativities in our lives to overwhelm us. Our all-consuming preoccupations mostly consist of worrying about life's many minor irritations without ever thinking how fortunate we are just to have a body that functions. Instead of thinking,

"How terrible, I put on another two pounds!" or getting up in the morning to see three more lines around our eyes, only to go back to bed, we need to capitalize on our opportunities to reap the benefits of spiritual practice while we can. The renowned yogi Milarepa (1040–1123), admonishes his listeners about this in the following verse:

> Oh you confused and worldly beings,
> You always waste your leisure, letting time slip by.
> Though your mind is ever saying, "I must practice Dharma,"
> Your life is wasted as the hours slip by.[4]

One of our biggest faults is the tendency to overlook the things that are important to us while we still have them. We only realize how precious something is once it's gone, but by then it's too late. According to the traditional Mahayana teachings, a human body is very precious and hard to obtain. We may think this is just a rhetorical statement, but if we look at the vast multitudes of insects in the natural world and compare that to the number of human beings, we can see that a human life is relatively rare. In this way, we need to broaden the way we think about possible states of existence. Shantideva (685–763) makes this point in the following verse from the *Bodhicharyavatara* (*spyod 'jug*):

> This is why Lord Buddha has declared
> That like a turtle that perchance can place
> Its head within a yoke adrift upon a shoreless sea,
> This human birth is difficult to find![5]

By appreciating our precious human body, we can transform it into a spiritual vehicle of unconditional meaning and joy. It is difficult enough to obtain a human rebirth from among the six potential realms of existence,[6] but it is rarer still to attain a human birth that has the attributes and leisure that properly define a "precious human body." This kind of existence is called *dal 'byor* in Tibetan (Skt. *kshana-sampada*), *dal* meaning "free of certain impediments" and *'byor* meaning "in possession of certain endowments." We must tame our fickle and distracted mind before it robs us of our good fortune, and heed Phadampa Sangye's (twelfth century) admonishment to his disciples:

> With its freedoms and advantages, human life is like a
>   treasure island;
> People of Tingri, do not come back an empty-handed
>   failure.[7]

The impediments consist of birth in an environment where there is abject poverty, where food is scarce and famine common, where there is constant warfare or where people have very short lives. That kind of birth would be full of immeasurable suffering, and everything would be stacked against us. Such an existence would barely afford the luxury of pursuing a spiritual path.[8] The freedoms we possess consist of being born human, having the leisure to pursue spiritual practice, possessing physical health and intelligence, contact with the teachings and the moral sensibilities to appreciate those teachings and feel compassion for others. In other words, our human body has all the capacities we need to cultivate a spiritual existence if we have a precious human rebirth. Many human beings do not have the endowments and leisure that are necessary for spiritual practice. You must remind yourself of these freedoms and endowments every time you practice and engrave them deeply in your mind:

"My life could very easily have been different. I might have died in infancy, be suffering from grave physical or mental deficiencies, be living in grinding poverty, or be experiencing any of the things that are anathema to pursuing a spiritual life. I am truly fortunate indeed!"

Impermanence

This precious human body is hard to attain and easily lost, for we are mortal beings and virtually begin our demise from the moment we are born. We can't keep on postponing and deferring spiritual practice in such a cavalier manner, immersing ourselves in trivial pursuits and refusing to consider the impermanent (Skt. *anitya;* Tib. *mi rtag pa*) and pernicious nature of our lives. People often think we should live for today and not worry about the future, because we don't know what will happen next—we might walk out the door and get run over by a bus. Such a fatalistic attitude can serve no purpose in our lives. Developing a sense of urgency about our existential predicament will quell our complacency and challenge our tendency to keep deferring our spiritual practice. As Jamgön Kongtrül states in his autobiography:

> As I wonder what to do and what is best,
> like a widow grieving for her husband dead and gone,
> will former karma and present circumstances cause
> some virulent disease, impossible to treat,
> and shall I die tonight? Or tomorrow early?
> Helplessness and impermanence
> have become my teachers, encouraging me to take heed.[9]

We need to reflect on what is worth pursuing and what we should eliminate from our lives. Too often we fail to prioritize our lives, ignoring what transforms our negative emotions into positive ones and energetically pursuing those deluded seductions that make us feel miserable and undermined. Conditioned existence (Skt. *samsara;* Tib. '*khor ba*) is ephemeral and transient, offering us no real sense of comfort or security, so unless we do something about our spiritual enrichment now, we'll only experience further suffering and misfortune. No matter how old you are, you can't expect your current opportunities to go on forever, which is why Phadampa Sangye fervently implores his listeners:

Life is so ephemeral, like the dew on the grass;
People of Tingri, don't yield to laziness and indifference.[10]

It is not only our own mortality that we need to contemplate: everything is subject to change and temporality. We think that objects such as mountains are so solid, immobile, and immutable, but even they are changing. Geologists say that the Himalayas are continuously growing as the earth's continental plates shift. The lojong teachings recommend we examine our physical environment and see for ourselves that nothing remains the same for even an instant. We should recite the following contemplation to develop a real appreciation of our own mortality and the tyrannies of impermanence:

"If even mountains are subject to change and dissolution, how much more so is my own body, which is susceptible to disease, breakdown, the elements, accidents, and all kinds of harm? I must utilize my opportunities now, before that chance is lost forever."

The Dissatisfactory Nature of Samsara

This contemplation is not trying to suggest that life is dissatis-
factory in itself; it is simply highlighting the truth that we'll
never find any real purpose or meaning in worldly pursuits. Due
to the misguided nature of our efforts, much of what we do to
bring meaning to our lives only leads to further frustration,
pain, and disappointment so that we simply go around in circles
repeating the same mistakes. Gaining another job promotion or
giving birth to a new baby or finding a new boyfriend or girl-
friend will never give us genuine fulfillment. It is not that such
events can't be enriching at one level, it's just that they are not
intrinsically enriching. Our worldly experiences and achievements will always be a source of dissatisfaction because of our
misplaced trust and hope. It is not hope and trust in general
that is being referred to here, but rather the hope and trust that
we might gain release from our samsaric malaise. Our underlying feelings of futility or entrapment only reflect the nature of
conditioned existence, and nothing that we do in a worldly sense
will ever really alleviate that. When we add the inevitability of
old age, sickness, death, and the sufferings of loss, separation,
and disruptive circumstances, we'll see that we need more than
worldly achievements to consummate our lives. Milarepa is quite
uncompromising about this point:

> Whatever one does brings suffering and is futile.
> Whatever one thinks is impermanent and is futile.
> Whatever one achieves is illusory and futile.
> Even if one has it all, it is futile.
> The dharmas of samsara are futile.[11]

We should never be in any doubt that the fulfillment of our temporary needs is quite different from the fulfillment of our more profound needs. If we don't recognize this distinction, we will constantly be frustrated by searching for illusory satisfactions that are intrinsically incapable of delivering such fulfillment. This is traditionally compared to trying to extract oil from sand and is the reason we wander aimlessly from life to life without any particular direction or purpose. We have to meet our temporal requirements through temporary measures and our spiritual goals through spiritual ones. As Shantideva says:

The high have mental suffering;
For the common it comes from the body.
Day by day, both kinds of suffering
Overwhelm people in the world.[12]

If we examine our experiences properly, it will become evident that when we are having a good time, it's never really enjoyable. Either the pleasure doesn't last or it's simply covering an underlying pain that only becomes more obvious when the pleasure wears off. As long as we are in samsara, seeming pleasures will only be pleasurable for a fleeting moment. It's like people who use drugs or alcohol and have to keep increasing their consumption to experience the same level of intoxication; most samsaric pleasures might begin as the cause of pleasure but quickly become the source of great pain. Our sensory experiences create distractions that we respond to with attraction, aversion, or indifference. When we desire something, we become entangled in our senses, and if we feel aversion, we generate disgust or indifference. These responses give rise to conflicting emotions and ensure that we never have any real sense of joy and peace. The following contemplation reminds us of the futility of trying to gain what we really want from things that were never meant to provide it:

"Most of my experiences are unpleasant, because my mind is completely unruly and disturbed by conflicting emotions. Even when I imagine I'm having a good time, it's really only a disguised form of pain. As temporal goals can only satisfy temporary needs, I will devote myself from this day forward to spiritual practice."

Karmic Cause and Effect

It is very important to contemplate the connection between our mental states and our actions. Our karmic patterns are formed and sustained by the intentional actions of the "three gates" of body, speech, and mind—everything we do, say, or think with volitional intention. Our actions and reactions form the cause and effect of action (Skt. *karma;* Tib. *las*) that in turn determines the kinds of experiences we have. As such, our mind has the potential to transport us to elevated states of existence or to plunge us into demeaning states of confusion and anguish. Our actions are not like footprints left on water; they leave imprints in our minds, the consequences of which will invariably manifest unless we can somehow nullify them. As the thirteenth Karmapa, Dudul Dorje (1733–97) states:

In the empty dwelling place of confusion,
Desire is unchanging, marked on the mind
Like an etching on rock.[13]

The thoughts and emotions we experience and the attitudes and beliefs we hold all help to mold our character and dispositions and the kind of people we become. Conditioned existence is characterized by delusions, defilements, confusions, and disturbances of all kinds. We have to ask ourselves why we experience so much pain, while our pleasures are so ephemeral and transient. The answer is that these are the karmic fruits of our negative actions (Skt. *papa-karma;* Tib. *sdig pa'i las*). Jamgön Kongtrül says:

> The result of wholesome action is happiness; the result of unwholesome action is suffering, and nothing else. These results are not interchangeable: when you plant buckwheat, you get buckwheat; when you plant barley, you get barley.[14]

This cycle of cause and effect continues relentlessly, unless we embark on a virtuous spiritual path and learn to reverse this process by performing wholesome actions (Skt. *kusala-karma;* Tib. *dge ba'i las*). It is our intentions that determine whether an action is wholesome or unwholesome, and therefore it is our intentions that will dictate the quality of our future experiences. We have to think of karmic cause and effect in the following terms:

"My current suffering is due to the negative actions, attitudes, thoughts, and emotions I performed in the past, and whatever I think, say, and do now will determine what I experience and become in the future. So from now on, I will contemplate the truth of karma, and pursue my spiritual practices with enthusiasm and positive intentions."

Conclusion

Any expedition requires proper preparation if it is to have some hope of success. If we fail to plan for our travels, we will quickly tire of the journey or abandon it and return home. The same hesitation and lack of endurance can tarnish the spiritual path, which is why it is imperative to thoroughly prepare ourselves for the journey. Practicing these preliminaries serves three functions: they are good at the beginning, good in the middle, and good at the end. At the beginning, these contemplations encourage us to propel ourselves into spiritual practice. In the middle, they help us to sustain our practice with diligence and vigor. And at the end, they become an aid to our spiritual fulfillment.

Many people think these contemplations are too negative and diminish our zest for life. However, this is a complete misunderstanding of their intended purpose. We are not trying to generate an attitude that will make us turn our backs on the world and lose interest in living. These preliminaries are a skillful method for teaching us to live a purposeful and meaningful life. It is precisely because everything is impermanent that we have the opportunity to bring about positive change in our lives. That's why we should try to create positive change while we can, instead of postponing it to some indefinite time in the future, when our circumstances might suddenly change.

From the Buddhist point of view, to live properly is to lead a life without regret. We will have no regrets if we learn to distinguish the essential from the nonessential ways we can conduct our lives and devote ourselves to the essential ones. A regretful life has "waste" written all over it, while a life fully lived carries all the marks of success. These preliminary meditations are daily reminders of what is important for a meaningful and purposeful life.

The Actual Practice: The Cultivation of Bodhichitta

This point contains the actual practice (Tib. *gngos gzhi*) of the cultivation of bodhichitta in formal meditation. This is the core of the lojong teachings and the theme that runs through all its contemplations and practices. The Tibetan term for bodhichitta is *bhang chub kyi sems'*. We can translate this as "enlightened heart," for *bhang chub* means "enlightened," and *sems* in this particular case means "mind" or "heart." *Bhang chub* carries two connotations: *chub* means "possessing the attributes and qualities of enlightenment," and *bhang* means "freedom from defiling tendencies." While we generally understand bodhichitta to be the benevolent concern for living beings, anyone who genuinely gives rise to it will possess both compassion (Skt. *karuna;* Tib. *snying rje*) and wisdom (Skt. *prajna;* Tib. *shes rab*).

The cultivation of bodhichitta, or an enlightened heart, has two aspects and two associated practices: absolute and relative. The traditional Mahayana analogy for the spiritual path is that it requires two wings to accomplish, just as a bird needs two wings to fly: the wings of wisdom and compassion. You could define absolute bodhichitta as the wisdom mind, and relative bodhichitta as the cultivation of a compassionate heart. While relative and absolute bodhichitta are ultimately inseparable, it's important that we first learn to distinguish them. The lojong teachings are predominantly concerned with the cultivation of relative bodhichitta, but we should never forget that absolute bodhichitta is the main frame of reference and therefore the basis of our training.

The cultivation of compassion is the veritable heart of the lojong teachings. Compassion is not just about alleviating the suffering of others; it is also a powerful tool for effecting our own spiritual transformation. We must learn to be compassionately concerned about others, because that concern is what enables us to go beyond our discursive thoughts (Skt. *vikalpa;* Tib. *rnam rtog*), conflicting emotions (Skt. *klesha;* Tib. *nyon mongs*), and self-obsessions (Skt. *atmagrha;* Tib. *bdag 'dzin*) and break down the barriers created by ignorance, prejudice, fear, uncertainty, and doubt.

Absolute bodhichitta, on the other hand, is our authentic and original state of being, and therefore relates to the wisdom aspect of enlightenment. Despite the fact that sentient beings experience a multitude of delusions and obscurations, an element of the mind remains uncorrupted. There is an open, empty, clear, spacious, and luminous clarity of mind that is beyond concepts, ideas, or sensations. It does not come and go because it never enters the stream of time and is beyond both experience and intellectualism. Alternative terms for this supreme aspect of bodhichitta are *emptiness, the natural state, buddha-nature, the nature of the mind, the ground of being, ultimate reality,* and *the primordial state,* depending on the context. They all refer to an innate wakefulness that is present even when the delusions and obscurations of the mind are at work.

While the main practice of lojong is the cultivation of relative bodhichitta, the ultimate aim is to realize a transcendental or absolute state. We are not simply trying to effect a psychological change in how we see and experience the world. While it is quite possible to have a direct, immediate glimpse of absolute bodhichitta, our compulsive and overwhelming tendency to indulge in virulent thoughts and emotions makes it very difficult for us to stabilize that into a permanent realization when we are starting out on the spiritual path. We need to convert our temporary glimpses into a stable realization of the natural state, for the ability to permanently rest in the natural state is the same as realization of absolute bodhichitta, or wisdom mind. It is the practice of compassion that leads to the actualization of the wisdom mind, for while the practice of relative bodhichitta does not cause enlightenment, it does help to lift the veils and remove the conflicting emotions that create obstacles to permanently actualizing the ever-present condition of absolute bodhichitta. Realizing the state of innate wakefulness also gives rise to the understanding that relative bodhichitta and absolute bodhichitta are really two aspects of the same thing.

Absolute Bodhichitta

Before we try to realize absolute bodhichitta by cultivating compassion in our meditation (Skt. *bhavana;* Tib. *sgom*), we need to establish ourselves in our own natural state (Skt. *bhutata;* Tib. *gnas lugs*). While this may seem paradoxical, it is not so difficult to learn to meditate on absolute bodhichitta, even if we cannot easily stabilize that state, for while resting and stabilization are by no means the same, they are intimately connected in the context of spiritual practice. We must learn to temporarily rest in our natural state through the contemplative method of tranquillity meditation (Skt. *shamatha;* Tib. *zhi gnas*) before we can practice relative bodhichitta. It is essential to understand this point, for even though we can't permanently access absolute bodhichitta, we *can* learn to temporarily rest in it during meditation. If we were to begin the lojong practices of relative bodhichitta before learning to rest in this open, empty, free, spacious, luminous clarity of mind, we would only increase our mental agitation, because our minds would not be sufficiently calmed to attempt any genuine assimilation of the practices.

This emphasis on remaining in the natural state is one of the hallmarks of our Kagyu tradition. Commentaries on lojong practice from other Tibetan traditions discuss absolute bodhichitta predominantly in terms of emptiness (Skt. *shunyata;* Tib. *stong pa nyid*). However, the Kagyu approach discusses absolute bodhichitta in terms of resting in the vast openness of wisdom mind, or the natural state, rather than emptiness, for ultimately we can't make any conceptual statements about emptiness. Consider B. Alan Wallace's explanation of absolute bodhichitta:

> The teachings on sunyata, or emptiness, are called a mystery because they are not evident to the senses. We cannot experience this view of reality by simply gazing about us and observing appearances, because the ultimate mode of our existence—of ourselves, our bodies, our environment— is contrary to how it appears. Although it is mysterious in this sense, nevertheless it can be experienced, and this experience radically transforms the mind.[1]

This distinction is quite significant, because it reflects the subjective emphasis of the Kagyupas on the luminous clarity (Skt. *prabhasvara;* Tib. *'od gsal*) of the mind as ultimate reality (Skt. *dharmata;* Tib. *chos nyid*) rather than the more objective emphasis of other schools that emphasize emptiness. For while emptiness is an objective reality, the natural state is part of our very being.[2] In the Kagyu tradition, "resting in the natural state" means that the mind should have mental spaciousness, luminous clarity, and stability. Resting in a state where these three qualities are present is equivalent to having a temporary realization of absolute bodhichitta.

Another way of understanding meditation on absolute bodhichitta involves the Buddhist idea of view, meditation, and action. These three should complement one another, for we can't meditate without the view, and we won't be able to transform our actions without the support of meditation. In the lojong context, we develop the view by meditating on absolute bodhichitta, we practice meditation by doing the relative bodhichitta contemplations, and we translate that into everyday action with the support of the other lojong slogans.

Tranquillity Meditation

Tranquillity meditation is a fundamental technique for calming the mind. After taking refuge in the Triple Gem and contemplating the four preliminaries, you sit cross-legged with a straight spine, your head tilted forward, eyes slightly open, and settle into the meditation posture. Your mouth should be slightly open, with the tip of your tongue lightly touching your upper palate. Rest your right hand over your left in your lap, with your thumbs slightly touching, and breathe evenly. It is important not to slouch or stretch your shoulders too much. Your chest should stick out slightly, and it is advisable to have a cushion beneath your buttocks to support your spine, because a straight spine is the most crucial aspect of the whole posture.

Our tendency to proliferate thoughts is so persistent that if we haven't first settled our mind by meditating on absolute bodhichitta, we will never succeed with the imaginative exercises that follow. We shouldn't manufacture mental calm by eliminating our thoughts and emotions, but should simply refrain from following or elaborating upon them. This technique involves paying attention to whatever thoughts arise, rather than investing time and energy in trying to suppress them. It is practically impossible, in any case, to force your thoughts to dissipate, and all attempts to do so will result in even more mental agitation. The proper technique is simply to focus your awareness on whatever is taking place in the mind, without trying to subjugate it to your will. The most common technique is to focus your attention on the breath or a visual object, a technique that has been described at length in numerous meditation manuals.[3]

We have essentially two options: we can relinquish our awareness and chase after thoughts or we can maintain an awareness of thoughts while they are occurring. When we remain aware of our thoughts, we are in our natural state of being, which is the state of absolute bodhichitta.

When we begin to practice tranquillity meditation, it may be difficult to maintain this awareness. That's why we focus on the exhalation and inhalation of the breath rather than on what is going on in the mind, because focusing on our thoughts and emotions is much more difficult. We can formalize this technique by counting the incoming and outgoing breaths, in whatever rhythm is natural for us. In the beginning, you count an exhalation and inhalation as one breath and continue counting until you reach seven breaths, before returning to the count of one again.

When we breathe out, we should know that we are breathing out, and when we breathe in, we should know that we are breathing in. When you're comfortable counting seven breaths, you increase the number to fifteen and then to twenty-one. When you can hold your attention on the breath for twenty-one cycles, you will have developed some proficiency in mindfulness.

Nine Methods of Resting the Mind

Tibetan Buddhist literature lists nine methods of resting the mind. This is only one way of describing them, but it is the most helpful in relation to lojong, because it emphasizes the notion of meditative concentration (Skt. *dhyana;* Tib. *bsam gtan*) rather than meditative absorption (Skt. *jhana;* Tib. *snyoms 'jug*). These nine techniques are not just methods of practice; they are also stages in the establishment of shamatha. With each succeeding stage, there is a further development.[4]

1. Resting the Mind

Although this stage is called "resting the mind," it doesn't mean that our mind is necessarily without agitation, drowsiness, or stupor, but rather simply that it doesn't have to be in a constant state of agitation. The key is simply to rest the mind for however long we are able. While any kind of settled state will not last long, we begin to experience calm. Prior to this, it might have seemed inevitable that our mind would be dominated by some kind of activity. When we can clearly detect this calmness, we call it "resting the mind."

2. Continuous Resting

We reach the next stage when we can slightly prolong this state of rest. We just persist with the practice of mindfulness by staying with the object of meditation. If the mind is distracted by agitation or drowsiness, we recognize that and return to the breath. Mindfulness is what allows us to detect what is going on in the mind. The notion of time is not important here, for if we are able to maintain that restful state for even a short while, we call that "continuous resting." If discursive thoughts disturb our concentration, we just recognize that they have arisen, and if there are no discursive thoughts, we simply recognize that also. Normally, we only recognize agitation after it has overwhelmed our mind.

3. Patchlike Resting

During meditation our mind constantly fluctuates back and forth from calm to agitation. By gradually becoming accustomed to exercising mindfulness, we come to see that the two main obstacles to shamatha practice are agitation and stupor. Agitation is more easily detected than stupor, because we can so easily mistake stupor for a state of calm. We call this stage "patchlike" because it is reminiscent of patches on cloth. We are still only able to maintain mindfulness for a minute or so, only to have it torn away the next, but the point is that we are beginning to recognize our discursive thoughts and to bring our mind back to a restful state. We remain in such states of restfulness until a discursive thought arises again, but if we can recognize the disruption with a sense of calm, the restful state will return naturally. In other words, when agitation arises, we maintain our mindfulness and awareness, and that very act of recognition will be enough to restore our tranquil state.

4. Close Placement

When we are no longer agitated by discursive thoughts, it becomes much easier to return to the object of meditation with mindfulness. As we struggle less with our mental activities, our agitation gradually subsides. However, other distractions will now start to arise, thoughts that are not necessarily associated with violent or upsetting emotions but are nonetheless discouraging to our meditation. Overwhelmed by boredom and apathy, we begin to think that we are no longer making progress, which in turn can weaken our motivation to go on.

5. Pacification

When we become bogged down by these concerns, the text offers two solutions: contemplating the benefits of meditation and considering the harm that results from avoiding it. Rather than forcing ourselves to practice with a complete lack of interest, or to practice through periods of depression, we should remind ourselves of the benefits of meditation: that it cools the heat of conflicting emotions, as well as that of aggression and passion, and provides a true and tested antidote to our lonely, agitated states of mind. By contemplating our emotions, character traits, and spiritual goals, then examining what happens to our mental states when we're not meditating, we are better able to appreciate the benefits of practicing shamatha in our daily lives.

6. Subjugation

Subjugation comes about through focusing on our negative thoughts and emotions as the object of meditation. We might recall an incident where we were angry and then examine how that caused tremendous harm to ourselves and others. We should do the same with other conflicting emotions, such as jealousy, envy, covetousness, lust, and so forth. We can remember how we've put ourselves through painful and demeaning situations in order to pursue our lust or ambitions, how we compromised ourselves or indulged in actions that brought us only misery and harm, or how we embarrassed ourselves in our efforts to win love, or used deceitful tactics to reach our goals. We should think about the sheer volume of our discursive thoughts and their total uselessness. It is not as if we have such thoughts once and then they disappear. Millions of thoughts pass through our mind. If we examine them, we'll see that they are full of suspicion, paranoia, fear, anxiety, worry, desire, and so forth. Understanding these imprints will revive our desire to practice shamatha, for it is only when we are meditating that we are really doing something to counteract all these negative emotions.

7. Thorough Subjugation

This level of meditation allows us to recognize different states of mind with mindfulness and awareness. The strengthening of mindfulness gives rise to awareness, so that even without trying to be mindful, we will become aware that a certain thought or mood has arisen; this indicates that a subjugation of the distracted mind has taken place. These positive qualities are the result of having reduced our discursive thoughts and conflicting emotions through shamatha meditation. However, at this stage we shouldn't become too preoccupied with our mindfulness and awareness. It is far more beneficial to simply rest in our natural state without really contemplating anything in particular.

8. One-Pointed Concentration

Practicing mindfulness and awareness and not wavering in our resolve will gradually lead to the ability to stay focused without getting overwhelmed by discursive thoughts and emotions. This doesn't mean that discursive thoughts or emotions will cease, it just means that they will no longer be a preoccupation and that we will be able to maintain an "unwavering sense of awareness" as they come and go.

9. Meditative Equipoise

At this final stage, even the notion of one-pointedness is no longer relevant, for that still implies a sense of deliberation in our mindfulness and awareness. Meditative equipoise (Skt. *samahita*; Tib. *mnyam gzhag*) is a sign of spontaneously resting in the meditative state, without any deliberate application or effort, a state where we don't have to be consciously aware of anything in particular in order to engage in cognitive awareness.

Mindfulness and Awareness

Mindfulness (Skt. *smrti*; Tib. *dran pa*) and awareness (Skt. *jneya*; Tib. *shes bzhin*) are distinct but related features of the mind. Mindfulness is something we apply more or less deliberately in order to become more cognizant, while awareness is a gentle way of simply being present. The meditation literature describes mindfulness as the opposite of forgetfulness. The Tibetan term *dran pa* means "remembrance," as in the ability to focus and pay attention to the object of meditation in an unwavering fashion. As the *Abhidharmasamuccaya* states, "The function is not to be distracted from letting what one knows slip away from one's mind."[5] Awareness, on the other hand, according to the *Abhidharmasamuccaya*, is a state of mental and physical pliability that gradually develops as we remove mental sluggishness and clear away all obscurations, drawing the mind toward a state of integration.[6] The Tibetan term *shes bzhin* is actually a verb rather than a noun, meaning "being in a state of awareness." The basic difference between mindfulness and awareness is simply that the former is deliberate and the latter spontaneous. According to Buddhism, being aware is not something we habitually tend toward; it is something we have to learn through meditation.

It is significant that the Kagyu and Nyingma traditions regard awareness as an innate (Skt. *sahaja;* Tib. *lhan skyes*) component of the mind, because the mind is aware by nature. They say that the nature of the mind is inseparable from intrinsic awareness (Skt. *vidya;* Tib. *rigpa*), but it is buried under the plethora of conflicting emotions and discursive thoughts that dominate our mind stream. These are the obstacles that the practice of relative bodhichitta helps to diminish so that we can perceive the awake, ever-present, innate, luminous clarity of the mind. This wakefulness is something that we have to retrieve, because if we were able to permanently rest in the luminous clarity of mind, we would already be enlightened. In one sense, we are already enlightened, we simply do not recognize this fact because of the obscuring veils (Skt. *avarana;* Tib. *sgrib pa*) of our conceptual confusion and conflicting emotions.

Insight Meditation

We can perform wholesome actions from a worldly perspective as well as from a transcendentally spiritual perspective. This is a very important distinction in Mahayana Buddhism, because it highlights the importance of always trying to convert our worldly spiritual actions into transcendentally spiritual ones. It is only possible to achieve that transformation by cultivating the perspective of insight meditation (Skt. *vipashyana;* Tib. *lhag mthong*).

The difference between worldly spirituality and transcendental spirituality lies in the distinction between simply doing good and engaging in transcendental actions that arise from having insight into the reality of things. Worldly spiritual actions involve the accumulation of merit (Skt. *punya;* Tib. *bsod nams*) through good acts, and as such help to improve our lives and make us less

afflicted and happier people. Transcendentally spiritual actions
demand more of us. Real spirituality is not just a matter of cultivating wholesome traits and positive thoughts and emotions; it
is about learning to distinguish between things as they are and
our present confusion about them, and thus gaining insight into
the nature of our own minds.

Our Buddhist practices have two aims: the immediate goal (Tib.
ngon tho) of personal eminence and the distant goal (Tib. *nge legs*) of
enlightenment. A life based on the stability of inner growth rather
than the contingent happiness of fortuitous circumstances will
lead to a more fulfilling existence in both this life and the next.
Enlightenment is the summum bonum of existence, an ambitious
aim that can only be reached by degrees, through a combination
of practice and learning. These two goals are closely linked to
help us attain transcendental awakening, as it isn't enough to op-
erate solely on the level of worldly spirituality. Unless we cultivate
the really penetrating wisdom that comes from insight meditation, we will never manage to transcend our worldly preoccupations and realize the full potential of our being.

The following five slogans are vipashyana meditations that
will allow a glimpse of absolute bodhichitta as we contemplate
them from the perspective of the natural state. These glimpses
are what provide the integrity for the practices of relative bodhichitta that follow.

2 • Regard all phenomena as dreams

This slogan is another contemplation on absolute bodhichitta,
our innate, ongoing wakeful state that is an expression of emptiness—the central Buddhist doctrine that reveals the phenomenal

world as having no tangible, self-existing, or substantial nature. This world is said to be like a dream, a mirage, a magical illusion, an echo, or a reflection on water. That same world, when purified of our obscurations, is seen to be an ornament of our natural awareness. For when we awaken to ever-present reality, the world is not a dream, it is an aspect of our enlightened body, our wisdom mind, and our compassionate heart. This is why we can have relationships and feel love and compassion. In other words, when the world is seen apart from buddha-nature, it is illusory, but when it is seen as an aspect of buddha-nature, it is quite pure. Before we can generate love and compassion in our meditation practices, we need to understand that our thoughts and emotions are also insubstantial. Dharmarakshita (tenth century) summarizes this view in the *The Wheel-Weapon Mind Training*, a text which earns its name because it equates a weapon with prajna's ability to demolish the superstructure of egoistic foundation:

> Like the plantain tree, life has no inner core. Like a bubble, a lifetime has no inner core. Like a mist, it dissipates upon close examination. Like a mirage, it is beautiful from afar. Like a reflection in a mirror, it seems as if it were really true. Like clouds and fog, it seems as if it were really stable.[7]

We shouldn't mistake this view of insubstantiality for a doctrine of nothingness or nonbeing. Some people have misconstrued this as a form of nihilism and completely distorted its existential import. I know of Westerners who have ceased to be Buddhists after misinterpreting emptiness to mean that nothing exists at all. This is in fact quite a prevalent misunderstanding among Western interpreters of Buddhism. Professor Paul Williams from the University of Bristol, a fine Buddhist scholar and student of the Tibetan

Gelugpa order for thirty years, justifies his recent conversion to Catholicism on the grounds that Buddhism has a problem with love and compassion on a relative level, in that there can be no real neighbor to love if that neighbor is made up only of *dharmas* (psycho-physical elements), *skandhas* (psycho-physical constituents), and *ayatanas* (psycho-physical sensory apparatuses). Furthermore, he says that on the ultimate level, there would be no ultimate other to reunite with—something that the Christian mystics have claimed throughout the ages, by the way—because emptiness does not love anyone, nor can we feel love and compassion for emptiness. He writes:

> Buddhism is vividly portrayed here as essentially a religion of the hole rather than the doughnut. For all its advocacy of compassion—a compassion which will take those who suffer to the bliss of freedom—the state of one who is enlightened, or the state of a Buddha, from his or her own side is one of complete and utter self-sufficiency.[8]

It's not very difficult to arrive at a rudimentary intellectual grasp of emptiness or at least an intimation of its real meaning. The doctrine of emptiness is not anathema to the idea of being or existence; in fact, the very point of emptiness—its raison d'être—is that it's beyond both being and nonbeing. It is only because things have this insubstantial nature that they can exist in a mutually interactive and dynamic process. This view of reality is predicated on the early Buddhist teachings of impermanence (Skt. *anitya;* Tib. *mi rtag pa*) and dependent arising (Skt. *pratityasamutpada;* Tib. *rten 'brel*). "Dependent arising" means that everything comes into being as a result of causality, the interdependent and contingent operation of causes and conditions. David Kalupahana, at the University of Hawaii, framed this insight in the following manner:

> When this is present, that comes to be;
> from the arising of this, that arises.
> When this is absent, that does not come to be;
> on the cessation of this, that ceases.[9]

Nagarjuna (CE 150–250) systematically expounded this formulation into the theory of emptiness in his magnum opus, *The Fundamental Verses on the Middle Way* (*Mulamadhyamakakarika*), where he explicitly states that the subjective consciousness and the material word are dependently arisen and represent the middle way between the extremes of nihilism and eternalism:

> Whatever is dependently co-arisen
> That is explained to be emptiness.
> That, being a dependent designation,
> Is itself the middle way.[10]

Far from repudiating all life, the doctrine of emptiness has always attributed a measure of existence to things, but only in the manner of a dream. It only says that phenomena are "like a dream" (Tib. *rmi lam 'dra ba*), because they arise and dissipate based on causes and conditions and have no essential nature of their own. It is the truth of causation that determines the insubstantiality of things, as His Holiness the Dalai Lama explains:

> Effectively, the notion of intrinsic, independent existence
> is incompatible with causation. This is because causation
> implies contingency and dependence, while anything that

possesses independent existence would be immutable and self-enclosed. Everything is composed of dependently related events, of continuously interacting phenomena with no fixed, immutable essence, which are themselves in constantly changing dynamic relations.[11]

We can see, then, that emptiness is nothing like nihilism, because it doesn't claim that things literally are a dream. In fact, as both Chandrakirti (600–650), abbot of Nalanda University and a disciple and commentator on Nagarjuna's work, and Nagarjuna point out, we can only make sense of things coming into existence in relation to emptiness, for if anything were to truly have some immutable substance, it must always have existed, and how could something that has always existed ever come into being? If our naive view of the world were true, nothing would pass away and nothing new could come into existence, thus assigning us to an unimaginably static world. We have made a great leap forward in our understanding of emptiness if we understand this point. As Aryadeva says:

> How can there be things with no duration?
> Being impermanent, how can they endure?
> If they had duration first,
> They would not grow old in the end.[12]

If we really analyze external phenomena, we'll discover that our innate supposition that things are separate and discrete is erroneous as well. We wrongly postulate an independent subject that is "in here" and a material world that is "out there" and is inhabited by other self-sufficient, independently existing beings. This assumption of "thingness" has to be analyzed. We examine an external object, such as a table, to discover for ourselves whether there is a single indivisible entity of that name in any true sense. Such an examination will reveal that a table is an aggregate of many elements, which can be broken down into smaller and smaller components until there is nothing substantial remaining. We will also discover through this method that there is no such thing as a "self" that can have suddenly sprung into existence of its own accord, for we are composites of many things—our many different body parts; our thoughts, feelings, moods, and attitudes; and even our feelings, moods, attitudes, and current emotional states, and it is very difficult to find anything we can actually grasp on to and say, "This is what I am."

As such, emptiness really denotes the lack of intrinsic existence (Skt. *nihsvabhava;* Tib. *rang bzhin med pa*) that characterizes all phenomena, including ourselves. If things had intrinsic existence, they could not be dependently arising, for they would exist in and of themselves without change or influence. While we see "self" (Tib. *bdag*) and "other" (Tib. *gzhan*) as intrinsically different, where the self is felt to be in need of protection and the other is seen as some kind of threat, this dualistic perception makes self and other occupy very fixed positions. The subjective notion of a perceiver makes sense only when there is an object to be perceived, for "perceiver" and "perceived" mutually engage each other. We therefore construct our ideas about self and other from a dynamic process of mutual interaction. The experiences we have in relation to self and other are perpetually in motion, just like a child's spinning top that appears to be unmoving at the center when it is actually revolving at great speed. When we look at things from our normal perspective, we may think that our vantage point is something unmoving, but closer examination reveals that everything is in a constant state of transition and that we can't occupy any kind of fixed position. The Dalai Lama elaborates on this point by relating our attributions of substance to the very structure of language itself:

> In our naïve or commonsense view of the world, we relate to things and events as if they possess an enduring intrinsic reality. We tend to believe that the world is composed of things and events, each of which has a discrete, independent reality of its own and it is these things with discrete identities and independence that interact with one another. . . . This view of the world as made of solid objects and inherent properties is reinforced further by our language of subjects and predicates, which is structured with substantive nouns and adjectives on the one hand and active verbs on the other.[13]

Appearance and ultimate reality, or emptiness, are inseparable in their nature, so how could we diminish appearance by recognizing reality? It is only the dualistic mind that can make such a categorical claim. The conceptual division that treats mind and matter as different kinds of entities, where mind is merely a function of the properties of the brain, might support this claim, but Buddhism speaks about dualism in relation to subject and object, not from the viewpoint of the Cartesian dualism of mind and matter that is favored in the West. As the philosopher-neuroscientist Christopher deCharms says:

> From the Buddhist standpoint there is nothing more or less material about subjects in comparison with objects, they share equal status in this regard. Buddhist thought posits that reality shares both sides of a nature, which

seems paradoxical from a simple Western perspective. The Tibetan tradition suggests that it is neither correct to suggest that reality is completely unified, nor that it is divided, and it can only be truly understood from this perspective.[14]

However, just having a philosophical understanding of the mutual dependence of the phenomenal world is not enough to have an awakened perspective. We need to have a stable and direct realization of emptiness by recognizing the luminous clarity of our nonconceptual wisdom mind, for it is this wisdom mind that perceives emptiness. Seeing dependent arising can help us perceive emptiness, but that is not exactly the same as realizing the ultimate nature of the phenomenal world. Awakening to the impartial, nonconceptual absolute bodhichitta can only take place in conjunction with meditative awareness. We need a direct, stable realization of the non-divisibility of emptiness and appearance, and of the suchness of everything. This awakening is not a thought, feeling, or sensation; it is the vast, ever-present luminous clarity of the nature of mind.

Beneath the world of mere appearance is the world of suchness. While seeing everything as interconnected is seeing how things are, the actual nature of the interconnectedness of all things is emptiness. It takes a deep realization, or deep awakening to reality, to realize emptiness. Reality itself cannot be described as interconnected. Interconnectedness is a way of describing the phenomenal world, but absolute bodhichitta is beyond conception, beyond "same" and "different."

Westerners always seem to be trying to equate emptiness with their own theories, but all of these modern theories, to use a Kantian phrase, are about the phenomenal world, not the noumenal world, so they will not lead to a realization of emptiness.

Many other Western commentators on Buddhism have found the Mahayana teachings on emptiness and compassion to be diametrically opposed as well. Heinrich Dumoulin (1905–95), the author of a two-volume history on Zen Buddhism, says that compassion and emptiness are completely incompatible. Dumoulin, an otherwise fine Buddhist scholar as well as being a Jesuit priest, had this to say about the unity of wisdom and compassion:

> The troubling feature of this vision is that it seems to leave no place for a rapport between human beings, since in their transitory human existence they are empty of any self-nature (*svabhava*). One is asked to help and save others in the awareness that really there is no one who helps and saves, nor is there anyone who is helped and saved, and this detachment from the illusion of substantiality is supposed to make one all the more energetic and free in the work of compassion. Is there not a logical contradiction here?[15]

The logic is that if nothing is real in the true sense, compassion too must be unreal, and if that is the case, it can have no value. They conclude that we need to have some notion of actual, distinct individuals going through unspeakable misery and torment if we are to give rise to compassion. On the basis of this, some Western scholars have argued that it is absurd to try to link compassion with emptiness. If everything were to be regarded as a dream, it would be very difficult to generate compassion because the compassion, the recipients of that compassion, and the suffering itself would all be illusory.

According to Mahayana adepts, however, the potency of compassion can never be diminished by the reality of emptiness. In fact, they maintain that it is only when we have an understanding of emptiness that we can be truly compassionate. We may feel a mundane form of compassion for others, but this will never have a liberating influence on the person it is directed toward. Compassion can only be liberating when it is fused with the wisdom of emptiness. Only this enables us to transcend the dualistic perception that phenomena are composed of discrete and independent subjects and objects. What really prevents us from generating compassion toward others is the fixed notions we have about self and other. Compassion only makes sense when there is a relationship, and a relationship can only exist between mutually dependent, contingently existing beings. Emptiness and compassion are therefore not only compatible, there is an intimate relationship between understanding that everything is a dream and the generation of compassion.

Setting aside the philosophical question about ultimate reality, we also need to ask ourselves the following question: how does regarding phenomena as a dream facilitate the development of genuine compassion? The answer is that all our misery comes from mental fixation (Tib. *'dzin pa*), and viewing phenomena as dreamlike will help us to relinquish our fixation on the world. If we don't put some effort into gradually weaning ourselves from this fixation on "self" and "other" as real, we will never succeed in being compassionate and will continue to invite pain and suffering into our lives. Even when we try to be caring, loving, considerate, and courteous, it will never be a fundamentally transformative experience, because we have not let go of our fixation. As Shantideva says:

> When doing virtuous acts, beyond reproach,
> To help ourselves, or for the sake of others,
> Let us always bear in mind the thought
> That we are self-less, like an apparition.[16]

Normally, our fixations continually escalate, causing our thinking to become more and more distorted, biased, and confounded.
We may not be conscious of these prejudiced perceptions, but they
are pervasive within our minds and spoil all our experiences. Seeing
phenomena as dreamlike will free us from this fixation and open
our minds to compassionate responses toward all beings, not just
the localized and sporadic compassion we usually feel for specific
people or animals. As the Hua-Yen Buddhist teachers say, it is the
feeling of interconnectedness with everything that allows us to feel
empathy with and sympathy for other beings. Francis H. Cook,
from the University of California, Riverside and an expert on the
Hua-Yen and Zen schools of Japanese Buddhism, has eloquently
linked Hua-Yen's vision of the interconnectedness of all beings
with the Buddhist emphasis on meditation and ethical life:

> Thus the Bodhisattva who begins to wend his way down
> the eons must do more than believe in his religion, and
> he must do more than gain an understanding of the na-
> ture of existence through a study of philosophical texts;
> he must act as if the Hua-yen vision were an indubitable
> reality. Buddhism therefore places a great amount of stress
> on meditation and the ethical life which is the outflow of
> this meditation, for both are at once practical means of re-
> alizing the Hua-yen *dharma-dhatu* and an acting out of the
> reality of that vision.[17]

This is not a purely philosophical or intellectual exercise but a
meditative way of thinking that enables us to see things more
clearly. Integration and disintegration are part of the phenomenal
world, and we can't hold on to any situation as real or formulate
any kind of basic pattern in relation to our experiences. While we

imagine we are perceiving stable patterns in our experiences, un-expected disruptions and anomalies are occurring all the time. We are taught to regard everything as a dream because whatever we perceive is in a state of flux, and the moment we try to arrest or seize the moment, it is gone. The Kadampa masters call this "try-ing to scoop up water with a net." Genuine compassion comes from seeing life in a nondualistic fashion, so that our experiences are not so strongly colored by thoughts of self and other.

3 • Examine the nature of unborn unawareness

While the aim of the previous slogan was to analyze the nonsub-stantiality of the phenomenal world, this slogan is about analyz-ing the nonsubstantiality of mind itself. It is very difficult to talk about mind in a lucid way, for what we normally mean by mind is what Buddhists call "the deluded mind" (Skt. *chitta;* Tib. *sems*). While this mind consists of myriad cognitive and affective states, it is not regarded as a "psychic substance." It is, however, imbued with an awareness that is unborn.

Unborn awareness is absolute bodhichitta; it is not a thought, not a feeling, not an idea, not a sensation, and not an experience. To say that absolute bodhichitta is experiential rather than a thought or concept is a step in the right direction, but it is not an experience either. Experiences come and go, but there is a vast, open, and clear spaciousness that does not come and go, that does not have a beginning, middle, or end, which is why it is "un-born." It never enters the stream of time, turmoil, and pain. That vast spaciousness and luminous clarity is what we awaken after the practice of relative bodhichitta has removed the obstacles to our ever-present unborn awareness. That is the innate, spontaneous, ongoing luminous clarity of mind.

This unborn awareness is our innate wisdom mind (Skt. *jnana;* Tib. *ye shes*), which enables us to apprehend the ultimate reality of emptiness. Furthermore, any distinction between wisdom and ultimate reality is only a heuristic one, because wisdom and ultimate reality are inseparable in their nature, like sugar and sweetness. A genuine realization of absolute bodhichitta involves the integration of both. That awareness is said to be unborn because it is inherent in the mind itself, not having been acquired through the diligent accumulation of learning or knowledge. Anything that is caused will cease to exist when the conditions that support it change or disappear. But this wisdom will continue to be wisdom, no matter how we try to understand it, because it is not contingent on anything. As Jamgön Kongtrül states:

> Since mind has no origin, it has never come into existence in the first place. Now it is not located anywhere, inside or outside the body. Finally, the mind is not some object that goes somewhere or ceases to exist. By examining and investigating the mind, you should come to a precise and certain understanding of the nature of awareness, which has no origin, location, or cessation.[18]

When we are unreflective, we mistake our thoughts and emotions for something real and tangible, whereas in truth they are very elusive and transient. When we try to grasp the mind, we find that it has no attributes or characteristics and that it is quite difficult to identify what is actually taking place. As soon as we recognize that a particular thought has been aroused, it has already vanished. When we closely observe and analyze our thoughts, feelings, emotions, moods, mental dispositions, predilections, and habit patterns, we make the liberating discovery that nothing is really going on in the mind at all. We peel these away, layer after layer, until we get to the very recesses of our mind, only to find that all that is left is a bare sense of awareness. That bare awareness is absolute bodhichitta, or buddha-nature. In Mahamudra and Dzogchen literature, this is called "the nature of the mind" (Tib. *sems nyid*). If we examine the faculty of awareness itself, we will also discover that there is nothing we can label as "unborn awareness."

We can't form any definite opinions about unborn awareness if we can't comprehend it conceptually. While we can develop an inferential understanding of it from reading, study, and deep contemplation, we will never recognize its existential import unless we experience it directly. The fact that we have it means that we don't have to think of ourselves as ignorant, depraved, and confused samsaric creatures, taking faltering baby steps toward enlightenment. We may be confused and given to violent bouts of emotions that lead us to indulge in negative thoughts, but deep down our capacity for enlightenment has never diminished. Our ability to generate genuine love and compassion will be bolstered by understanding that we already possess the wisdom mind that naturally manifests the qualities of compassion.

4 • *Even the remedy is free to self-liberate*

The remedy in this case is analysis, the principal method of the previous vipashyana exercises. While analysis dismantles the object of fixation, the lojong teachings advise us that analysis has no reality of its own either, and that while it's a convenient tool for revealing the nature of emptiness and the nature of unborn awareness, it doesn't, in itself, possess wisdom or superior mental faculty. Because analysis can't dissect itself any more than a knife can cut itself, we eventually simply let go of whatever answer we come up with in vipashyana meditation and rest the mind in the natural state. As Jamgön Kongtrül points out:

> When we look at the presence of the remedy itself, these thoughts about the absence of true existence, there is nothing for the mind to refer to and they subside naturally on their own.[19]

5 • Rest in the natural state, the basis of all

After returning to shamatha meditation in the previous slogan, we continue with the following instruction: The basis of all (Skt. *alaya;* Tib. *kun gzhi*) can be understood in two different ways: as basic consciousness (Skt. *alaya-vijnana;* Tib. *kun gzhi rnam shes*) and as wisdom consciousness (Skt. *alaya-jnana;* Tib. *kun gzhi ye shes*). Basic consciousness is the storehouse of all our delusory experiences, while wisdom consciousness is the actual ground of both our delusory and our nondelusory experiences. Milarepa realized this when he said:

> I understood that in general all things related to samsara and nirvana are interdependent. Furthermore I perceived that the source consciousness is neutral. Samsara is the result of a wrong point of view. Nirvana is realized through perfect awareness. I perceived that the essence of both lay in an empty and luminous awareness.[20]

There have been ongoing discussions about whether the phrase "rest in the basis of all" means to rest in the basic consciousness or to rest in the wisdom consciousness. Most Kagyupa commentators interpret it to mean that we should rest in the wisdom consciousness, which is the same as absolute bodhichitta or unborn awareness. Jamgön Kongtrül says that the basis of everything "is pointed out by the term 'noble buddha-nature.'"[21]

According to the Kagyu and Nyingma traditions, the basic consciousness underlies the whole structure of our cognitive processes, which can be broken down into eight forms of consciousness. There are the five sense consciousnesses as well as a sixth consciousness, which is the seat of reflexive awareness, the center of our rational thought processes. Then we have a seventh, "egoistic" consciousness (Skt. *mano-vijnana;* Tib. *yid kyi rnam shes*), which is the seat of our perception, for whatever we perceive here becomes incorporated into our self-identity. Finally, there is the basic consciousness, which contains traces of all the memories, habitual tendencies, emotional reactions, self-perceptions, and apperceptions that have been processed by other levels of consciousness. These traces come from the karmic imprints (Skt. *vasana;* Tib. *bag chags*) that result from this interaction between the eight forms of consciousness and determine our experience of things, thinking patterns, emotions, attitudes, and character traits. Nothing that has been processed by consciousness is wasted; it all gets retained in the form of sedimented karmic formations. All of these things are happening all the time, yet we remain completely unaware of them.[22]

It is said that the seventh, egoistic consciousness misperceives the basic consciousness to be the self, because it is the repository of all our experiences and memories. Everything that gets processed through the other seven levels of consciousness leaves imprints in this basic consciousness, and these imprints give rise to further experiences that are structured around the conceptions of "me" and "mine" by the egoistic consciousness. All eight forms of consciousness must be operational for us to experience anything, and together constitute our total sense of self. Jamgön Kongtrül expresses it this way:

> The mind that grasps, too, is not located anywhere externally or internally and does not exist concretely with a color or shape. From the continuity of ego clinging, which mistakes that which isn't (i.e. a self) for something which is, comes the eight consciousnesses, which are like sky-flowers, empty from the beginning.[23]

This state of bare awareness is the basis of absolute bodhichitta, or our wisdom consciousness. It is traditionally compared to the flickering of a lamp on a windless night. We can rest our minds in many different ways, contrived or natural. For the natural way of resting, we simply maintain a sense of bare awareness without thinking about anything or forcing the mind into a concentrated state.

6 • *In postmeditation, be a child of illusion*

The way to elevate and liberate ourselves on the spiritual path is by maintaining the perspective of the insubstantial nature of things in our everyday activities. Instead of viewing people and things as discrete and unique, we need to bring the understanding of dependent arising to our everyday lives. If we contemplate this view properly, we will develop a very different perspective. It

is very easy to become emotionally stirred up when we are practicing lojong and thereby confuse our feelings of love and compassion with more negative emotions. The lojong masters warn
us how easy it is to allow our more universal feelings of benevolence to slide into personal narratives of self-pity, hopeless-
ness, resentment, and anger. To guard against these illusions, they
advise us not to take our lives too seriously and to maintain a balance between our feelings for others and our self-absorbed in-
volvements in everyday life.

The word *illusion* in this instruction doesn't imply that things
are a hallucination or fabrication of the mind. It simply means
that we normally misperceive issues by making them too real. A
more propitious way of behaving would be to relinquish this
habit of fixation. The traditional example for this is to mistake a
rope for a snake. When we react with fear and dread, it does not
imply that the rope itself is an illusion, but rather that we are simply experiencing the result of an error of perception. In a similar
way, the teachings on emptiness claim that when we perceive others as independently existing, self-enclosed individuals, we are
making an error of perception that has the potential to give rise
to equally disturbing emotions—the stronger the illusion of self
and other, the greater our fixation and emotional arousal.

The lojong texts describe this world and the sentient creatures that inhabit it as a container (Tib. *snod*) and its content
(Tib. *bcud*), because all the living beings within that container are
constantly moving, interacting, acting, and impacting on one another's lives. When we recognize how both alike and unalike we
are, the qualities of loving-kindness and compassion will naturally arise in our being. Applying this understanding to postmeditation situations as an adjunct to our vipashyana exercises will
help us to maintain a proper perspective, one that is based on our

understanding of absolute bodhichitta. This view will protect us from our tendency to pollute our altruistic attitudes with unsavory emotions. This is called "adopting the right view." We are learning to think in a different way rather than trying to stop thoughts from arising. Right view and compassion are the two main practices of lojong. If we can maintain the perspective of absolute bodhichitta in meditation, even artificially, we will add a profound resonance to our relative bodhichitta practices.

Relative Bodhichitta

Relative bodhichitta is the cultivation of compassion. Compassion is like the moisture that allows for the growth of other virtues, so it follows that if we behave in a self-centered and uncaring way toward others, these other virtues will never take root in our being. The practice of compassion is about cultivating a nonegoistic understanding of the world and learning to evaluate ourselves from that perspective. Egoistic perception is always deluded perception and the cause of our emotional afflictions and deluded mental states.

Practicing relative bodhichitta trains us to develop the intelligence that is capable of transcending egoism. The panoramic perspective required for this transformation comes from the practice of absolute bodhichitta, which is why it is so important to remember that relative bodhichitta is based on the insights of vipashyana meditation. Just being a good person or having a good heart is not enough to become a spiritual person. We must distinguish between mundane acts of goodwill and transcendental states of consciousness that imbue our compassionate acts with intelligence and impartiality.

The authoritative works of the great Mahayana masters, such as Nagarjuna, Aryadeva (second century) and Chandrakirti (seventh century), the founders of the Madhyamaka school and Asanga (fourth century), and Vasubandhu (330–400), the founders of the other major Mahayana school known as Yogachara, profoundly affected the development of Buddhism. It is significant that Chandrakirti doesn't begin his *Entry to the Middle Way* (*Madhyamakavatara*) by paying homage to the Buddhas and bodhisattvas, as was the convention of his time, but by singing praises to compassion:

> The Shravakas and those halfway to buddhahood are
> born from the Mighty Sage,
> And Buddhas take their birth from Bodhisattva heroes.
> Compassion, nonduality, the wish for buddhahood for
> others' sake
> Are causes of the children of the Conqueror.
>
> Of buddhahood's abundant crop, compassion is the seed.
> It is like moisture bringing increase and is said
> To ripen in the state of lasting happiness.
> Therefore to begin, I celebrate compassion![24]

Meditating on love and compassion is equivalent to making the preparations for a journey, and practicing the paramitas of generosity (Skt. *dana;* Tib. *sbyin pa*), patience (Skt. *ksanti;* Tib. *bzod pa*), vigor (Skt. *virya;* Tib. *brston 'grus*), and moral precepts (Skt. *shila;* Tib. *tshul khrims*) is equivalent to actually taking that journey. As the preliminary practices point out, if we haven't really thought the journey through and prepared ourselves properly, we may well be unsuccessful in our endeavors and meet with insurmountable obstacles. We need to train ourselves to think in a certain way before we can implement the bodhisattva principles in everyday life. When Tibetan Buddhists want to emphasize the thinking mind, we use the word *lo*, so we could say that lo-*jong* practice is designed to train the mind to think in a different way. *Lodro* (Tib. *blo gros*) means "intelligence," and a very fine intelligence is called *lodro chenpo*, which means "great intelligence." Lojong practice is not just a method of contemplation but a means for changing the whole way we see, think, feel, perceive, and so on.

That's why relative bodhichitta has two aspects: the intention to work for the benefit of others and the actions themselves. The former, contemplative aspect is related to the thought of compassion in meditation, and the active aspect is related to the demonstration of compassion in everyday life. Buddhism does not make a sharp distinction between contemplative compassion and active demonstration because our actions can only be truly compassionate if we have first generated bodhichitta in our thoughts. Intention has to take precedence over action, because the cultivation of relative bodhichitta relies upon pure intention. Shantideva draws the following analogy to making a journey:

Bodhichitta, the awakening mind,
In brief is said to have two aspects:
First, aspiring, *bodhichitta in intention*;
Then, *active bodhichitta*, practical engagement.

Wishing to depart and setting out upon the road,
This is how the difference is conceived.
The wise and learned thus should understand
This difference, which is ordered and progressive.[25]

We cultivate a compassion that encompasses all beings, not just the ones that are suffering in a visible way. No one is free from the troubles of living, so we must direct compassion toward everyone, taking care that the nature of our compassion remains impartial, without degenerating into the type of blind emotions that compel us to act. Compassion has to be imbued with intelligence. Just caring for others is no guarantee that our intentions will be expressed wisely. We therefore make a distinction between ordinary forms of compassion and that one that is motivated by bodhichitta, the latter being called "great compassion" (Skt. *maha-karuna;* Tib. *snying rje chen po*).

The necessary condition for this transformation is the recognition that it's just as important to think about love and compassion as it is to do loving and compassionate acts. We shouldn't underestimate the importance of this thought of love and compassion. We will never be able to engage in compassionate acts until we accustom ourselves to a radically different way of thinking. We generally understand the word *compassion* to mean something like "suffering with others," but that is definitely not the Buddhist understanding. Buddhism defines compassion as wishing that others "may be free from suffering and the cause of suffering," and we generate compassion by imagining that people are in fact free of their physical ailments and mental torments. As Shantideva so eloquently describes:

> May I be a guard for those who are protectorless,
> A guide for those who journey on the road.
> For those who wish to go across the water,
> May I be a boat, a raft, a bridge.
>
> May I be an isle for those who yearn for landfall,
> And a lamp for those who long for light;

For those who need a resting place, a bed;
For all who need a servant, may I be their slave.[26]

Simply thinking in an imaginative way with love and compassion can have a transformative effect, even if those wishes for all intents and purposes are unrealizable. The fact that you can't be transformed into a bridge and so forth is not important; it is the wish that you could be of benefit to others that is the key. If we make wishes of that nature, love and compassion for people will arise naturally within us. This is very different from the way we normally approach things, where we assume that if something is unrealizable, there is no point in thinking about it. The point here is that compassionate action will arise from having compassionate thoughts.

The cultivation of relative bodhichitta is first and foremost a method for reversing our self-centered attitude and changing it to one that regards "the other" as equal. Once we generate this attitude, which is the very foundation of lojong practice, we won't need to reduce our egoism deliberately, because our narcissistic tendencies will naturally diminish. The Kadampa masters claim that the real problem is that we continually blame other people for our misery. By selfishly pursuing our own needs we manage to be completely indulgent of our egoistic minds and never tire of the abuse we subject ourselves to. Rather than improving our sense of self-worth and happiness, this tendency to be obsessively concerned with our own welfare only magnifies our feelings of loneliness and disconnection. The issue isn't about desiring happiness or not, it is about gaining it at the expense of others.

The understanding that hurting others to protect ourselves is quite destructive to ourselves is the fulcrum of mind training practice. The only way to change the emotional impoverishment

of our own lives into something more fulfilling is to reverse our
attitude and to focus instead on wishing for the happiness of
others. As Yangonpa, a great Tibetan master, says in his *Instruction
on Training the Mind*:

> Train your thoughts to ponder others' well-being; this
>   essential point
> Ensures that everything you do becomes Dharma practice.[27]

Once we understand the significance of this point, we will see
that lojong practice is also a means of lessening our own misery.
Harboring negative attitudes about others is a self-destructive
habit, and obsessing over our own needs will only ensure we are
discontented, which is why we need to reflect on our experiences
and be quite clear about the motivation (Tib. *kun slong*) behind
our actions. Understanding relative bodhichitta teaches us how
wrong it is to think, "I will sometimes be required to harm others for the sake of my self-preservation." If we can learn to reverse
this attitude, it will not only be beneficial for others, it will also
result in a vastly improved quality of life for ourselves as well.

Westerners tend to value action over everything else, but Buddhism sees the motives behind an action as being far more important. Our motives can essentially be broken down into the desire to
help and the desire to harm. However, these two motivations often
run parallel to each other and can easily become confused, so that
even when we mean well, there is always some dubious agenda shad-
owing our good intentions. All our motives come about as a result
of discriminatory judgments and always involve whatever we think
will promote our own happiness and reduce our suffering. Even
the actions we commit with a bad intention have this as their goal.
We need to become fully conscious of the different intentions and

motives that are at work in our minds if we wish to penetrate the self-deceptions that lurk behind our actions.

7 • *Train in sending and taking alternatively, these two should ride the breath*

Sending and taking (Tib. *tong len*) is the contemplative practice of relative bodhichitta. This practice is counterintuitive to the way we normally understand our experiences, which is to reject everything we don't want and cling to everything we do want. We undertake *tonglen* because our physical actions are a direct result of our mental habits. Unless we transform these negative mental habits, we'll never be able to manifest compassion, either in our actions or in our thoughts. Shantideva gives a series of examples for developing an attitude that encourages recognition of the other:

> May those who lose their way and stray
> In misery, find fellow travelers,
> And safe from threat of thieves and savage beasts,
> Be tireless, and their journey light.[28]

In tonglen, we are trying to adopt a radically new way of looking at things. Tonglen is called "exchanging oneself for others" because it involves giving away everything that is good in our lives and taking on everything that is bad in the lives of others. It is a training in courage, because the whole point of doing it is to train ourselves to be less fearful and anxious. Our capacity to feel love and compassion for others, and our courage to take on their suffering, will increase if our tonglen practice is working. This practice is so extremely beneficial because we're training ourselves to stop thinking about everything from a defensive posture. The more selfish and egocentric we are, the more defensive we become. If we think about sharing our happiness, we will become less self-obsessed, and our conflicting emotions will naturally subside. In *The Thirty-seven Practices of Bodhisattvas*, Gyalsay Togme Sangpo (1295–1369) advises:

> All suffering comes from the wish for your own happiness.
> Perfect Buddhas are born from the thought to help others.
> Therefore exchange your own happiness
> For the suffering of others—
> This is the practice of bodhisattvas.[29]

Self-obsession is not just about overevaluating our own worth, it also includes our feelings of inadequacy and self-criticism. Contrary to our fears, mentally taking on the suffering of others does not compound our pain; it enriches our lives, releases us from the nagging problems that normally plague us, and has a transformative effect on our psyche. Whereas self-obsession diminishes our being and keeps us trapped in inner turmoil, tonglen—an antidote to all forms of self-obsession—enables our mind to become elevated and expansive (Skt. *arya;* Tib. *'phags pa*). As Shantideva says:

> Do not be downcast, but marshal all your strength;
> Take heart and be the master of yourself!
> Practice the equality of self and other;
> Practice the exchange of self and other.[30]

When we do the actual practice, we begin by taking refuge, contemplating the preliminaries, and resting in the natural state.

This is followed by the vipashyana exercises of the previous slogans and returning again to rest in the natural state. We then do tonglen from within that state. We think of others purely in terms of their suffering and undesirable experiences, imagining the distress of illness, the pain and suffering of loss, the deprivation and affliction of poverty, the confusion and torment of mental illness, and the disabling distress of emotional conflicts. Then we inhale all that suffering into ourselves. We think of ourselves purely in terms of our own happiness, imagining everything that we hold dear, the special moments we cherish when we experienced love or intimacy or moments when we were at ease with ourselves, and we breathe that out to others.

We also breathe in the causes and conditions of all the suffering in others' lives and breathe out the causes and conditions for their happiness. There is the actual experience of suffering and then there are the debilitating effects that we suffer due to our conflicting emotions, which strangely, are the causes of the same suffering and pain. These conflicting emotions are both the cause and the effect of our suffering, and thereby are what create the vicious cycle that is samsara. We include all of this within our tonglen practice, breathing in everything that is debilitating for others and breathing out everything that would be the cause of joy.

Lojong practices train the mind, just as we would train the body. The way we try to maintain our health can be quite erroneous. We think we have to constantly feed ourselves and get plenty of rest, but that is not necessarily a healthy solution. If the body is pampered and unconditioned, it will become more and more sensitive to discomfort until the least irritation becomes a great privation. When our body is fit, we can walk for miles with ease, but when it is not fit, just getting out of the house becomes a difficult task. The more we fear discomfort and sickness, the greater that discomfort becomes and the more extreme the effects of our ill health will seem. For example, if we get the flu and our mental conditioning is weak, it can be very draining and painful, and we may even pick up more life-threatening forms of illness. In the same way, if our mind is not trained, it becomes lethargic and lazy, and any little unpleasantness is perceived as a dangerous affront. Again, Shantideva makes this point in the following verse:

> To the extent this human form
> Is cosseted and saved from hurt,
> Just so, just so, to that degree,
> It grows so sensitive and peevish.[31]

Just like people who undergo physical endurance tests in their training to climb Mount Everest, the mental training of tonglen practice is meant to instill courage and determination. If we are psychologically prepared to take on difficulties, our trials and pains might not be so troubling. The samsaric mind is very weak and easily provoked, but when the mind is strong, its capacities are greatly enhanced. In lojong practice, everything else is supplementary.

People new to tonglen have many trepidations and doubts. Some people think, "If I do tonglen, I'll be totally miserable, because I'll always be thinking about the suffering of others." Others think that when things go wrong, it's a direct result of tonglen practice. Both these fears are completely misplaced. It is impossible to invite misfortune and disruption into our lives through tonglen. We have to remind ourselves that we do not engage in the practice of sending and taking in order to share the suffering of others. For example, if someone is suffering from cancer and we take on his or her suffering in tonglen practice, we should not think, "Now I will get cancer." Once we have visualized taking on others' suffering, it immediately dissipates within us.

Other people think they just don't have a lot of love to give. I often hear people say, "I feel so empty; it's like I have nothing inside." This is a common experience for most of us, because we have been self-obsessed since the day we were born. If we have siblings, we may remember that when we were children, we not only wanted to eat our share of the food but theirs as well. We wanted our sister or brother's toys, and if we did not get them, we threw a tantrum. The emptiness we feel is a lack of love and compassion for others. If we had those wholesome emotions, we would not experience this existential crisis of nothingness. We feel nurtured when we are nurturing. Only a nurturing person can nurture, and a nurturing person is nurtured by his or her own caring attitudes. If you can develop these qualities, you will no longer have to go around like a sponge, soaking up the drops of love others leave behind.

Buddhas have gone beyond suffering, so how can they share in the suffering of others? There is no such thing as a Buddha that suffers with us or shares in our suffering. Having been human beings, they know what it means to suffer, which is why their compassion is endless and infinite. It is not because Buddhas are enlightened that they know about suffering, even though they no longer experience suffering. This transcendence of suffering is the key point in Buddhism. Suffering is the combination of pain and attempting to avoid that pain. Once we rid ourselves of grasping and avoidance, we are only left with our pain, which is not the same as suffering. If you were still suffering after attaining enlightenment, all the mind training and arduous spiritual practices would have been for nothing.

Nothing is literally given away and nothing is literally being taken on when we do tonglen. When we breathe in, we are not afraid to take on the illness, grief, distress, physical ailments, or mental torment of others. When we breathe out, we are not afraid to send out loving thoughts and caring attitudes to others, or to imagine that we are strong enough to be of help to them.

Some people assume that tonglen can't possibly have an impact on anybody else's life because it's only a mental exercise. From a Buddhist point of view, the interconnected nature of everything suggests there will be some impact on others. Just as our selfishness and neediness has an adverse impact on others, our positive attitudes will also impact on others in a tangible way. Lojong practice is ultimately for oneself, however; it is not a method for solving the world's problems. Even if we diligently breathe out affirmations with the wish to solve the world's problems, these will have no actual effect on the world. However, breathing out wonderful virtues and breathing in terrible sufferings will have an actual and very powerful effect on our own transformation. All the difficulties and painful experiences that we have in life come from our fixation on the notion of self and other. When we exchange ourselves for others, we experience self-transcendence, because we have gone beyond the parameters of our own egoistic mind. We experience a release from the imprisonment of our conventional egoism and become something greater than ourselves. If we have the lojong attitude, many of the problems that once seemed so overwhelming will cease to matter. When we are grateful to other people for providing us the opportunity to develop these transformative abilities, we realize that we are the real beneficiaries of tonglen practice.

Postmeditation

After practicing tonglen, we return to shamatha meditation and rest in the natural state. The life we return to at the end of our session is called "postmeditation," because our everyday activities must be ancillary to our meditation practice. We bring the mindfulness and awareness of our meditation and the other-regarding attitude of tonglen into everyday life. People often mistake awareness for self-consciousness. They wonder, "How am I responding to this situation, person, or interaction?" and focus on what is going on in their heads. Self-consciousness just means becoming conscious of our perception of other people's responses to us and is simply another form of self-obsession, because we are still the center of our own attention. In postmeditation, lojong advises us to notice our responses to other people and situations so that we understand our own actions within the context of their needs and expectations. When we integrate these experiences within our meditations and prayers and make aspirations about the well-being of others, we transform our own attitudes.

In postmeditation, this is called *monlam* (Skt. *pranidhana;* Tib. *smon lam*), or an "act of aspiration." The concept of aspiration is an unusual one for Westerners, but it's very important to understand this very powerful psychological and spiritual technique. *Monlam* is sometimes translated as "prayer," but this interpretation is possibly misleading, for Buddhist prayers are not directed toward anyone. Their power doesn't come from outside our own thoughts but through an accumulation of positive intentions and practices. By directing that psychic energy through an act of aspiration, we draw whatever we want to realize in the future closer to us.[32]

There are three more slogans that directly help us maintain our awareness in postmeditation activities.

8 • *Three objects, three poisons, three seeds of virtue*

We tend to group people into three general categories in daily life: those we get along with, those who we don't get along with, and those who are of no real interest to us. We have great attachment, love, and affection for the people we get along with, and we don't want any harm to come to them. We have nothing but scorn and condemnation for the people we are averse to and are prepared to revile them at every turn. And the third category comprises the majority of people, who are unknown to us, so we don't have any opinion about them at all. However, even the feeling of indifference is a form of feeling, thus our response is not completely neutral or innocuous so these people are always potential objects of attachment or aversion. According to the Buddhist view, the people we have great affection for are the objects of our desire; the people we have aversion to are the objects of our anger, and the people who are strangers and don't interest us are the objects of our ignorance. The "three objects" are those groups of people. The "three poisons" are our desire, anger, and ignorance. And the "three virtues" are non-desire, non-anger, and non-ignorance.

This slogan says that we can transform the objects and poisons into virtue. Instead of seeing virtue as something totally unconnected to vice, we can cultivate virtue from the soil of our negative tendencies by relating to the object of our emotions in a different way. If we can maintain an awareness of these three "objects," we will be able to recognize that our relationship to friends, foes, and strangers does not form in a vacuum. Someone is a friend, foe, or stranger depending on a variety of factors, circumstances, and existing conditions. It is very profound to view our interpersonal relationships in this way, because no one is a friend or foe in essence, and our relationships to others can change very quickly. Someone whom we considered a friend might turn into a hated enemy, and our enemy can just as easily turn into our best friend, while people who have never provoked any strong feelings in us can become either.

Becoming aware of these shifting relationships will make it easier to develop love and compassion. It doesn't mean that certain people are not our "friends" while others appear as "enemies"; it just means that we can go beyond these temporary perceptions and view all our relationships as dependently originated. Keeping the dreamlike quality of everything clearly in our minds helps us resist our habitual tendency to fixate on the substantiality of others. Other people want to overcome loneliness, despondency, depression, despair, frustration, and unimaginable suffering and pain just as we do. Failing to view everything as a dream will result in losing our panoramic perspective. This balance between absolute and relative bodhichitta is essential for any true capacity to sympathize with others. Therefore we gradually try to extend our love and compassion toward a broader range of people, first toward strangers and then toward our enemies or the people with whom we find difficult to deal. Shantideva says:

Thus, when enemies or friends
Are seen to act improperly,
Be calm and call to mind
That everything arises from conditions.[33]

We don't grow as human beings only through having good friends; we also grow when other people seem hell-bent on creating difficulties for us or putting obstacles in our path. In other words, we don't develop virtues in the absence of vices; we develop virtues by dealing with our vices, which is why this kind of meditation is so important. We might still have problems dealing with our attachment, anger, or indifference in everyday life, but if we try to deal with them in a positive way during meditation, we will sow the seeds of virtue.

We can also do imaginative exercises in postmeditation to facilitate this process. For example, if you meet someone you feel strong desire toward, you can try to remember someone you were extremely attracted to in the past where that attraction turned into something unpleasant or painful. Think about all the problems that came from your excessive feelings of desire and then think that other sentient beings may have gone through a similar experience as a result of their obsession. Imagine you are absorbing all their pain, relieving them of their anguish. Then make the following mental aspiration: "May I and all sentient beings be free of the pain associated with excessive desire and attain the virtue of nonattachment." The key point of the exercise is not just having the willingness to take on the suffering of others, but using that to transform our own poisons into the corresponding seeds of virtue through the force of our aspirations. Sometimes people have problems understanding the whole mechanism of this practice, but if we actively use it, it is actually very profound.

9 • Use sayings to train in all forms of activity

Pithy sayings in our daily activities can help us steer our minds in the right direction. We should try to memorize as many slogans as possible, not just the ones that are included in the lojong manual.

For example, Jamgön Kongtrül Rinpoche quotes Shantideva here, because he was famous for pithy sayings such as this one:

While their evil ripens in me,
May all my virtue ripen in them.[34]

It's not a matter of simply parroting these slogans once we've developed familiarity with them; we have to use them to bring about a real change in our outlook. Words and phrases can have a positive or a negative impact on us, depending on their content. If we really think about these slogans and understand their profound subtleties, they will help to maintain our bodhisattva attitude and interrupt our negative flow of thoughts. According to the lojong teachings, we cannot underestimate the power of these sayings. Every time we remember a slogan, it will automatically help us not to react to things in our usual habitual way.

This slogan is essentially about the concept of rejoicing. It is very easy to harp on the negative. For instance, whenever something bad happens in our world, the media considers it newsworthy, yet many good things happen that we never get to hear about. Good news is no news for most people. Bad news is more appealing; perhaps because it makes our bad-news life seem more like good news. Often we can't help ourselves: if we hear some good news involving somebody who might have suddenly come into a sum of money, found love, or received a work promotion, we automatically think he or she is less deserving than we are and resent the good fortune. The last thing we do is rejoice. If we use the lojong slogans properly, we'll only have to invoke the relevant slogan to find ourselves rejoicing in their happiness, and if we can feel happy for others, we will also learn to be happy ourselves.

This is one of the key strategies of lojong: a kind of trick to make us happy. If someone's beauty reminds us of our own ugliness, or someone's wealth reminds us of our poverty, or someone's successful children remind us of our own child's bad grades, we should learn to rejoice in their good fortune rather than wallowing in our own failures. Our misery is created by our reaction to their happiness, so if we can change our reaction to a positive one, we will be able to share in their happiness instead of cutting ourselves off from their joy. This is how we overcome our negativities and how lojong can be beneficial to our own as well as others' well-being.

Buddhists believe that everything we think, feel, and do will result in karmic imprints. The kinds of imprints we leave in our minds through meditation are extremely important, because they redirect the mind in a positive way. That's why we need to think about these slogans and burn their messages deeply into our minds. If we can do that properly, the lojong slogans will pop up automatically in postmeditation situations and will change our mood. This mental "self-talk" or internal dialogue is very important. It is a form of mental conditioning, because we become what we think and we think what we become. We talk to ourselves all the time anyway, but often that is just a form of negative feedback. These lojong exercises will help us to correct that defeatist habit. Transformation doesn't come from changing our mannerisms or our way of talking; it comes from learning to think about things differently.

10 • Begin the sequence of exchange with yourself

Self-obsession is a solipsistic state. The word *solipsism* pertains to the belief that only our own experience exists, and that there is nothing truly outside of us. However, there is no comfort, ease, or respite in such a state. We should constantly be thinking, "May I have the power to go beyond this solipsistic state of self-absorption and engage with others." If we don't free ourselves from our self-obsession, we will remain stuck in the painful emotional states we've created for ourselves. In that self-enclosed world, we think our perceptions are incontestable and believe unconditionally in our own reality. That unshakable belief in our world is what prevents us from overcoming our conflicting emotions and delusory mental states. The only way to dismantle solipsism is to take the following advice from Dharmarakshita about exchanging ourselves for others:

When I become enmeshed in selfishness, I will offer
   my own
happiness to living beings so as to counteract it. In the
   same way,
should a companion be ungrateful to me, I will be content
in knowing that this is in retribution for my own
   inconstancy.[35]

The best way to begin this exchange is to think about all the painful things other people are going through, instead of painful things that we are experiencing. Considering other people's experience is a way of moving away from our self-obsession. We begin by trying to experience the emotions and feelings of others, instead of worrying about our own emotions and feelings. We all know that too much self-absorption is destructive. Take the example of an anorexic person who has become so engrossed in his or her own reality that a distorted fear of being overweight has actually become life-threatening. According to Buddhism, we all behave like this in varying degrees; that is what characterizes the samsaric world. If we want to evolve, we need to find a way to break out of that, and the best way is to put ourselves in somebody else's shoes. We can never really experience what someone else is going through, but we can try to imagine it. This is how we become transformed, because we begin to see that the experience of others might actually be more painful and distressing than our own. Shantideva says:

> Those desiring speedily to be
> A refuge for themselves and other beings.
> Should interchange the terms of "I" and "other,"
> And thus embrace a sacred mystery.[36]

For instance, we have all known times when we were feeling overburdened by heavy responsibilities, overwhelmed by the enormity of others' suffering, or had some kind of psychological resistance to letting go of our own misery. At such times, it can be helpful to jump start the process by directing compassion toward ourselves first in order to generate some genuine self-acceptance and expunge any feelings of inadequacy or self-loathing. Therefore, we begin by using ourselves as the object of sending and taking: we breathe out the cause of our suffering and pain—our conflicting emotions and self-obsession—and breathe in the capacity to go beyond egoism and develop positive emotions.

The Kadampa tradition encourages us to develop this attitude in relation to inanimate objects as well. Along with trying to exchange ourselves for others in daily life, we have to learn to treat all people and things with respect. There is a large amount of literature on bodhisattva conduct that tells us how we should clean our teeth, wash our plates, greet people out in the street, close doors and windows, prepare our bed, fold our clothes, and so on. Shantideva dedicates a number of verses to advice such as the following:

> When eating do not gobble noisily,
> Nor stuff and cram your gaping mouth.
> And do not sit with legs outstretched,
> Nor rudely rub your hands together.[37]

We should not just throw our clothes on the floor, but fold them away neatly. Our food is organic, so we should treat it with love. When we cook, we should not just throw something together, overcooking or undercooking it; we should make the effort to get it just right. "Cooking with gentleness" is the Kadampa expression. When you chop onions, for example, you chop them with care, not with a sloppy attitude. This applies to everything else in your environment as well. We should keep our possessions in working order, without neglecting anything or wasting it. We should keep our house neat, tidy, and well maintained with a sense of care, love, awareness, and presence. All of this is training in mindfulness, awareness, and conscientiousness. If we have no regard for inanimate objects, our neglect will expand to our dealings with other sentient beings.

Exchanging self for others is a way of strengthening our self-confidence and establishing ourselves in a more genuine and authentic way of being. The more authentic we become, the more confident we will feel about our endeavors. Far from undermining our sense of self-worth, as many Western commentators have maintained, this approach actually strengthens our confidence.

Those who accuse the philosophy of Buddhism of undermining self-worth and who maintain that psychotherapy is a more effective method of personal growth than the practice of meditation often have no practical suggestions for how people can help themselves. They often simply analyze the psychodynamic causes of a person's lack of self-confidence, for example, blaming the person's parents, without actually clearly identifying what "confidence" truly consists of. The remedy, according to them, is to see our own opinions as important and to develop confidence by asserting those opinions without regard for the views of others. However, such self-assertion does nothing for one's self-esteem on a fundamental level. The real way to build a sense of well-being in the world is to love and be loved by others. If we don't recognize the fragility and interdependence of our samsaric identities, we will never achieve a genuine sense of confidence, because all of our hopes for happiness will be focused on maintaining an identity that doesn't actually exist in the first place.

Conclusion

We begin our meditations on absolute and relative bodhichitta by taking refuge, meditating on the preliminaries, resting in the natural state in shamatha meditation, contemplating the vipashyana exercises of absolute bodhichitta, and then returning to the natural state once again. We practice tonglen from the perspective of the natural state, then return to rest in it once again at the conclusion of the sending-and-taking practice. We finish off the meditation session by reflecting on the three poisons and exchanging self for others. If you have any time after this, you can contemplate other slogans, going over them again and again, thinking about their meaning and the commentaries you have read about them. None of the other lojong slogans will take root in our being unless we have established ourselves in the formal meditation.

The lojong teachings are connected to the bodhisattva way of life. Along with transforming our self-obsession, we also learn to treat people and things in a different way than we have up until now. We have to aim high, but it is also very important not to push ourselves too hard, because the mind has to adapt itself to this new way of thinking. We practice what we can and gradually push ourselves to take on more in tonglen so that the practice will expand our mental horizons, capacities, and resilience. We should not practice lojong in isolation, but complement it with other Buddhist practices. Lojong is a way of reconditioning the mind and gradually overcoming our negative tendencies, without deliberately trying to suppress them. If we simply lessen our preoccupation with these afflictions, they will cease to be a problem. In other words, we can develop positive qualities before we overcome our negative ones. This is one of the methods of Mahayana Buddhism. Tackling our problems head on, especially if a problem is intractable, has the potential to cause more damage than good. If our attention is switched to something else, however, such as focusing on the antidote instead, the problem often diminishes without our even noticing.

POINT THREE

Transforming Adversity into the Path of Awakening

We now come to the instructions on how to train our minds amid the unfavorable and unwanted circumstances of our lives. We have been born into an imperfect world, characterized by unpredictability and adversity, as finite human beings that have foibles, make mistakes, get confused, and think irrationally. There is much to contend with, and our ability to prevent or circumvent difficulty is quite limited. We aren't omnipotent beings, and while we try to protect ourselves and maintain order in our lives, we simply don't have the ability to safeguard ourselves from its disasters.

It is self-evident that the natural world doesn't behave in a predictable way or do our bidding. We can see this in the recent examples of the Indian Ocean tsunami and the hurricane that decimated New Orleans. Natural disasters have occurred repeatedly in the past and are likely to continue to do so in the future. Millions of people have lost their lives, are losing their lives, and will lose their lives to disease: the typhoid, cholera, dysentery, and bubonic plagues of the past; the HIV epidemic of the present; and so on. Even at a personal level, many things go awry, and our efforts to complete projects are constantly thwarted and disrupted by sickness, mental distress, and all kinds of deception and mistreatment by others.

Adverse circumstances and situations are an integral part of conditioned existence. They tend to arise as sudden interruptions, so we shouldn't be surprised that natural calamities and upheavals occur in both our private and our public lives. Buddhists do not believe in divine authorship or omnipotent governance of any kind; things just happen when the proper conditions and circumstances come together. As Shantideva tells us in his chapter on patience, "Conditions, once assembled, have no thought/ That now they will give rise to some result,"[1] but our ignorance about this process doesn't change the fact they are interdependent. The importance of understanding dependent arising cannot be underestimated, because we have to be realistic about what we can and cannot do. As Padma Karpo (1527–92) writes:

> If you look closely at your normal activities
> You will discover that they do not deserve the trust you
>   accord them.
> You are not the agent in power but the victim of your
>   projections.
> Don't you think you should look closely into that?
> Please turn your mind within and reflect on this.[2]

We can't tailor the world to suit ourselves, or force it to fit into our vision of things. This doesn't mean we shouldn't aspire to make things better. The bodhisattva ideal specifically recommends trying to improve our world to the best of our ability, but that ideal is based on a realistic recognition that the world is imperfect and likely to remain that way. Things may sometimes work a little better, sometimes a little worse, but so long as there is ignorance, hatred, jealousy, pride, and selfishness, we will all be living in a world that is socially and politically imperfect. Shantideva counsels equanimity in the face of life's changing circumstances:

> If there is a remedy when trouble strikes,
> What reason is there for despondency?
> And if there is no help for it,
> What use is there in being sad?[3]

If things are interdependent, as Buddhists say, we can never expect to protect ourselves against unexpected occurrences, because there is no real order to existence apart from the regularity of certain natural processes. The fact that anything and everything can and does happen would then come as no real surprise to us. The question then becomes not so much why these things happen, but what we can do about them once they do. We cannot control the environment in any strict sense, so we must try to change our attitude and see things in a different light. Only then will we be able to take full advantage of our situation, even if it happens to be a bad one. While it often seems there is nothing we can do in the face of insurmountable obstacles, the lojong teachings tell us this is not true. The imperfect world can be an opportunity for awakening rather than an obstacle to our goals.

Sometimes things just happen, and there may be nothing we can do to change that, but we can control our responses to events. We don't have to despair in the face of disaster. We can either continue to respond in the way we've always done and get progressively worse, or we can turn things around and use our misfortune to aid our spiritual growth. For example, if we suffer from illness, we should not allow despondency to get the better of us if our recovery is slow. Despite seeing the best doctors and receiving the best medication, we should accept our situation with courage and fortitude and use it to train our minds to be more accommodating and understanding. No matter what situation we encounter, we can strengthen our minds by incorporating it into our spiritual journey. Another text on mind training known as *The Wheel-Weapon Mind Training* states that our selfish actions create a sword that returns to cut us. This text advises us to accept adversity as both the repercussions for our own negative actions and the method for removing the self-obsession that caused them. As the text says:

> In short, when calamities befall me, it is the weapon
> of my own evil deeds turned upon me, like a smith killed
> by his own sword. From now on I shall be heedful
> of my own sinful actions.[4]

Atisha, one of the greatest Kadampa masters, was invited to Tibet during the second propagation of Buddhism (eleventh to fourteenth centuries). A story associated with Atisha tells how he brought a very difficult Bengali attendant as the object of his mind training, because he'd heard the Tibetans were extremely nice people. However, it wasn't long before he sent the attendant home. When asked why, he replied, "I don't need him anymore. I have you Tibetans." Such stories are common in the Kadampa tradition because they demonstrate that lojong practice is about strengthening the mind, instead of giving in to despair in the face of adversity.

We grow more quickly if we are open to working with difficulties rather than constantly running away from them. The lojong teachings say that when we harden ourselves to suffering, we only become more susceptible to it. The more harsh or cruel we are toward others, the more vulnerable we become to irritation or anger that is directed at us. Contrary to our instincts, it is by learning to become more open to others and our world that we grow stronger and more resilient. It is our own choice how we respond to others. We can capitulate to the entrenched habits and inner compulsions deeply ingrained in our basic consciousness, or we can recognize the limitations of our situation and apply a considered approach. Our conditioned samsaric minds will always compel us to focus on what we can't control rather than questioning whether we should respond at all. However, once we recognize the mechanical way in which our ego always reacts, it becomes possible to reverse that process.

The great strength of the lojong teachings is the idea that we can train our minds to turn these unfavorable circumstances around and make them work to our advantage. The main criterion is that we never give up in the face of adversity, no matter what kind of world we are confronted with at the personal or political level. When we think there is nothing we can do, we realize there is something we can do, and we see that this "something" is actually quite tremendous.

11 • When beings and the world are filled with evil, transform unfavorable circumstances into the path of enlightenment

Mind training enables us to utilize adversity instead of allowing misfortune to drive us into a corner with no answers. This tendency to adopt a defeatist attitude in the face of evil is the biggest obstacle to our everyday lives and the greatest hindrance to the attainment of our spiritual goals. We need to be vigilant about the acquisition of more skillful ways to deal with our difficulties and thereby circumvent the habit of waging war on ourselves. Responding with fortitude, courage, understanding, and openness will yield a stronger sense of self-worth and might even help to mend or ameliorate the situation. This is also how we learn to face unfavorable circumstances and "take them as the path" (Tib. *lam khyer*) so that we are working with our problems rather than against them. Because fighting with others and ourselves only exacerbates our problems, we continually need to examine our negative responses, to see whether they serve any real purpose or whether they're capitulations to the unconscious patterns that habitually influence us.

It is not only when things are going our way and people are kind to us that we can benefit from others. We can also benefit from them when they're not treating us well. This is a very delicate point, especially in the West, where people are quite sensitized to the notions of abuse and victimhood. People sometimes misconstrue this slogan to be promoting a form of exploitation, as if the victim were being told to willingly participate in the continuation of his or her abuse, but that is not its intent at all. This purpose is actually to strengthen our mind, so that we can step outside our solipsistic state and freely enter into the wider world.

If we are skillful and precise about generating love and compassion, it will make us a person of significance—with integrity, dignity, depth, and weight—rather than someone who adds to another's sense of self-inflation or advances his or her own reputation by eliciting a positive response from others.

Dharmaraksita's *The Poison-Destroying Peacock Mind Training* states:

Just as he pulled the sinner out of the well when he was
the monkey bodhisattva, so you too should guide evil
   people

compassionately without expecting good in return, even to one's detriment.[5]

This slogan is about the development of compassion. In Mahayana Buddhism, compassion is identified with "skill in means" (Skt. *upaya-kausalya;* Tib. *thabs mkhas*) rather than self-sacrificing or self-serving acts. It is altruistic motivation merged with insight, as John Schroeder, a scholar of early Buddhist studies at Saint Mary's College of Maryland, explains:

> Very generally, upaya refers to the different pedagogical styles, meditation techniques, and religious practices that help people overcome attachments, and to ways in which Buddhism is communicated to others. [It] arises from the idea that wisdom is embodied in how one responds to others rather than an abstract conception of the world, and reflects an ongoing concern with the soteriological effectiveness of the Buddhist teachings.[6]

The lojong teachings list three "skills in means" for transforming adversity into the path of awakening: (1) the skillful means of relative bodhichitta, (2) the skillful means of absolute bodhichitta, and (3) the special skillful means. We should be careful not to impose a victim mentality on ourselves when contemplating any of the following slogans.

The Skillful Means of Relative Bodhichitta

When we suffer from events that are beyond our control, it makes our suffering infinitely worse if we regard ourselves as victims.

Since most of our emotional experiences are the direct result of how we interpret and personalize the events in our lives, the real factor in determining how things affect us is the skill with which we handle our own responses. It is easy to see that no two individuals ever respond the same way to a given situation, so we need to ask ourselves how one person can remain largely untouched by an event when someone else is completely devastated by it. The explanation lies in their respective responses. For example, while it is quite common to experience some envy at first when hearing of another's success in an area where we feel ourselves weak, that experience will affect us even more profoundly if we continue to dwell on it, for it is really our fixation that intensifies any negative impact. That's why it is so important to investigate the real causes of our suffering rather than assume that our initial responses are always undeniably true and correct. As Chandrakirti claims:

Attachment to one's own belief,
Aversion for another's view: all this is thought.[7]

A life without challenges and difficulties would hardly be worth living. While we know this to be true, we all still tend to drift into laziness rather than approach life with a courageous and expansive attitude. However, even when we manage to pamper ourselves, it never seems enough; we continue to rail against our misfortunes and find fault with what we have, focusing on what we don't have. People who have experienced a few knocks and difficulties and have learned to handle them effectively usually survive much better than people who have been spoiled from the beginning. It is only when we tame our egoistic drives that we can disrupt our ingrained behaviors and develop real character. Handling difficulties and coming out of them a better person are the whole purpose of the lojong teachings, but we can only do that if we aren't constantly defending our egos. Because the ego is unable to face difficult situations, preferring to indulge instead in emotional dramas and negative states of mind, it blames everyone else for its problems. And it is in that sense that the degree to which we experience pain and suffering depends on us rather than on the external circumstances themselves. When we blame others, we are really only giving them power over us, and completely disempowering ourselves as a consequence. Taking responsibility for our own lives, on the other hand, empowers us and cures our tendency to victimize ourselves in any given situation. The following two slogans address the way in which we handle adversity by dealing directly with our self-obsession; the first relates to ourselves, while the second relates to others.

12 • *Drive all blames into one*

As ordinary sentient beings, we are governed by our own selfish needs. Our history books are filled with well-known personalities who ended in ruin as a direct result of the lying, cheating, murder, and theft they engaged in to serve their own perceived needs and desires when their extreme lust, greed, jealousy, and hatred failed to deliver the good fortune they were hoping for. If we examine our own lives, we'll see that our egoistic drives have actually attracted the difficulties that beleaguer us, a fair indication of the foolishness of our behavior. We might stay in an abusive relationship or exhibit a shameless and reckless disregard for everybody including ourselves. Some people even place their own lives at risk in the pursuit of their selfish desires. The more we become self-absorbed, the more we become entangled and confused. These delusions are actually self-deceptions, because at a certain level we mislead ourselves into thinking they are good for us. Shantideva clearly states:

> O my mind, what countless ages
> Have you spent working for yourself?
> And what weariness it was,
> While your reward was only misery![8]

Even though we don't possess the kind of influence that ultimately makes people change their behavior or attitudes, an awareness of our own egoistic drives can help eliminate the obsessive fixations that cause us, and other people, so much harm. Our egoism endlessly promises satisfaction, but never gives us any real return. We invest, we try hard, we do all the things it directs us to do, but the return is not there.

Many people take this teaching the wrong way at first, thinking, "Now I have to blame myself for everything!" However, the lojong teachings condemn only our egoistic, deluded mind, not the totality of our being. Blaming the ego is not the same as blaming the whole self. If that were all we were, then once that mind was transcended, we wouldn't be able to function. But we are also in possession of unborn awareness, or buddha-nature, and we don't annihilate ourselves when we turn away from self-regarding attitudes. Buddhism acknowledges a structural formation of self-identity, with many different types of identification based on various levels of consciousness and distinctive levels of being, but it doesn't endorse a separately existing "self." When we blame the egoistic mind for our misery, we are just blaming that particular aspect of our identity. We need to understand that it's possible to think independently of our ego. It is not essential that the ego assume the role of commander-in-chief. As Dharmarakshita says:

> Since that's the way it is, I seize the enemy! I seize the
> thief who
> ambushed and deceived me, the hypocrite who deceived me
> disguised as myself. Aha! It is ego-clinging, without a
> doubt.[9]

If we regard ourselves as a unity, we might mistakenly feel that it is useless to try to effect any change. When we come to understand the destructiveness of the ego, we sometimes believe that we are simply wretched creatures. However, this is an incorrect view and will only interfere with our mind training and spiritual goals. We are wretched in one way only, and that is in our egoistic self-obsession. When something undesirable happens, rather than blaming somebody or something else, we should look at how we might have contributed to the event. Because our perceptions are not always correct and may not be a genuine reflection of what has taken place, we should always ask ourselves, "Maybe this isn't how things really are. It might just be my own biased, egoistic mind projecting something onto the situation."

If we examine how we constantly personalize everything, we'll see that the real source of our misery is this failure to manage, educate, and transform our mental states. Whenever something goes wrong, we look for someone or something external to blame, and become completely outraged by whatever we decide is responsible for our discomfort. That is really no solution to our predicament, for even if we do find someone or something to blame, it only inflames our anxiety, frustration, and resentment. We might think that the act of blaming others releases us from unfair responsibility, but it really only disempowers us. We'll have to spend our entire lives trying to stop other people from causing problems for us, something that realistically can never be done. In order to cure an illness, we need to make the correct diagnosis. The lojong perspective is the correct diagnosis for our samsaric condition and is the exact antidote to the incorrect diagnosis, which is thinking that other people are to blame. As Shantideva points out, dealing with our own reactions to things is a far more practical way to mitigate our suffering:

To cover the earth with sheets of hide—
Where could such amounts of skin be found?
But simply wrap some leather around your feet,
And it's as if the whole earth had been covered![10]

When the lojong teachings say that we should look at our own egoistic mind, and blame everything on that instead of blaming everybody else, it is not denying that other people influence us. In fact, this is why the lojong texts say that we ourselves will become great if we consort with great beings, whereas consorting with evil people will ensure that we are contaminated by evil. The Mahayana teachings use the myth of a gold mountain and a poisonous mountain to make this point. In this myth, the gold mountain turns the surrounding area into gold, while the poisonous mountain turns everything to poison. As Gyalsay Togme Sangpo advises:

When you keep their company your three poisons increase,
Your activities of hearing, thinking, and meditation decline,

And they make you lose your love and compassion.
Give up bad friends—
This is the practice of Bodhisattvas.[11]

We'll never gain insight into the real source of our suffering until we truly understand our existential condition. The ego always adopts some kind of defensive posture; however, this will guarantee a certain level of paranoia by always trying to determine whether a situation is for or against it. In fact, this is another way in which there is a clear link between negative states of mind and our experience of suffering and pain. On so many levels, our habitual way of thinking is very taxing and undermining. This is why we need to train in the mental strengthening of lojong and stop thinking that every time we have a painful experience it is someone else's fault. If we don't critically analyze things, we become lost in a world of make-believe that has very little correspondence with reality. Shantideva compares self-obsession and its attendant conflicting emotions to a demon:

All the harm with which this world is rife,
All fear and suffering that there is,
Clinging to the "I" has caused it!
What am I to do with this great demon?[12]

The Buddhist definition of a demon is something harmful. In fact, self-obsessive emotions are listed as one of the "four demons" of the Mahayana tradition.[13] Self-obsession is not an isolated experience that only takes place in our own mind: it drives us to do all kinds of very unwise acts. Thus the Mahayana teachings advise us that if somebody completely loses control, "blame the poison, not the person," because the poison is what is driving him or her to that extreme behavior. If we understand this, we can cultivate a different perspective in the way we respond to others. We will cease to be provoked by their actions and stop thinking the worst or expecting the worst from other people, or we can at least give them the benefit of the doubt. Aryadeva states this clearly:

> Just as a physician is not upset with
> Someone who rages while possessed by a demon,
> Subduers see disturbing emotions as
> The enemy, not the person who has them.[14]

Some Western Buddhist authors have presented this slogan with a slight twist: They play down the need to relinquish our fixation on our personal stories, anguish, and resentments, claiming that Westerners have fragile egos and thus need to build a healthy ego first before they can deconstruct it.[15] That sort of logic is total nonsense. The lojong approach has nothing to do with weakening the part of us that helps us function. Only people with a genuine belief in themselves could work with adverse circumstances and situations in this way. What Westerners need is to relinquish their overfocus on their own personal desires and problems, because they have a tendency to dwell on their own stuff far too much. It is easy to misunderstand the Buddhist notion of egolessness. Put simply, Buddhism makes the radical observation that there is no fixed, unchanging, singular, separately existing entity, and that applies to all phenomena, including the ego. It is quite true that, in the relative world, we cannot just casually get rid of our ego, for the ego is a vital part of us that has a function. However, we can train ourselves to harness the ego's energy on the spiritual path, and in the process of doing so, we transform a problematic aspect of our lives into something transcendent and inspiring.

13 • *Meditate on the great kindness of everyone*

From the cradle to the grave, other people do things for us, even if we think we are neglected and unloved. If they had not helped us, especially when we were babies, we would never have survived. We continue to survive because other people are still helping to maintain our world. Whether we think our upbringing was good or bad, people provided us with some kind of education and made sure we didn't go hungry. Practically all of the pleasure, joy, and happiness that we experience come to us because of the presence or activities of others. The food we eat is available to us because many thousands of people are involved in producing, packaging, and distributing it. The same applies to the water we drink, the clothes we buy, the electricity and gas we use, and any number of other things. Waiters bring us food in restaurants, hotel receptionists greet us, sometimes even by name, and bus drivers take us to our destination and exchange pleasantries with us. We must rely on others if we are to have any quality of life. It's not only those near and dear to us toward whom we should feel grateful, although the kindness of our loved ones often goes unrecognized the most.

Our habituated responses are disempowering, because they make everything look and feel as if it were working against us. If we can shift our focus from our rigid, narrow, and habituated points of view, we will empower our ability to embrace situations in a new way so that every situation will start to seem more workable. Because we tend to think other people are taking advantage of us whenever they get the opportunity, we become unceasingly self-protective and suspicious. We need, therefore, to remind ourselves, over and over again, not to take anything for granted and to appreciate the kindness of others.

There will always appear to be circumstances, situations, and people that create difficulties and obstacles for us. This slogan specifically instructs us to think about the kindness of others when we are confronted with negative situations, remembering that we only mature spiritually and psychologically when we are tested. We should endeavor to think good thoughts about people who have in fact made our lives quite difficult at times and try to turn these negative situations to our own spiritual advantage, so that we become wiser and stronger. As Shantideva says:

So like a treasure found at home,
Enriching me without fatigue,
All enemies are helpers in my bodhisattva work
And therefore they should be a joy to me.[16]

This is also true in relation to bad situations in general. The Kadampa masters say that every time we overcome an obstacle or an adversity, we become that much more intelligent and resilient, for it's the accumulation of diverse experiences that enriches our lives. Both Christian and Buddhist masters emphasize the importance of dealing with difficulties, instead of allowing them to get the better of us. This may be expressed in different ways and with different recommendations, but they all say that it's through difficulty that we grow. Saint John of the Cross describes what he calls the "dark night of the soul," exhorting people not to give in to the darkness but see it instead as a portent of light. In the same way, our difficulties shouldn't be viewed as something that will automatically destroy us. The metaphor used in the Kadampa teachings, again and again, is that the manure of experience becomes fertilizer for the field of *bodhi* (enlightenment). Dharmaraksita says, in *The Poison-Destroying Peacock Mind Training*:

> If we don't put on the armor of the bodhisattvas who
> willingly embrace others' ingratitude, happiness will
>   never come
> to those in cyclic existence. Therefore, willingly accept all that
> is undesirable.[17]

If we see that it is our response to difficulties that determines what kind of impact they have on our lives, we'll naturally begin to move toward a more meaningful engagement with our lives as they are. For example, blaming ourselves about our negative habits and mistakes often causes more unhappiness than the actual situation. It is also important to learn from the mistakes of others, so that we don't repeat their errors and compound our own confusion. If we think somebody has done something reprehensible, rather than blaming that person, we should pay attention to our own behavior and resolve not to imitate such actions. We may be constantly enraged by other people's behaviors, but if we examine our own responses, we'll often find that we've acted in the same way ourselves, but with a more lenient explanation of our own behavior. Keeping things in perspective through honest introspection is the way to heed the lojong emphasis on refraining from fixation on others. We'll then view the behavior of others more objectively and open up the possibility of learning something positive from them. Each of us has our own karmic history and has to suffer the karmic consequences of our actions—nobody gets away with anything. It is fruitless to set ourselves up as the arbiters of other people's actions, making judgments about what they do. This doesn't mean that we shouldn't take an interest in social issues, only that we should maintain our spiritual perspective. The only thing we really have any control over is our own experience, and this control is reinforced by learning how to deal with difficult circumstances and situations without anger or bitterness. Chandrakirti states:

> If you respond with anger when another harms you,
> Does your wrath remove the harm inflicted?
> Resentment surely serves no purpose in this life
> And brings adversity in lives to come.[18]

The Skillful Means of Absolute Bodhichitta

Sometimes we generate too much emotion in our lojong practices and run the risk of being overwhelmed. We become so absorbed in our feelings about others that we are swamped by sadness and helplessness and end up thinking, "There's so much suffering out there; I just can't do anything about it." If these negative feelings become too strong, they might become injurious to our lojong practice, so we have to counterbalance that tendency by focusing on the perspective of absolute bodhichitta. This equilibrium between absolute and relative bodhichitta underlies the lojong teachings and is the framework for Mahayana Buddhism in general. As Atisha points out, skillful means and wisdom are the two essential ingredients for overcoming conditioned existence:

> Wisdom without skillful means
> And skillful means, too, without wisdom

Are referred to as bondage.
Therefore do not give up either.[19]

In the Buddhist teachings, the notions of both love and compassion are infused with the qualities of detachment (Skt. *amoha;* Tib. *ma chags pa*) and equanimity (Skt. *upeksha;* Tib. *tang snyim*). If we lose sight of that relationship, we may begin to think that equanimity and compassion are completely different states of mind or that it's impossible to have loving feelings when we are dwelling in a state of detachment. Detachment doesn't equal indifference, and equanimity doesn't mean we don't experience any emotion at all. We are simply trying to combine the two in order to maintain a sense of equilibrium in our emotional responses. The Mahayana masters all say that a blending of the two is far more effective than just generating one without the other. Relating to people only with detachment would not be a genuine Mahayana approach, and relating to people with a love that hasn't been tempered by equanimity would leave us vulnerable to dramatic emotional upheavals.

Compassion doesn't just entail a great outpouring of emotion; it's about skillfully channeling our positive attitudes. In order to express our emotions skillfully, we need to be focused, with our senses intact and our wits about us. While it is important not to suppress our emotions, we have to learn to express them intelligently. That's why it's important to infuse them with detachment and equanimity. This combination is the very definition of compassion. As the *Skill in Means Sutra* makes clear:

Venerable Lord, Bodhisattva great heroes guard against all attachments. They are like this: Dwelling in skill in means that is inconceivable, they course in form, sound, smell, taste, and touch—all of which are occasions for attachment—yet are not attached to them.[20]

When we fixate on other people as autonomous beings, we lose our equanimity in regard to the propelling force of emotion and thereby mentally solidify others' sufferings into seemingly insurmountable obstacles. Meditating on wisdom is the antidote to that problem. We have to remind ourselves that the sentient creatures we care about are also dependently originated, just like us; their real nature is emptiness. Even the confusions that prevent us from perceiving phenomena in a more fluid way are an expression of emptiness, for ultimate reality is not separate from our thoughts and emotions. This approach is about learning to deal with anger and jealousy as well as other conflicting emotions. We aren't expected to eliminate them completely, but by learning to relinquish them with greater ease, we won't be so predisposed to pursue and perpetuate their habitual tendencies.

This integration of absolute and relative bodhichitta, or emptiness and compassion, is an expression of the Buddhist middle view. Some people argue that our emotions will always lead us astray and that we have to be rational at all times in order to counteract their effect. Others maintain that our capacity to feel is paramount and that an overreliance on abstract thought threatens to impoverish our lives. The Buddhist view lies somewhere between these two views. The Buddha himself constantly emphasized the middle way:

Katyayana, everyday experience relies on the duality of "it is" and "it is not." But for one who relies on the Dharma and on wisdom, and thereby directly perceives how the things of the world arise and pass away, for him, there is no "it is" and "it is not." "Everything exists" is simply one extreme, Katyayana, and "nothing exists" is the other extreme. The Tathagata relies on neither of these two extremes, Katyayana; he teaches the Dharma as a Middle Way.[21]

Bodhisattva practice is about trying to love and care for all people. All the sentient beings in samsara are suffering in one way or another. As Buddhism says, the mighty and powerful suffer too. The arrogant person is afflicted with arrogance, the disdainful person with disdain, and the rich person with wealth. Shantideva goes to great lengths to describe how painful it is to accumulate, hang on to, and lose wealth, as well as to be obsessed by the constant fear that others are coveting it:

> The trouble guarding what we have, the pain of
>   losing all!
> See the endless hardships brought on us by wealth!
> Those distracted by their love of riches
> Never have a moment's rest from sorrows of existence.[22]

Some people try to shift the emphasis of mind training toward some kind of political or social activism. Mind training's sole concern is to train the mind; it has nothing to do with activism. This doesn't mean we shouldn't engage with the world and support different causes, but when we do, we have to adopt a broader spiritual view. Our view has to be as wide as the sky, but our actions have to be directed precisely to whatever comes to hand.

14 • *To see confusion as the four kayas,*
the protection of emptiness is unsurpassable

The *kayas* (Tib. *sku*), or "aspects of Buddha's being," help us to maintain an enlightened perspective on our world. The *nirmanakaya* is the physical appearance of a Buddha's being, the *sambhogakaya* is the embodiment of the wisdom qualities, and the *dharmakaya* is the transcendental aspect. Dharmakaya is inseparable from ultimate reality, because everything that we perceive has the nature of emptiness. Sambhogakaya represents the interconnectedness of all things, because the mental and physical are not totally independent of each other; everything that exists—good or bad, beautiful or ugly, sacred or profane—is part of the pattern of events and processes. Nirmanakaya is how we see everything that is presented to our senses as a manifestation of emptiness. Normally only three kayas are mentioned in Mahayana literature, but sometimes a fourth is included to illustrate the inseparability of these three aspects. This is called *svabhavivakaya*, which is not a fourth "body" so much as a unifying concept. It signifies the fact that we should not think of the physical, mental, and transcendental aspects of a Buddha's being as three separate entities, but as an inseparable whole that is interdependently coalescent. Atisha discusses this co-emergent quality in terms of emptiness and compassion:

> Between the dancing waves and the vast ocean,
> None has observed any separation or division.
> Similarly from the spontaneous coemergence of emptiness
> Arises compassion that touches beings and stirs the
>   heart.

When compassion arises, it does so from emptiness,
And when it ceases, it does so in emptiness, too, my son.[23]

The physical, mental, and transcendental are only distinguishable on the conceptual level of understanding. From the perspective of a Buddha's own being, there is no such separation. Just as water can be either liquid or ice, the three aspects of Buddha's being can manifest as identifiable qualities while remaining fundamentally indistinguishable from one another. It is therefore possible to understand the four kayas from both an objective and a subjective standpoint. When we understand them objectively, we are talking about a fully enlightened being that is separate from ourselves. We can also understand the four kayas from a transcendentally subjective perspective, which is quite different from the egoistically subjective one. The Mahamudra and Dzogchen teachings, for example, describe the aspects of a Buddha's being from this subjective position. In their teachings, the four kayas are understood in relation to ourselves. This lojong slogan is also advising us to apply the four kayas to our own experience, so in this way, too, it seems amenable to this subjective interpretation. By reminding ourselves of the three kayas, we can let go of the fixation that solidifies the mind. As Phadampa Sangye says:

Your notion of outer and inner derive from the mind
    within;
People of Tingri, let the solid ice melt into liquid.[24]

In this subjective interpretation, we understand the nirmanakaya aspect as the thoughts, emotions, and feelings that constantly take place in our own consciousness. We can connect the sambhogakaya aspect to our cognitive capacity—the heart of our consciousness, often called luminosity—and the dharmakaya aspect to the empty nature of the thoughts, emotions, and cognizance of consciousness that are all empty by nature. The svabhavikaya is the recognition that all three kayas are united as one reality. In relation to our meditative experiences, our thoughts are the nirmanakaya aspect. While thoughts normally run wild in a complete state of disarray in our meditation practice, we might occasionally observe one that has some clarity, some "inexplicable brilliance" as the text says. That is the sambhogakaya. However, even though that thought may be vividly present in the mind's eye, it has a very intangible and elusive quality that we simply can't hold on to. That non-graspability is the dharmakaya. These insights will enable us to remain in a state of equanimity, without becoming too aroused by our emotions.

We have to understand that our confusion doesn't just include negative emotions, but also positive ones, because even these are always tainted with some ulterior motive, expectation, or hidden agenda. We don't need to condemn ourselves for that, we just need to recognize that our emotional responses are always mixed. We develop equanimity by seeing that there is clarity in confusion. Confusion does not obscure reality, as we might tend to think, and reality is never far away, even amid our confusion. Ngotrup Gyaltsen, a great Tibetan meditation master, describes the unencumbered mind in these terms:

Discursive thoughts are like waves in the ocean.
Although they arise, their essence is empty.
How joyful, this birth of the unborn![25]

From the Mahayana point of view—especially from the Kagyu-Nyingma perspective—appearance and reality are inseparable. We tend to think that appearance is some kind of outer facade and reality is hidden behind that. We then imagine that this facade is full of distortions while the hidden reality is completely free of any impurities. Ultimate reality is often understood this way in the philosophical traditions of both East and West, but that is not the Buddhist understanding of the nature of existence. For a Buddhist, there can be no separation between appearance and reality, which is not to say that appearance and reality are the same, just that there is no possibility of separating them. If we have the perspective of absolute bodhichitta, we will realize that the reality of confusion is not perplexity, for confusion is only an appearance. The reality of confusion is emptiness. If we have this perspective, we won't get churned up by our negative emotions and latch on to them when they arise, because we'll understand that their reality is also emptiness. That's why emptiness is the best protection and why Shantideva can say:

> Wandering beings, thus, resemble dreams
> And also the banana tree, if you examine well.
> No difference is there, in their own true nature,
> Between the states of suffering and beyond all sorrow.[26]

Reminding ourselves of this puts us in touch with the purity of things, from the absolute point of view. On the relative level, conditioned existence is characterized by dissatisfaction, frustration, suffering, and pain, but from the absolute standpoint, there is an equalization (Tib. *snyoms pa*) of everything. Trying to develop some understanding of that is very helpful for utilizing adversity as part of the path.

The Special Skillful Means

We generally regard all adversity as disruptive and will do any-thing to avoid it. Yet we often misunderstand the circumstances of our lives and perceive some things to be harmful when noth-ing of the kind is actually happening. We also misinterpret cer-tain things in our lives to be beneficial, when in reality they are quite ruinous. For example, we may derive a great deal of enjoy-ment from the so-called pleasures that occur in the form of dis-tractions. We might be immediately drawn to the dubious activities of someone of bad character, or regard an event as wonderful when in reality it is going to have a devastating impact on our lives, such as a business opportunity, a financial windfall from an unexpected source, or anything else that bedazzles us. Padma Karpo encapsu-lates this point:

> You want to have a good life but always do the wrong
>   thing to get it
> And look for the causes of suffering to create a con-
>   tented life.
> You have become a slave to your impulses.[27]

We have also been deceived many times by circumstances and people. We may think we have met a knight in shining armor or a goddess in human form, but the knight turns out to be a char-latan and the goddess a witch. Such distractions put us in a hyp-notic state, and we invariably begin to act foolishly. It ends up causing us a great deal of pain and misery, and our lives are over-come by regret, self-denigration, self-loathing, and despair. If we don't perceive things properly, adversity has the potential to in-flict pain and suffering on us. Therefore, we have to find a way to deal with this predicament in our everyday lives by dealing with the special skill in means—remedial measures that are reserved for our actions in everyday life. There are two slogans involved with this method.

15 • *The four applications are the best method*

This particular adversity is called "bad conditions" (Tib. *kyen ngen pa*), the idea being that the bad conditions that arise are only a temporary occurrence—they just happen on the spot. What does linger and cause difficulty for us is not the situation itself but the emotional turmoil that results from our mental fixation on our suffering. It is really this grasping that we need to counteract. Painful situations will continue to arise in our lives, for the simple reason that negative conditions will always bring about unwanted experiences and situations, but they don't need to be the cause of major negative reactions in our minds if we are able to mentally free ourselves from them in the moment.

Lojong offers four very Buddhist practices for dealing with the suffering that comes from misinterpreting adversity and fixating on our misfortunes: (1) the accumulation of merit, (2) confession, (3) ritual offerings to evil spirits, and (4) ritual offerings to the Dharma protectors.

1. Accumulation of Merit

Despite the fact that Buddhism emphasizes the notion of merit, it has proven a very difficult concept for Westerners to grasp. People normally think of merit as some kind of accounting system or bank balance, where we either deposit or withdraw merit to create a situation of surplus or deficit. The accumulation of merit is not really like that, for it doesn't represent something we can own or lose so much as something that can really transform energy.

In Buddhism, the notion of merit refers to psycho-spiritual dispositional properties. We need to understand the importance of developing these properties if we want to enrich our lives and stop feeling so empty and vacuous. It is the accumulation of merit that determines the kind of human beings we will become. This doesn't only refer to the psychological dispositions that form our character traits but also to a form of spiritual competence that is hard to convey. Much of the difficulty in translating this term comes from the fact that we can't use theistic language to translate Buddhist concepts. This makes the loss of their spiritual component somewhat inevitable, because we reduce our translations to the secular ideas of the West. This is quite unfortunate, because Buddhist concepts such as "merit" have a very strong spiritual dimension. The whole concept of merit works something like this: great merit (Tib. *bsod nams chen pos*) enables us to avert obstacles and prevent adversity, a sufficient amount of merit enables us to overcome adversity, and very little merit (Tib. *bsod nams chung chung*) actually attracts adversity into our lives, just as having a weak body attracts illness. Merit is the cause of all the happiness we possess, whether in the form of material wealth, good fortune, or our positive qualities and attributes.

We don't "just happen" to have these things or attain them through luck, determination, or a few benevolent acts; we have acquired our good fortune through the merit we have earned in previous lives. As Padma Karpo tells us, "You obtain this body through merit, not through accident."[28] We accumulate merit by engaging in virtuous actions and cultivating wholesome mental states with a kind heart. Stocking up on merit ensures that our lives will become immune to negative phenomena and that positive energies are drawn our way. On the other hand, if we constantly view things from a negative point of view, even when something good has happened, we will deplete our merit and attract negativity into our lives by leaving ourselves open to all kinds of upheavals and disruptions.

In Tibetan Buddhism, we are instructed to adopt a two-pronged approach (Tib. *mchod sbyin*). *Chod* literally means "offering," and *sbyin* means "giving." We offer services to special beings, and we give ourselves over to the service of sentient creatures. We perform services for elevated beings like the Buddhas and bodhisattvas, making donations to Dharma centers, and commission offerings of thangkas, reliquaries, statues, and texts. We perform services for ordinary sentient beings by not neglecting our body, speech, and mind. We should not devote our lives to the service of great beings and neglect ordinary sentient beings like ourselves, but instead perform services for enlightened and deluded beings alike with acts of equal kindness, strength, and intensity. It is because of this approach that Aryadeva can say:

> The Tathagata said that the merit
> Gathered constantly through skillful means
> For a very long time is immeasurable
> Even for the omniscient.[29]

2. Confession

Confession (Tib. *bshags pa*) has a unique meaning in Buddhism. Instead of confessing to someone else, such as a lama or teacher, we acknowledge to ourselves whatever we feel ashamed about or that has been gnawing away in the back of our minds.

To understand the notion of confession, we need to have a general understanding of the way karma operates. We generate demerit when our past motivations have been tainted by thoughts of aggression, anger, egoism, jealousy, and resentment. When our physical actions spring from aggression, or we gossip with malice and rejoice at hearing about somebody else's difficulties, we create imprints that go underground and become latent karmic tendencies. When we fail to act in an aware and considerate fashion, these negative karmic imprints accumulate and fester, hidden from our consciousness until appropriate circumstances trigger them and they find their expression in the form of bad experiences.

Luckily, for us, the karmic causal nexus is not a mechanical, predetermined operation, but is instead quite malleable. We are not condemned to suffer its consequences. Buddhism doesn't entertain the notion of any kind of moral law. The reference to a "karmic law" is a Western concept that has been introduced into Buddhist thinking. The relationship between cause and effect is far too complex and indeterminate to be a "law." There is some kind of karmic causal nexus, but there is no such thing as a cosmic law, because cause and effect is all about human action. In previous centuries, Western thinkers used to speak about moral laws and natural laws in political and moral philosophy, but nobody seems to favor this interpretation anymore. Even in physics, people are speaking less and less about natural laws. Hinduism does promote the belief in a universal cosmic order, which for them is encapsulated in the notion of karma. However, if the cosmos were indeed orderly, behaving in compliance with it should be enough to prevent disruptions or unexpected events from occurring. But that is not what happens in fact.

We can, however, change or ameliorate our karma through confession. By acknowledging our negative actions and bringing the slightly volcanic activity of karma to the surface, we can avoid a much greater volcanic explosion later on. In order to discharge the latent karmic tendencies our negative actions have created, we must generate a genuine sense of regret when we confess. Whether we consciously acknowledge it or not, whenever we have done something terrible, the thought of it continues to nag at us in the form of guilt, making us "feel the pangs of conscience," as a Christian would say. This is an uncomfortable experience and has the potential to cause very negative experiences for us in the future. However, unlike guilt, which tends to fixate on the past and compel us to repeat the same mistakes, genuine regret is a highly effective preventative because it involves making a commitment not to behave that way again in the future. As Patrul Rinpoche explains:

> The power of regret comes from a feeling of remorse for all the negative actions you have done in the past. There can be no purification if you do not see your misdeeds as something wrong and confess them with fierce regret, without concealing anything.[30]

It is also important to bring a witness to the whole process of our acknowledgment of regret. For this we invoke the Buddhas and bodhisattvas, imagining that they are present, and confess to them, "I did this and that and I fully acknowledge my actions. I'm not trying to hide from it, and I'm not trying to deny I did it. I'm not trying to make any excuses for it." There are confession formulas that you can chant if you wish. We then imagine that the Buddhas and bodhisattvas receive our acknowledgment of regret and allow us to unburden ourselves of the karmic weight.

3. Ritual Offerings to Evil Spirits

According to Tibetan Buddhism, there are two different kinds of harmful beings or forces: those that cause disruption in our lives and those that we owe some kind of debt to. For example, traveling somewhere to meet someone very important, and falling ill halfway through the trip, despite being in perfect health before you departed, could be interpreted as the intervention of a negative force. There are also our "unresolved debts to others" (Tib. *lan chags*), which means any kind of debt that has not been paid. We have had dealings with so many people in the past, particularly if we believe in rebirth, that it is quite likely we have behaved, either deliberately or accidentally, in a way that incurred some debt to them.

While it isn't essential to believe in rebirth, evil spirits, or ghosts to practice lojong, we can't entirely discount the possibility that they do exist. That would be quite presumptuous. When one disaster after another occurs, it's possible to think that ghosts and evil spirits are trying to cause us harm or instigate some kind of disruption in our lives. Many people believe this quite strongly, and because Buddhism has something to offer everyone, it has a remedy for this kind of interference as well. The practice of ritual offerings appeases these negative forces we might have attracted into our lives. If you think nonhumans (Tib. *me ma yin*) might be trying to harm you because you are indebted to them in some way, you can give them "offering cakes" (Skt. *balingta*; Tib. *torma*).

Dharmaraksita informs us that ultimately it doesn't matter how we view appearances:

> Some may arise as enemies and demons, but regard
>   them not at all.
> Trample on attachment to self and aversion to others
>   without
> conceiving of them in any way. View memory and
>   perception like
> the wrathful Yamantaka.[31]

Even if evil spirits don't actually exist, if you perform this ritual as if you really did believe in them, it will still bring some psychological relief. Sometimes when people feel really depressed, vulnerable, or edgy, they fall back on an assumption that something nasty and otherworldly is hovering around them. The famous Tibetan yogi Milarepa says that if we are frightened, evil spirits will arise, regardless of whether they are real or imagined. There is a story about how one day Milarepa returned to his cave to find it filled with spirits. Initially frightened, he tried to subjugate them, demanding that they leave, but to no avail. Only when he generated bodhichitta and sent waves of compassion toward them did they vanish. In the song called "Red Rock Agate Mountain," he sang:

> Demon, if you were to stay here longer, that would be
>   fine with me.
> If you have friends, bring them along.
> We will talk of our differences.
> AH TSA MA! I feel compassion for this spirit.[32]

Etymologically, the word *torma* means "something that smashes or annihilates things." Thus, such offerings and rituals are intended to completely remove the negative forces that arise from unwholesome emotions, karmic traces, and dispositions, as well as inauspicious circumstances and situations. It is not necessary to make a proper ritual cake. You can offer anything or just imagine that you're making some form of restitution. There are also short ritual liturgies that you can recite. It is not the ritual that is important here, but the psychological process of saying, "Come in, have some cake, and stop bothering me." This is not an exorcism, where we are trying to wage a war with evil spirits or exorcise demons or something of that nature.[33] We shouldn't allow ourselves to become too superstitious, seeing invisible hands at work everywhere, but the truth is that we don't really know what does or doesn't exist. The whole point of the practice is to be open and expansive, even to what we might not understand. We make the following prayer and imagine it has taken effect, for the act of offering torma will reverse our tendency to be negative: "Whatever I owe any sentient being, either living or dead, I want to settle it now, for the last time. Whether I incurred these debts through deliberately manipulative acts, through an oversight, or through negligence, I want to settle them. I have no issue with you, no malice, no grudges, no problems with you whatsoever."

4. Ritual Offerings to the Dharma Protectors

The Dharma protectors (Skt. *dharmapalas;* Tib. *chos skyong*) are benign or enlightened beings, perhaps the Buddhist equivalent to angels, which protect us from adverse circumstances and situations.

We invoke their protection with torma offerings when things go wrong and when we want to enlist their assistance in averting a disaster. For example, there are times when things have become so difficult for us—perhaps we have become sick, are experiencing bankruptcy, or are faced with a personal tragedy—that we begin to lose our resolve to go on. The wisdom of making ritual offerings to the protectors is that it is an alternative strategy that gives us something to do against adversity when all else fails. There are many ways to understand evil spirits and Dharma protectors, even within Tibetan Buddhism itself. The great hermit-yogi Godrakpa (1170–1249) informs us:

> When there's no realization, these confused appearances and
> apparitions of demonic impediment are gods and
> ghosts.[34]

Machik Lapdron (1055–1149), an exceptional female teacher who made the practice of Chöd famous in Tibet, points out in her Chöd instructions that evil spirits can be seen as our psychological states on one level and external beings on another. As she explains in her *Complete Explanation*:

> That which is called devil is not some actual great big black thing that scares and petrifies whomever it sees. A devil is anything that obstructs the achievement of freedom. Therefore, even loving and affectionate friends become devils [with regard to] freedom. Most of all, there is no greater devil than this fixation to a self. So until this ego-fixation is cut off, all the devils wait with open mouths.

For that reason, you need to exert yourself with a skillful method to sever the devil of ego-fixation.[35]

This is also true of the Dharma protectors, who can be regarded as a reflection of our wisdom consciousness. While we can try to appease or supplicate them outwardly, it is more important that we understand them internally. Understanding things in this way doesn't mean we automatically discard their external manifestation, because the outer and the inner go together. It is only our dualistic and scientific ways of thinking that divide the two into separate domains. From a Buddhist perspective, the inner and the outer worlds are a seamless whole, without any hard and fast lines between what is really out there and what is in our own minds. We shouldn't necessarily regard these as the same, nor are they as different as we might assume.

16 • *Immediately join whatever you meet with meditation*

This slogan refers to the practice of transforming adverse circumstances and situations into the path of awakening. It is a reminder not to respond to things in a habitual way, but rather to respond with understanding, openness, and courage by maintaining a sense of awareness. We shouldn't think of meditation as something we only do if we're sitting on a cushion, but should treat everyday situations as meditations by focusing our mind on whatever arises. There's nothing we can't utilize for our own and others' benefit if we use both fortunate and unfortunate circumstances to train the mind. Godrakpa sings about joining experience with meditation in this verse:

A yogi is like a sword,
I sever instantly whatever thoughts arise,
happy to take the encounter as the path.[36]

If we merely follow our old habitual patterns whenever unfavorable circumstances arise, we'll inevitably make things more difficult for ourselves. The lojong masters say that when we are egoistic, selfish, arrogant, domineering, and manipulative, we may think we are in charge of our lives, but we are really fighting a losing battle. It is only by adopting a meditative response, by not allowing whatever has arisen on a particular occasion to distract or overwhelm us, that we can really empower ourselves and maintain presence of mind. It's so important to develop the qualities of fortitude, courage, and vigor to rise above whatever situation is at hand, even those situations that seem to be going our way and thus seem to negate any need to train our minds. We have to start seeing everything that arises in our lives as an opportunity to improve ourselves, rather than something that has robbed or seduced us away from that opportunity.

Conclusion

If we have the right lojong spirit, we'll always find a way to derive benefit from our experiences, no matter how difficult the situation, and transform everything into a source of merit. We have to feel confident that we can reverse our adverse circumstances and situations and step outside our constant self-obsessions. When we have concern for others and engage positively with the world, instead of remaining ensnared in our own solipsistic state, we'll start to do things that are worthy and admirable. Dwelling on our own experiences will never empower us. We are so habitually prone to negative ways of thinking and interpretation that we have to consciously and deliberately do something to reverse this tendency. The best way to transform adversity is to resist personalizing our experiences and scripting them into our own narratives. If we try instead to become more outwardly oriented and resist the tendency to get enmeshed in our own dramas, we'll not only avoid the enormous suffering and pain that attends adversity, we'll start to develop a meaningful engagement with our lives. This is not just a practical way of dealing with adversity; it is a way of using the Dharma as an antidote to our problems. Whatever we do in a non-Dharmic way can only be a temporary solution, because samsara can never be fixed. Trying to seek perfection in samsara—through political, social, economic, or technological means—will never work. The only real comfort and ease comes from taking refuge in the Dharma.

Maintaining the Practice for the Duration of Our Lives

The fourth point of the lojong practice is concerned with the constant reminders that we should concentrate on when we are alive and the things we should do at the time of death. We learn how to practice well and how to deal with the various situations of life properly through the use of five powers—five that we can utilize while we are alive and five that are important at the time of death. While the five powers are the same in each situation, their application is slightly different. Applying these five powers throughout our lives and at the time of our death is to utilize the essence of the lojong teachings, which itself is the "essence of the essence" of the Buddhist instructions.

17 • A summary of the essential instructions, train in the five powers

The pith instructions on this point present two aspects: what to practice while we are alive and what to practice at the time of death. The following five powers (Skt. *pancendriya;* Tib. *dbang po lnga*) represent the quintessential instructions to be followed throughout our lives, because they show us how to implement the vital instructions on the spot. This slogan encompasses both formal meditation and everyday conduct, and while there will never be a perfect match between our meditative experiences and everyday life before we attain enlightenment, we can aim to lessen the gap between them by following the methods outlined in the following five powers.

1. The Power of Aspiration

Whenever we do formal meditation practice or some activity that's beneficial, worthy, and constructive, it is important to begin by making an aspiration for the benefit of others as well as ourselves. According to the lojong pith instructions, it's extremely important to be clear about our future goals when we undertake any spiritual activity and not just begin our practices in a haphazard manner. The main goal of lojong is the generation of relative bodhichitta and the realization of absolute bodhichitta. If we begin spiritual and worldly projects by aspiring to generate the enlightened heart for the benefit of all beings, it will generate an enormous amount of positive energy. Patrul Rinpoche makes a clear distinction between worldly good actions and spiritual ones, based on the power of aspiration:

> No conditional good actions have a direction of their own,
> So make vast prayers of aspiration for the benefit of beings.[1]

This is sometimes is called "the propelling power," because it projects us into a better future state than what we might otherwise experience. If we harness our concentrative power and energy and imaginatively direct it into the future as the consummation of our goal, this attainment will be drawn toward us in the present. It's possible to generate a tremendous amount of positive energy by seizing our current mental state and converting it into a virtuous one. Just as an accumulation of negative mental energy can gain its own momentum and attract negative experiences, the creation of positive mental energy can generate an immense amount of concentration that has the power to magnetize and attract the fruition of our more distant goals. Following is an example of how to begin each spiritual and worldly activity:

"May what I'm about to do yield beneficial results. May it give me the power to be of real benefit to others. May it help me overcome my defilements and delusions. May it clear away the obstacles on the path. May it propel me to the future state of enlightenment."

We can apply this power to any commitments we might undertake. We may want to become a fully ordained or novice monk or nun, we may want to take the five precepts on a short retreat or undertake the uncommon preliminary practice—whatever the activity, the power of aspiration is about fully and sincerely committing ourselves so that the results will be beneficial for everyone. The power that is generated by this commitment is projected to the future realization of our goals. It is especially important in retreat situations to generate positive psychic energy by making these kinds of aspirations about the fruition of our efforts. Shantideva is very clear about the power of aspiration:

Aspiration is the root of every virtue,
Thus the Mighty One has said.
And aspiration's root in turn
Is constant meditation on the fruits of action.[2]

We can apply the power of aspiration to our daily lives by paying particular attention to our first thoughts in the morning and our last thoughts before sleeping. Our daily life is bracketed by these two moments, and they have an enormous impact on how we approach our waking hours. It's important to project positive thoughts into the future immediately upon waking instead of just getting out of bed and performing our daily routines like an automaton. We need to wake up feeling inspired by a fresh and enthusiastic attitude toward our day's activities. It's important to make plans for both our general goals and our more immediate goals and project positive aspirations into the day, such as, "I resolve to achieve the goals I've set for myself in this life, no matter what it takes." It's very important to learn how to relinquish yesterday's worries and plan our day with freshness and optimism, resolving to undertake our goals with the spirit of lojong. As Patrul Rinpoche advises:

When you wake up in the morning, do not suddenly jump out of bed like a cow or a sheep from its pen. While you are still in bed, relax your mind; turn within and examine it carefully.[3]

When we retire to bed, we shouldn't just drift off to sleep in an anxious and agitated state, but deliberately empty our minds as we review our day. We should ask ourselves whether we were able to fulfill the day's commitments and examine how well we maintained our lojong spirit. If we feel we lapsed into our deep-seated habitual patterns and lost the spirit of mind training, it's very important not to become too disheartened or judgmental toward ourselves, but rather vow to pay closer attention to our mental states tomorrow. If we reaffirm our commitment while we drift into unconsciousness, we will experience a more restful sleep, because our positive mind-set will prevent our worries and anxieties from resurfacing in the form of dreams or nightmares.

The psychic energy that we invest in our activities by projecting our positive determination into the future has a tremendous influence on the quality and direction of our lives, making every day seem new, fresh, and full of potential. It isn't true that every day is a repeat of the preceding one; it just seems that way if we lack initiative and insight. Allowing negative thoughts to proliferate and overwhelm us will make every day seem like a repetition of the last. But if we seize the moment to focus our energy in a positive direction, we'll transform our lives into a spiritual journey of significance.

2. The Power of Habituation

This power necessarily follows from the previous one if we truly want to bring things to fruition, because even when we successfully generate and project positive psychic energy into the future, there are often obstacles in the way. These obstacles are not caused by any particular character flaw on our part but are simply the result of our being creatures of habit. Human beings are distinguished by their tendency to repeat whatever appeases their needs and anxieties until it becomes an entrenched pattern of behavior. Anything we do repeatedly will create imprints in our consciousness that shape our mental outlook. Many of our habitual tendencies are so self-defeating and unconstructive that the task of breaking them can be quite onerous. For example, we may invite misery into our relationships or bring tremendous grief to ourselves by indulging in substance abuse, yet we don't seem able to learn from our mistakes. This process of habituation goes on continually, and these habits are almost always negative because their formation is taking place unconsciously. Failure to restrain and manage this process ensures that our self-obsessions will keep us mired in conditioned existence ad infinitum. As the Kadampa master Chokyi Gyaltsen (1121–89) advises:

> How long have you been wandering in cyclic existence in general and in the three lower realms in particular? This is brought about by cherishing your self and desiring its happiness.[4]

Sometimes habits such as substance abuse can be eliminated with a focused approach, but most habits are only eliminated over time. From a Buddhist standpoint, we are born with these habits. Our only option is to acknowledge their strength and recognize that we have to wean ourselves from their negative influence through more positive orientations. The power of habituation is also known as "the power of familiarity," because we must familiarize ourselves with new ways of behaving. As Shantideva says:

> There's nothing that does not grow light
> Through habit and familiarity.
> Putting up with little cares
> I'll train myself to bear with great adversity.[5]

Even though we don't have the necessary resources to defeat our negative habits with one stroke, we can still learn how to skillfully transform ourselves over time, turning our aggressive habitual moods into love and compassion for others.

Mind training is all about utilizing the modus operandi of consciousness to create positive imprints in the mind. Instead of launching a frontal attack on our habits, we approach them indirectly by putting our energy into activities that act as an antidote. By gradually introducing these new activities and increasing their frequency over time, we will, by extension, begin to erode our negative mental tendencies. Because old habits are formed from repetition, repeatedly countering them in this manner will eventually overpower them. This is much better than attempting to introduce too many changes at the beginning, for that can frustrate our efforts, causing us to resume the old habits. Thus, it is important to start with something small and manageable and gradually extend our capacity. We shouldn't be discouraged by any seeming inability to effect change, for that would be capitulating to old habits and only increase our self-loathing, cynicism, and apathy. If we treat ourselves gently, we'll profit more from our positive actions and will gradually garner sufficient strength to mount a real challenge to our old habits. Chandrakirti elegantly observes:

As when a sturdy potter plies his wheel
And labors long and hard to get it turning well,
It later spins without his further work,
And pots are seen to be produced thereon.[6]

We free ourselves from the tendency to indulge in negativity when we use our positive attitudes and feelings to establish new patterns of behavior. If we look at how we respond to situations—the kinds of words we use, our tone of voice, our gaze, how we carry ourselves, how we eat, and so forth—we'll gradually bring about significant changes. A true change in our habit patterns will produce a change in our character traits, and changing our character traits will result in our becoming a different person.

We may not always feel good about our progress, because karmic imprints will continually trigger periods of difficulty or rekindle old issues that we'd thought were resolved. These karmic delusions and obscurations are etched so deeply within our consciousness that it's unrealistic to think that any practice will eradicate them completely. Spiritual practice doesn't work that way. But if we keep chipping away at them, our delusions will gradually decrease. Sudden interruptions and neurotic explosions may still occur, but they'll be increasingly less potent and the ride less bumpy and bruising as we move ahead. Jamgön Kongtrül himself says:

> Whatever occupation or activity you are engaged in—virtuous, nonvirtuous, or indeterminate—maintain mindfulness and awareness strictly and train again and again in keeping the two aspects of bodhichitta ever in mind.[7]

The importance of augmenting our spiritual practices with the power of habituation can't be underestimated, for our commitments will remain shallow and superficial if we just perform them with our usual states of mind. From the beginning, we have to aim high with our practices. No matter how difficult or complicated the task, it becomes easier through the power of habituation. If we aren't prepared to aim high, by deepening our practice and habituating our minds, we'll only dabble in spiritual transformation, manufacturing all kinds of unrealistic expectations and detrimental states of mind. We must apply this power throughout the course of our lives so that we are perpetually open to learning new ways of doing things. In that way, the power of habituation will help to bring us closer to our goal by planting virtuous seeds in our minds. And this leads us into the next power.

3. The Power of Planting White Seeds

It's necessary to reorient our minds to a more positive outlook if we are going to effect any real change in our mental habits. When we're ill, our body will manufacture healthy cells to counteract the diseased cells, thereby bringing about a remission. Our delusions will also be rescinded if we plant the positive seeds of awareness, thoughtfulness, conscientiousness, caring, fortitude, courage, vigor, and energy. There are black seeds and there are white seeds, or negative imprints and positive imprints, in this schema. By constantly planting black seeds, negatively judging whatever we see, hear, smell, taste, or touch, we will put a negative slant on our emotions, which will, in turn, leave a lasting residue in our minds. As *The Treasury of Precious Qualities* states:

> When the eagle soars up, high above the earth,
> Its shadow for the while is nowhere to be seen;
> Yet bird and shadow still are linked. So too our actions:
> When conditions come together, their effects are clearly
>   seen.[8]

We plant white seeds by observing our thoughts and emotions, as well as paying attention to how we speak and use our bodies, continually asking ourselves if the three gates of our body, speech, and thoughts are beneficial to others. Without them, we would have no way of interacting with other beings or the world. Each gate leaves karmic imprints in our unconscious, habituating us physically, verbally, and mentally. It's not enough to modify our minds if we wish to effect holistic change; we need to modify our speech and physical behavior as well. Atisha verifies this in his *Lamp for the Path to Enlightenment:*

> I shall purify all my bodily
> And my verbal forms of activity.
> My mental activities, too, I shall purify
> And do nothing that is non-virtuous.[9]

Every thought, word, and deed leaves lingering imprints entrenched in our mental continuum. For example, if someone plants the seed of suspicion in our minds about a friend, that suspicion may grow, whether we want it to or not and despite our having no real proof of the accusation. On the other hand, if our words are positive, other people may become heartened, feel appreciated, and even overjoyed. Many words spoken with kindness have a wonderful effect on those around us, and we ourselves become the major beneficiaries of our positive communication. It's so important to make a concerted effort to think kind thoughts instead of always focusing on the negative. Even when someone has done something good, we often manage to find fault with it. This attitude is the source of our misery, because it poisons our outlook. Chandrakirti points out:

> Meager in compassion and with harsh and ruthless
>   minds,
> Beings seek their self-regarding gain;
> And yet the riches they pursue, and the healing of
>   their ills,
> Are fruits of generosity alone.[10]

We shouldn't think that everything we do has to make a big impact or attract attention. As the word *seed* implies, it is important at first to focus and persevere with smaller actions. When we practice in this way over a long period, the self-doubt connected with our practice will diminish, for every time we do sitting meditation and generate loving-kindness toward somebody, we plant virtuous seeds in our mental continuum. In the song called "Milarepa and the Dying Sheep," Milarepa says:

When you forsake the "big" estate
And till your own small land [of self],
You must obey the rules of farming.
Should you expect big harvests quickly,
You will fall into the world once more.[11]

Nothing goes to waste when we plant positive seeds with even the smallest positive intention. In this way it is important to start paying attention to our every action instead of indulging in negative self-talk. Whether something is small or large is not the issue, it's about what we're trying to cultivate and whether it takes root in our mental continuum or not. Practices such as generosity, patience, vigor, meditation, or loving-kindness have to take root in our mind streams to be effective. All virtuous qualities develop from small beginnings, but once they take root, we can never lapse or backslide. Patrul Rinpoche again illustrates this point:

Do not take lightly small good deeds,
Believing they can hardly help:
For drops of water one by one
In time can fill a giant pot.[12]

Planting white seeds will not only free us from the negative habits that invite misery and pain but also attract the goodwill of others. If our physical gestures, posture, and demeanor are not aggressive and our speech pleasant and encouraging to others, then others will respond to us in kind. Even when we feel something positive about someone, we are often withholding and aloof. The more negativity we allow ourselves, the more we'll feel distant and disconnected, but by planting white seeds, the cold separations that define the negative mind will gradually melt through the warmth of love, compassion, and joy.

Until we attain enlightenment, our efforts to evolve should never cease. It's important not to dismiss our positive and negative attitudes as "just thoughts" and fail to exercise vigilance in cultivating white seeds.[13] These thoughts are the product of deepseated habitual tendencies, and every time our minds are given over to their influence, we encourage destructive tendencies and negative mental habits. We shouldn't limit ourselves by only thinking positively for a short period of time. Positive thinking can also take root in our mental continuum and become entrenched habits of mind. The point of this third power is that the powers are dependent on one another. The power of aspiration is aided by the power of habituation, which will only progress properly if its supported by the power of planting white seeds.

4. The Power of Exposure

Our tendency to hide our more undesirable qualities or embarrassing behaviors requires a more candid appraisal. Trying to ignore our pain will not make it go away, but will only bury it in the recesses of our consciousness, where it will fester and grow in unpredictable ways. *The Sutra of the Wise and Foolish* says:

> Do not take lightly small misdeeds,
> Believing they can do no harm:
> Even a tiny spark of fire
> Can set alight a mountain of hay.[14]

These denials cause us to distort reality and project our fantasies onto the phenomenal world. Our mental projections are often so compelling that we allow ourselves to be completely seduced, convincing ourselves that something is true, when there is no real ground beneath our perceptions. By fixating on all kinds of fanciful notions, even when deep down we know they're not true, we fall victim to painful experiences over and over again.

If there's no encouragement to reflect on our situation, we tend to assume that meaningful acts are harmful to us and harmful acts are worthwhile, causing us to pursue situations that constantly undermine us instead of bringing us the happiness we're asking for. In order to penetrate the layers of self-deception we've created around ourselves, we need to undertake regular self-reflection, or we'll never be free from negative mental states and emotions. A Kadampa maxim relating to this point says that we must carry a torch powerful enough to illuminate our own depths. The Mahayana teachings refer to our self-deceptions as "thick veils," as if we're literally wearing a shroud that obscures and distorts our vision. It is our responsibility to penetrate the depths of our own self-deceptions, for no one else can completely identify what we need to expose in order to liberate ourselves.

The power of exposure will reveal the false reality we have constructed for ourselves. This is called "exposing false reasoning" (Tib. *sun 'jinpa*) in Tibetan, a phrase that is often used in the context of Buddhist logic. Fantasies appear real to us because of the twisted logic we use to convince ourselves that our illusions are real. The power of exposure is the ability to break down our experiences and review them for what they are, so that we can gradually curtail perverse reasoning and gain insight into our mental states. Shantideva stresses the importance of exposing our unsavory impulses in this verse:

> For this is how so many times
> You have betrayed me, and how long I've suffered!
> Now my memory is full of rancor;
> I will crush your selfish schemes![15]

If we can recognize when we are becoming overexcited or agitated and then relax our fixation, it will become possible to expose our self-deceptions. We also create enormous problems in our lives by clinging to what has upset us and going over and over our negative responses until we become overwhelmed and dysfunctional. Sentient creatures have countless lifetimes, and this has an enormous impact on who we are and how we view the world. It isn't only psychotherapists who acknowledge this fact; Buddhism also accepts that the kind of person we are and how we think and behave is a product of our past. This makes it very difficult for us to know how we are thinking or feeling at any given moment, yet we still assume our thoughts, feelings, and experiences are reliable indicators of what's going on in our lives. Phadampa Sangye strongly advises us to develop greater honesty through self-examination:

> You say such clever things to people, but don't apply
>   them to yourself;
> People of Tingri, the faults within you are the ones to
>   be exposed.[16]

Trying to resolve issues through the use of violence, or thinking we have the right to be angry at all, are examples of the
twisted logic we bring to our lives. We distort the truth as a
defense strategy or protective shield, despite the fact that these
distortions don't offer any real protection to the integrity of our
egos. It's important that we take an honest look at the harmful-
ness of these strategies. Until we are convinced that there is no
benefit in externalizing negative emotions, we'll never embark on
a genuinely spiritual path. We are deceiving ourselves if we imagine that directing anger, resentment, or hostility toward others is
a legitimate method of self-defense; such a premise only arises
from the confusion caused by our discursive thinking. This isn't
a good way of approaching our own self-interest, because we're
the ones who are most harmed by these reactions. We may have
lingering doubts about being able to survive without selfishness,
thinking that people will take advantage of our weakness if we let
our defenses down. This is another example of deluded thinking. There is no evidence that selfishness is a legitimate form of
self-protection or advancement, while there is ample reason to
think that selfishness turns us into our own worst enemies, di-
minishing us as individuals as well as causing pain and suffering
in our lives. That's why it's so important to look into the hidden
recesses of our minds and to be clear about our motivations. As
Atisha points out:

> The best teacher is one who attacks your hidden faults;
> The best instruction is one aimed squarely at those hid-
>   den faults.[17]

This is another gradual process of seeing through the self-
deceptions we have created and hung on to for so long. Rather

than trying to rid ourselves of our self-deceptions all at once, we have to see that they wreak terrible havoc on our own being as well as causing disruption to the lives of others. While we can't overcome these conflicting emotions completely, we can lessen their impact and gradually diminish their power by recognizing them when they arise. We have to invest time and energy into penetrating the thick veils we have created around ourselves, and expose the whole situation for the sham it is. Simply reading that we live in a world of make-believe will never really change anything; we need firsthand experience to be convinced of the negative effects of our conflicting emotions and the liberating effects of overcoming them.

5. The Power of Dedication

Just as we use skillful methods for transforming adverse circumstances into the path of enlightenment, we can use skillful mental attitudes to expand a good situation into an even better one. If we include the thought of others in any joyful or positive experience, instead of selfishly consuming it, the benefits of that experience will be amplified. Merit has the capacity to magnetize and attract all kinds of positive situations into our lives. The power of dedication creates merit along with the possibility of positively impacting others. Cultivating this magnanimous attitude in our everyday lives will ensure that what we do for others and ourselves will always bear fruit. Whether it is meditation, a spiritual activity, or just something we feel really good about, we should seal it with a dedication. This is why so many great masters have echoed the sentiments expressed by Atisha in *Jewel Rosary of Bodhisattvas:*

Whatever virtues are collected in the three times,
Dedicate them for the unsurpassable great awakening.[18]

Since the purpose of lojong practice is the cultivation of bodhichitta, particularly relative bodhichitta, we dedicate the merit
of our good action to others so that they will realize relative bodhichitta in their mindstreams by saying the following formula:

"May whatever I have done, no matter how small, have a rip-
ple effect and influence the lives of other beings in a positive way
so that they can develop bodhichitta in their mind streams and
become freed of resentment, bitterness, hostility, and hatred. May
they find comfort and ease through the practices of love, compassion, joy, and equanimity."

The power of dedication works in quite subtle ways. In the usual
Mahayana understanding of merit, we start to exhaust our positive
karma at the point where we enjoy the fruits of our actions. As
Shantideva proclaims, "All other virtues, like the plantain tree, produce their fruit, but then their force is spent."[19] The merit that we
enjoy is in direct correspondence to the action we have performed
through our body, speech, and mind. Once we consume the fruit
of our actions, it is exhausted, but if we develop this joyful way of
sharing that fruit with others, we will continually re-create and re-
plenish that merit, which is why Patrul Rinpoche cautions us:

Never forget to perform the dedication at the end of any
meritorious act, great or small. Any source of merit not
dedicated in this way will bear fruit only once and will
then be exhausted. But whatever is dedicated to ultimate
enlightenment will never be exhausted, even after bearing
fruit a hundred times. Instead, it will increase and grow
until perfect Buddhahood is attained.[20]

By projecting the positive aspiration that others may share our merit into the future, we build up a psychic momentum that allows whatever we wish for to be drawn closer to us, just as we did with the power of aspiration.[21] The *Treasury of Precious Qualities* describes the magnetizing aspect of merit in the following terms:

This kind of dedication acts like an alchemical process, transmuting base metal into gold. With such an aspiration, our merit will convey us to enlightenment. This is an extraordinary teaching, expressive of the skillful means of the enlightened ones, and is unknown outside the Buddhadharma.[22]

Each of these five powers is used for specific purposes. If we think we lack something, we make use of the power of aspiration to develop it. If we wish to stabilize the fluctuations that result from our emotional states, we try to apply the power of habituation. If we notice that there are certain negativities we need to abandon or overcome, we try to make use of the power of exposure. We can utilize the power of dedication in relation to the other four powers so that every time we are able to exercise any one of the powers, we dedicate it for the benefit of everyone. If we apply these five powers in our meditation and our daily lives, virtuous seeds will take root and germinate.

18 • The Mahayana instructions on how to die are the five powers

Death is certain; it's only how and when that are uncertain. We can die peacefully or horribly, suddenly or slowly, but there's no way of knowing which of these will occur or when. That death will eventually overwhelm us when we face old age, ill health, or disruptive circumstance is not the issue, it's the manner in which we die that concerns us. Just as the whole purpose of life is to live well, it's important to depart this life in the proper spirit. If we've practiced mind training and the five powers during our lives, we'll be more prepared to face our demise when the time comes. Even if we haven't practiced these contemplations, it's never too late to introduce the five powers to support our dying process, for they enhance the effectiveness of everything we do and will therefore facilitate a more easeful death. If we haven't lived well, or as well as we would've liked, we can still have a good death if we approach it properly.

If we're fortunate, we'll have all our sensibilities and mental faculties intact and recognize that the time of death has arrived. When the signs are all there that death can no longer be averted, we shouldn't indulge in self-deception and fixate on false hopes that we'll somehow be revived. At this point it's extremely important that we maintain a very clear mind and prepare ourselves for death. We use the same five powers as before, but in a slightly different manner.

1. The Power of Planting White Seeds

This power relates to overcoming our tendency to indulge in feelings of self-reproach and remorse at the time of death, hanging on to resentments toward others and ourselves and thinking, "I wish I'd done this, I wish I hadn't done that." We need to learn to forgive ourselves and others and turn our minds toward the generation of love and compassion. This power also relates to attachment to loved ones and worries about unfinished business, such as organizing our estate and drawing up a will to dispose of our wealth and possessions. We should try to be very clear ahead of time about how our property and possessions are to be divided so that when it is time for us to depart, we can let go more easily. Our parting has to be a positive one, instead of an occasion for fear and despair. We need to plant white seeds, as well as meditate whenever possible, thereby resolving and reducing the potential for any anxiety, fear, anger, or resentment that might disturb our minds. It's very important to depart this world without longings or attachments. Phadampa Sangye is very clear about this point:

The very thing you feel attached to, let go of it, whatever—
People of Tingri, there isn't anything you need.[23]

Setting things in order and relinquishing our attachments and resentments plant white seeds in our mental continuum and help us at the time of death, bearing in mind that the results of our positive and negative actions follow us into the next life even though their effects might not be immediately evident. We should pray to ourselves:

"Through the power of the white seeds I have accumulated in the past, may I never forget to train in the cultivation of bodhichitta in all future lives."

The ability to let go is what it means to "plant virtuous seeds" in the context of death. We must learn to say farewell to the living and to all our possessions and assets. A portion of our assets should be donated to spiritual and religious activities. In order to increase our feelings of connection to other beings, we should in addition offer to the Buddhas, bodhisattvas, and hosts of enlightened beings our virtuous and beneficial thoughts and actions, and whatever merit we've accumulated from these. We should maintain an altar at our bedside, on which are placed symbolic representations of the things we'd like to offer as a farewell gift to the enlightened ones. Shantideva shows us the importance of such activities here:

> In fear that merit might be all consumed,
> We should at once cast far away
> Our mind's attachments:
> Tinder for the fiery flames of hate.[24]

2. The Power of Dedication

It's important to make certain aspirations while we're dying, without feeling too much anxiety, fear, or trepidation. Whenever we finish our tonglen or mind training practices during meditation on our sickbed, we dedicate the merit and project our virtuous actions and positive karma into future rebirths. If you don't believe in rebirth, you can dedicate your merit to the dying process itself. This is a very powerful method for steering ourselves in a positive spiritual direction. We make the following aspiration:

"May my death be a good one, based on the worthy and beneficial actions I performed during my life. May I dwell in a state of peace and contentment, never parting from that state during death, the intermediate state, and all future lives."

We regret anything hurtful, upsetting, or damaging that we've done to others and dedicate anything compassionate, worthy, or beneficial to a death free from suffering and pain. We also aspire to a rebirth free from emotional conflicts, a state conducive to the development of bodhichitta that will exist for the benefit of all. Aspiring to encounter wise and loving spiritual friends as a source of inspiration is also important, as is the wish to receive the blessings of the Buddha, Dharma, and Sangha in all future lives. Atisha encapsulates this power in the verse:

> Whatever virtues you gather through the three times,
> Dedicate them toward the unexcelled great awakening.
> Disperse your merit to all sentient beings,
> And utter the peerless aspiration prayers
> Of the seven limbs at all times.[25]

3. The Power of Exposure

The time of death is the time to make amends; it's not the time to hang on to old resentments. If there are people toward whom we still feel angry or resentful, this is the time to forgive them, make a proper and honest assessment of our hidden shortcomings, and expose these to ourselves. Gaining self-knowledge at the end of our lives is an important part of dying in a meaningful way. Even if we see qualities or characteristics we dislike, just acknowledging these limitations goes a long way toward overcoming their negativity. That acknowledgment itself has a redemptive quality and will have a purifying effect on our mental continuum. We need to recognize that our deluded states originate in our egoistic self-obsession and take this opportunity to relinquish our self-centered attitudes. We make the following prayer whenever we can:

"I've been hanging on to these obstacles for so long without any of them serving any purpose. They've only made my life and the lives of others more difficult. Today I'm letting go of all of them. May I be forever free of egoistic self-obsession and its attendant suffering and pain."

The aspect of regret is very important here, because regret includes the determination not to repeat an action in the future. When we examine ourselves, we may come to see that we overreacted in certain situations, conveniently blaming someone for something we now realize was our own fault. It's never too late to acknowledge our own shortcomings and mistakes. Patrul Rinpoche writes:

> The power of regret comes from feelings of remorse for all the negative actions you have done in the past. There can be no purification if you do not see your misdeeds as something wrong and confess them with fierce regret, without concealing anything.[26]

It's important to rejoice in this decision to let go of our grievances, acknowledge our shortcomings, and relieve ourselves of this burden. Feeling joy and relief is a vital part of the power of exposure. These acknowledgments should also be applied to all the unresolved issues in our lives. If there is any way to amend, restore, or heal some rift, this is the time to do it. The potency of dying with a clear mind has such value that we ought to do everything in our power to free our minds by resolving the issues and misunderstandings that have arisen during the course of our lives. Interestingly enough, even if we've experienced real difficulty letting go of our issues while living, we'll find it easier to forgive and make amends if we try to let go when the decisive moment arrives.

4. The Power of Aspiration

We apply the fourth power in order to relieve the pain and discomfort of our physical demise at the instant of death and during the intermediate state between this incarnation and the next. Instead of wallowing in our misery and fear of dying and becoming angry and frustrated at our pain, we should send out loving-kindness to everyone and should practice the four infinities, sometimes translated as the four immeasurables, of love, compassion, joy, and equanimity. We send that positive energy in all directions, feeling that we have only bodhichitta in our hearts, and make the aspiration that this will benefit all beings. If we can eliminate the unwanted intrusions of negative thoughts and resentments and resolve not to carry any extra baggage or unresolved issues, we'll be able to concentrate solely on bodhichitta. We project the thought of bodhichitta into the depths of our being while making the following aspiration:

"May I never be separated from the four infinities and the other wholesome qualities that will enable me to be a source of comfort and ease to everyone who encounters me in the future. May I never again be parted from these altruistic thoughts."

These aspirations will alleviate the tremendous mental anguish and torment we inflict upon ourselves and will help to transform our minds on the spiritual path. We should model our thoughts after the following words of Shantideva:

The pain and sorrows of all wandering beings—
May they ripen wholly on myself.
And may the virtuous company of bodhisattvas
Bring about the happiness of beings.[27]

5. The Power of Habituation

Whether we have a few weeks, a few days, or only a few hours left till the moment of death, there's still time to rehabituate our minds by looking forward rather than dwelling on the past. We should forget the kind of person we were and use our remaining time to steer our minds in a more positive direction by trying to familiarize ourselves with how to have a peaceful and meaningful death. Drukpa Kunley, a crazy Tibetan yogi of the Drukpa Kagyu order who lived in Bhutan for many years, is quite specific about the importance of honesty in our spiritual practices:

> Although I am unable to order my behavior
> In harmony with the regimen of the quarters of the day,
> I vow to avoid a hypocritical front and self-deception—
> Keep this vow in your hearts, my friends![28]

We prepare ourselves for the after-death experience because the attitude we have when we die will impact whatever takes place subsequent to that. We try to remain in a positive frame of mind by employing familiar lojong techniques to bring our minds clearly into the present moment and resist the temptation to indulge in our suffering. Any physical pain should be viewed as an opportunity to generate the following type of positive thoughts:

"May the pain I'm experiencing now alleviate my negative karmic inheritance. May other sentient beings be spared from experiencing pain as a result of my own endurance of it."

This thought will help to recondition the mind and keep it from reeling off in the wrong direction. We can also practice the meditation techniques we know to reduce our physical pain and mental anguish. It's also quite important to sit up and meditate whenever we can physically manage it. If possible, when we sense we could die at any moment, we should adopt the meditation posture of Vairocana, so that we are sitting upright with our spine in alignment and our hands in our lap, the right hand resting on the left hand with the thumbs touching. If that isn't possible, we can adopt the posture Buddha took at the time of his parinirvana in Kushinagar, called the "lying-down lion posture," which entails lying on our left side with our left hand underneath our head and our right hand resting on our hip.

When we think that the actual moment of death has arrived, we practice tonglen. We give away all our happiness and joy as we breathe out and take on all the suffering and pain of others as we breathe in. Imagining all the while that this is alleviating the suffering of others, we continuously contemplate love and compassion as we die, and pray that we'll take this wholesome mental state into our next rebirth.

Conclusion

We apply the five powers during life and at the time of death as a skillful means for cultivating the mind's inherent force and capability. When our mind is focused, all of its power and energy can be concentrated and projected forward with a clear intention. The power of aspiration gives that activity a positive direction whenever we begin something. The powers of habituation, planting white seeds, and exposure help us make the most of our opportunities for spiritual transformation. When we complete the activity, we dedicate the merit we have accumulated, praying that it will bear positive fruit. Instead of indulging in conflicting emotions and negative attitudes at the time of death, all five powers can be used to approach it with a positive attitude. The main focus of these pith instructions involves making the most of our time while we are alive. Life is short and there are so many demands on us, so it's important to make the most of our opportunities while we can. Godrakpa, the hermit of Go Cliffs, echoes this sentiment:

In degenerate times there's no serenity.
Seeing there's no time to stay long,
I put aside the words and practiced the meaning.

I could die now and have no regrets.[29]

Measuring the Success of Mind Training

We may want to assess our mind training practice from time to time in order to evaluate our progress. The four slogans contained in this point are dedicated to measuring our progress on the path by establishing whether our minds are becoming more other-centered or whether they are simply mired in more subtle habitual perceptions of the world. We need a balanced approach to this lojong point, because an obsessive concern over our progress is just another form of fixation, while failing to attend to it at all is equally detrimental. Committing these sayings to memory will make them a self-regulatory aspect of our practice. Each of these slogans is a pithy, succinct, often enigmatic saying that reveals its depths through repeated contemplation. They are known as the four methods of appraisal for evaluating our ability to exchange self for others on the lojong path.

19 • All Dharma has a single purpose

The word *Dharma* (Tib. *chos*) does not literally mean "teachings," but it has come to be synonymous with the Buddhist teachings themselves. This is because the Buddhist teachings deal with "knowable things," and the full Tibetan expression for the word *Dharma* is *shes bya chos,* where *chos* means "phenomena" and *shes bya* means "knowable." The Buddhist canon describes knowable things in the context of physical and mental phenomena and also in the context of confused and enlightened states of being. The reason for this is that the whole soteriological thrust of the Buddha's message is that only through understanding knowable things can we come to understand the key aspects of our existence. Questions such as "What are ignorance and wisdom?" "What does it mean to be in the confused state of samsara?" and "What does it mean to attain liberation from that samsaric state?" are all rendered comprehensible through an examination of knowable phenomena. In other words, knowledge of conditioned existence is only gained from insight into knowable things.

The Dharma is very vast, even if we are only referring to the sheer volume of the teachings. It's not like the Bible or the Koran or the Old Testament, which are able to be contained in one volume. The Buddhist teachings are so extensive and diverse that we might easily assume that its various numerous streams have different purposes, leading to dissimilar goals. However, this simply isn't true; all of the Buddhist teachings have an equivalent purpose and intent, leading to exactly the same quality of liberation from the same type of imprisonment.

The goal of all the Buddhist teachings is to overcome our state of ignorance. Our delusions obstruct our vision so that we draw all kinds of spurious conclusions from our experiences and cause ourselves immeasurable suffering. The main component of our delusory mental states is our egoistic preoccupation. The more we fixate on our experiences from that perspective, the more unmanageable our delusory mental states become. The more depressed our mood, the more we indulge in all kinds of projections onto other people, convincing ourselves that nobody really cares about us. Our self-obsession fans our negative emotions and compels us to obsess over our inner turmoil until we're incapable of seeing anything clearly. Dharmaraksita explains:

> Since your ego is your enemy, against whom shall you
> fight?
> Since your ego itself is the protector, whom shall you
> protect?
> It is the very witness of all you have done and left
> undone.
> When you have tamed your ego, you shall be liberated.[1]

All the Buddhist schools agree that the source of our ignorance comes from our conviction that there is a self-sufficient, discrete self and a substantial, immutable other. The conviction in a self comes from thinking we possess some kind of psychic substance, and the conviction in phenomena comes from thinking things have inherent existence. According to all Buddhist teachings without exception, these mistaken beliefs cause us to wander aimlessly in a distorted and improbable world. The single purpose of this slogan is therefore to reduce our delusory mental states through meditation and realize selflessness. Buddhist meditation is not just a psychological mechanism for producing certain psychic states, but a way to transcend our egoistic preoccupations. The Tibetan hermit Godrakpa sings of this transcendence of ego:

> In the darkness of illness and suffering
> I lost the path leading to liberation,
> But was guided on the path by the sun

Of the removal of impediments.
Self-interest was lost, but I've no regrets.[2]

In classical Buddhist literature, this notion of selflessness is traditionally demonstrated by the example of a chariot. A chariot is made of wood, shafts, spokes, metal rims, reins, a seat, and so on. When all the parts are put together, we have a chariot, but when all the parts are strewn about in separate locations, no such chariot can be found, proving that neither the parts nor the whole can be understood to inherently exist as something called chariot. Chandrakirti outlines this argument:

> Now if the chariot consisted of the mere collection of
>   its parts,
> The scattered fragments likewise would comprise the
>   chariot.
> But if there is no owner of the parts, there are no "parts,"
> And neither can the shape, or simple pattern, constitute it.[3]

Using this analogy, the early Buddhist teachings enumerated five "psycho-physical constituents" (Skt. *skandhas*; Tib. *phung po*) that constitute a person. These are physical form, psychic propensities, feeling, cognition, and consciousness. When all of these parts come together, we have the concept of a self, but just like the chariot, which is only a cohesive entity when all the pieces are put together in a specific formation, no "self" can be found independent of its constituent parts. Through analysis, we gradually understand there is no such thing as a self-sufficient, discrete, and immutable self. In fact, that belief in such an entity is the wellspring of ignorance. As Rupert Gethin, from the University of Bristol, elucidates in *The Foundations of Buddhism*:

The occurrence of physical and mental events is not just arbitrary or random; on the contrary there is a deep and real relationship of causal connectedness between events or phenomena. And it is the concern with the nature of this causal connectedness that lies at the heart of Buddhist philosophy and which is seen as validating all Buddhist practice.[4]

In Mahayana literature, the selflessness of persons is extended to encompass the selflessness of phenomena. We learn to deepen our understanding of selflessness through an understanding of dependent arising, which says that we can form the concept of a self only if there is the concept of an "other," for self and other are mutually defining and contingent. A discrete, autonomous entity that is unconnected to anything other than itself is completely untenable and invalidates any claim external phenomena may make toward the status of inherently existing entities. The selflessness of phenomena is coterminous with emptiness, which insight, for the Mahayana teachings, is the ultimate antidote to ignorance. Patrul Rinpoche illustrates this point with the following story from the Kadampa tradition:

> Drom Tonpa once asked Atisha what was the ultimate of all teachings. "Of all teachings, the ultimate is emptiness of which compassion is the very essence," replied the Master. "Realization of the truth of emptiness, the very nature of reality, is like a very powerful medicine, a panacea which can cure every disease in the world. It is the remedy for all the different negative emotions."[5]

All Buddhist teachings have the same purpose: to put an end to ignorance by realizing there is no such thing as a self-sufficient, permanent, substantial "self" or "other" in phenomenal existence. As long as we entertain the belief in this poorly constructed falsehood, we'll be immured in a state of suffering. As soon as we develop an appreciation of the nonduality of subject and object, appearance and reality, deluded consciousness and wisdom consciousness—we'll start to gain a proper insight into our true condition. That insight is the purpose of all the Buddhist teachings, because it leads to liberation. The way that this slogan helps us to appraise the success of our mind is by assessing how well we are able to relinquish our egoistic preoccupations. Konchok Gyaltsen makes this point very clearly:

> Therefore if your spiritual practice in general, and your practice of mind training in particular, fail to counter self-grasping, then [the realization of] mind training has not arisen in you. For whether mind training has arisen in your heart is determined by whether it has become an antidote to self-grasping.[6]

20 • *Of the two judges, rely on the principal one*

We can't inhabit our lives without paying attention to who we are and what we might wish to become. There are two types of opinions that shed light on who we are—the opinions we hold about ourselves, and the opinions others hold about us. When we question whether we're making any real progress with our practice, our tendency is to ask others whether they can perceive changes in us. Other people's opinions are very often not the same as our opinion of ourselves. It may be that people fail to see our inner qualities and judge us harshly, or it may be that we are being overly critical of ourselves while others see us in a very understanding and forgiving light. It is more often the case, however, that we have the more positive opinion of ourselves.

While we should not disregard others' perceptions of us entirely, we shouldn't give credence to their perceptions over our own. This is a very complex issue, because it depends on many subtle variables. Nagarjuna said that knowing whether someone is really a good, genuine person or not is as difficult as knowing the inside of a mango. We may think someone is wonderful and then find out he or she is quite mean-spirited in fact. Other people may seem surly or rough at first, but reveal themselves to be very tenderhearted. In Nagarjuna's words:

Know that men are like the mango fruit—
Unripe but appearing ripe;
Ripe but appearing unripe;
Unripe and appearing unripe;
Ripe and appearing ripe.[7]

While other people's opinions of us are important, this is not where the true matter lies, so we should rely more on what we think, because only we can really judge ourselves. We still need to follow the Abhidharma recommendations to observe shame in relation to ourselves and decorum in relation to others. The lojong teachings are not advocating "individualism" here, encouraging us to reject other people's opinions as completely irrelevant and assuming we can do whatever we like so long as we are minding our own business. This is a very common attitude these days, but the people who profess to hold it still act as if other people's opinion matters when it suits them, for example when they want to romance someone, or need to attend a court hearing when

they are caught breaking the law. At those times they're quite prepared to conform to all manner of social expectations and pro-
prieties. Rather than promoting this kind of hypocrisy, the lojong
teachings are simply advising us not to regard other people's opinions about us as more important than our own. Patrul Rinpoche
extends this warning:

> You might feel slightly disenchanted with samsara, develop
> a vague determination to be free of it, and take on the sem-
> blance of a serious Dharma student to the point that or-
> dinary folk are quite impressed, and want to be your patron
> and disciples. But at that point, unless you take a very rig-
> orous look at yourself, you could easily start thinking you
> really are as other people see you. Puffed up with pride,
> you get completely carried away by appearances and start
> to think that you can do whatever you want.[8]

There are two parts to how we go about our self-assessment.
The first is to know what we are really like in spite of our delusions, limitations, and self-deceptions. We aren't trying to judge
ourselves, to determine whether we're a good or a bad person. We're
trying to assess how to overcome certain negative habits or work
with our tendency to harbor negative thoughts and attitudes. The
fact that we have those negative habits and tendencies doesn't make
us bad people. The second part of our self-assessment has to do
with how we can recognize our true character and qualities, given
our delusions, limitations, and self-deceptions. How do we know
we are becoming better people and not just deceiving ourselves?

The first part of the exercise involves making a genuine and
heartfelt self-assessment of who we really are. We may see ourselves

quite differently on a deeper level than we do on the superficial, social level that we project to others. While the social level of awareness represents a self-assessment of sorts, this slogan is concerned with what we think about ourselves at a deeper level of self-analysis, where we can make an honest assessment of our real motives and opinions. Shantideva advises:

Examine yourself thus from every side.
Note harmful thoughts and every futile striving.
Thus it is that heroes in the bodhisattva path
Apply the remedies to keep a steady mind.[9]

We'll always have certain limitations as ordinary human beings, because only a Buddha can fully know himself or herself. However, a genuine effort to determine what we think and feel about ourselves will ensure that our self-knowledge is more accurate than anybody else's opinion of us. Other people may see good or bad qualities in us that we fail to recognize, and we may sometimes make errors of judgment about ourselves, but only we can really judge our true character. Self-deception is a very strong tendency. We can fool ourselves that we're better or worse than we really are, but despite this tendency, it's possible to learn to make an honest assessment of ourselves if we persevere with our meditation practice. This isn't an easy process, and we may remain a mystery to ourselves for a very long time, but our self-deceptions are not really intractable problems. They are relatively easy to overcome once we recognize that their comforting illusions are unnecessary. If we're already familiar with the power of exposure, we'll be practiced at making an honest assessment of ourselves. Se Chilbu Chokyi Gyaltsen puts it in these terms:

What, then, is the principal [witness]? Regard it as not becoming the object of your own disapproval. You should be able to feel that, even if you were to die this evening, you could have done nothing more.[10]

The second point is about assessing how we know whether we've changed for the better. If someone is singing our praises, for example, only we will know whether their assessment is actually true or not. We shouldn't assume we've changed just because someone else perceives a change in us; we need to look deeply into ourselves to see if we really are transformed. The lojong teachings say that a simple method for determining whether such perceptions are actually true is based on whether there's been some kind of fundamental shift in how we see ourselves and others. If there has been a genuine shift from being self-obsessed to more other-regarding, the lojong practice has taken effect. If we have simply changed on a personal level, making everyday alterations that mean nothing, there has been no real progress in our mind training. We'll be lost if we overemphasize the opinions of others and try to please them or conform to their opinions without giving serious thought to what we feel about ourselves. Konchok Gyaltsen says:

> Others may recognize you as a good practitioner merely on the basis of some positive behavior or some pleasant speech or because you happen to conform to their expectations. Of the two witnesses, therefore, the principal one is the assurance that you are not faulted by your own mind.[11]

Human beings are never stationary; we're always going somewhere, despite our feelings of imprisonment in samsara. We are constantly changing and developing new qualities and habits, both good and bad, so we need to look for the signs of a genuine, spiritual transformation in the way that we relate to others. Without that sign of genuine change, we'll never be able to eradicate our doubts about whether we are deceiving ourselves. As ordinary sentient beings, we'll never completely rid ourselves of egoistic thoughts and desires; it's more a question of making an honest assessment of our qualities and gradually reducing our self-obsessive tendencies. If we can appraise our attitudes as more open, tolerant, loving, and compassionate toward ourselves and others, we don't have to question the effectiveness of our mind training practices.

21 • *Always have the support of a joyful mind*

Another measure of success with mind training is whether we have grown more at ease with others and ourselves through the practices of lojong, tonglen, and cultivating relative bodhichitta. Our natural tendency is to react to others on impulse in a haphazard and agitated fashion, becoming easily overwhelmed by fear, anxiety, sadness, and loneliness, often for no apparent reason. Thinking about other people's needs, aspirations, and dreams, rather than our own broken dreams and frustrated ambitions, will transform that tendency. We can therefore assess our progress by asking ourselves whether we are less irritated and bothered by all the trivial things that go on in our lives and whether we've found some way to remain cheerful, despite our trials and tribulations. As Sangye Gompa (1179–1250) says in his "Public Explication of Mind Training":

In brief, whatever undesirable situations befall you, without any distress, learn to turn them into conditions favorable for training the mind, and whatever adversities occur, abide in joy so that its impact is magnified by your meditative equipoise.[12]

It's quite difficult to practice love and compassion toward others when we're not habituated to spontaneous surges of positive emotions toward all beings. While there is an element of hardship in cultivating this benevolent mind, thinking about the suffering of others should make us more cheerful, rather than compounding our feelings of depression and incapacitation. If we develop a more positive demeanor by cultivating love, compassion, and other-regarding attitudes, we'll transcend our own self-centered needs and generate more life-affirming attitudes. Shantideva highlights the importance of a happy state of mind:

So come what may, I'll never harm
My cheerful happiness of mind.
Depression never brings me what I want;
My virtue will be warped and marred by it.[13]

We're trying to develop an underlying sense of cheerfulness, one that doesn't fluctuate between happiness and despair at a moment's notice. It's our internal monologues and expectations that make it difficult for us to maintain a sense of optimism. We're always thinking about what we think we need for a good life, making lists of things we require and becoming extremely disappointed and frustrated when they fail to materialize. These expectations are based on our mental projections rather than on any kind of realistic assessment of our goals and compel us to race in hot pursuit of what we think we need, whether that is material, situational, or interpersonal. We can't enjoy the life we have, because we're constantly trying to amass more of something, yet never managing to have enough. No matter how many conditions we fulfill, we'll always want something that seems more essential for our happiness, and we will be forever subject to fears about not getting the things we want, or getting what we don't want and losing what we already have. Nagarjuna encapsulates our predicament in this verse:

> Amassing wealth, guarding it and making it grow
> will wear you out;
> Understand that riches bring unending ruin and
> destruction.[14]

The best way to maintain a sense of cheerfulness is to aim high, but without overextending ourselves through unrealistic expectations. We should always try to push the boundary of what we think we can and can't do, while at the same time recognizing that what we do in any given situation will always have its limits. This kind of balanced attitude will guard against disappointment and failure and help us to focus on the kind of person we want to become, rather than becoming distracted by temporal goals. We're encouraged to take everything in a step-by-step manner, which is why this approach is called the graduated path. Shantideva's celebratory verse reflects the power of this approach:

> For mounted on the horse of bodhichitta,
> That puts to flight all mournful weariness,

Who could ever be dejected,
Riding such a steed from joy to joy?[15]

We also derive inspiration from past and present masters, such as His Holinesses the Dalai Lama and Karmapa, who have the capacity to benefit many beings and impact enormously on other people's lives. We aspire to become more like these people, and we try gradually to chip away at ourselves until we have attained our desired goal, without getting carried away by fanciful thoughts of great realizations or attainments. We need to determine whether we are any happier as a result of engaging in lojong practice for ourselves. Happiness doesn't mean never feeling sad or distressed; rather, it is reflective of a general optimism toward ourselves and others.

Our potential to extend ourselves and reach for ever-higher goals is always present. Systematically achieving what we set out for ourselves in our lojong practice will give us an increasing sense of satisfaction, which in turn will boost our sense of well-being. Milarepa sings:

Having won the best conditions for Dharma practice,
    I am happy;
Having ceased from evil deeds and left off sinning, I
    am happy;
Treading the Path of Merits, I am happy;
Divorced from hate and injury, I am happy;
Having lost all pride and jealousy, I am happy;
Understanding the wrongness of the eight worldly
    dharmas, I am happy;
Using the mind to watch the mind; I am happy;
Without hope or fear, I am ever happy.[16]

22 • *You are proficient if you can practice even when distracted*

After practicing lojong meditation and tonglen for some time, we'll gradually become familiar with positive mental attitudes, which will, in turn, start to become a habit rather than something we are trying to manufacture. Not all habits are bad. Lojong practices are also habit-forming, so if we do them consistently, they will gradually become part of our psychological makeup and personality traits. Where once we became distracted by moments of depression, bitterness, or hostility, we'll now, through mindfulness and awareness, become less self-obsessed and more cheerful. Jamgön Kongtrül uses the following analogy to illustrate the spontaneous application of mind training:

> A skilled horseman does not fall from his horse, even when he is distracted. In the same way, if you are able to take adverse conditions that suddenly develop as aids to mind training even without expressly directing your attention to do so, then you are proficient in mind training. The two bodhichittas arise clearly and effortlessly along with everything that appears—enemies, friends, troublemakers, happiness, or suffering.[17]

The fact that our minds become naturally inclined toward mindfulness and awareness is an indication of how much we have changed as a result of our meditation practices. The phrase "to practice even when distracted" means that we're automatically practicing lojong as we go about our business, without even noticing that we're doing so. An example of this might be Tibetan children, who are taught from a very young age not to harm insects, and who automatically refrain from harming them when they're playing outside. Even as adults, the things we repeatedly do over a period of time become part of our character. Konchok Gyaltsen elaborates on this point:

> This does not refer merely to not being overtaken by adversities you encounter through the deliberate practice of mind training. Rather it refers to the ability to practice mind training spontaneously, without the need for deliberate effort as an antidote, when obstructions arise suddenly and unexpectedly. With deep familiarity, this is certainly possible. For do not afflictions like anger arise spontaneously due to the force of your beginningless habituation to self-cherishing? Do not the afflictions arise immediately in response to any old circumstance?[18]

Our samsaric logic tells us we'll feel better if we tolerate a constant discomfort over a long time than if we confront intense pain for a short time, similar to using some kind of balm to soothe a toothache rather than going to the dentist to remove the cause of the pain. The lojong masters, on the other hand, tell us that enduring a chronic, dull pain in order to avoid an acute, sharp pain is totally mistaken. The pain of wisdom and insight is an intense and penetrating experience, but it has a surgical effect on our mind, which relieves it of its own pain. Empathizing with the pain and suffering of others can be sharply distressing, but the samsaric mind would rather put up with the drudgery of samsaric existence than expose itself to this. However, as Sangye Gompa explains:

In all interactions with others, accept the loss and offer them the gain. If you grant others what is most desirable among the mundane excellences and accept upon yourself what is least desirable, then even if you experience disappointments like the person who goes to the land of jewels but fails to find even a piece of rock that can be used against a dog, this [act of giving and taking] will still become a cause for buddhahood. In this sense, whatever you encounter is immediately applied to your practice. In contrast, if you lack this [habit], all your vast learning, refined meditation, and so on become endeavors of the "I."[19]

We should focus on thinking that nothing is insignificant, no matter how small or unimportant it may seem. If we keep doing something with consistency, even if it is very small, those actions will accumulate. The main point is to be satisfied with the results, without becoming self-satisfied or complacent. We should be satisfied to the extent we're moving forward and that these practices are having an impact on us. We also shouldn't set our expectations too high, or we'll always feel that our practices should be making more of a difference than they are.

Instead of deriving comfort from the suffering of others and drawing pleasure from all the wrong places, we need to generate mindfulness and awareness and take pleasure in living with the right view. If we can respond to others with less spite, jealousy, and egoism, and can demonstrate more kindness, appreciation, and compassion, we will be making progress with our mind training. This view is self-generating, according to lojong, so this method of appraisal will clarify how well our practice is transforming our habits of mind.

Conclusion

Remembering these slogans from time to time will help us gauge our progress in mind training. If we are giving too much credence to other people's opinions, for example, we invoke the slogan "Of the two judges, rely on the principal one," and remind ourselves to make an honest assessment of ourselves. These slogans will then help us to see what we need to do to correct and direct our lojong practice. It's important to practice mind training without thinking of other people as the recipients. Even though many of the benefits of lojong practice may not at first be visible or tangible, we should have confidence that everything we do leaves an impression in our mental continuum and will continue to exert an influence. Lojong practice will definitely leave positive imprints in our unconscious, and we'll continue to receive benefits without necessarily realizing it. The goal of all Buddhist practice is to transcend our egoistic obsession and dispel ignorance. As Milarepa says:

> It is said you can tell whether someone has just eaten by how red his face is. Similarly, you can tell whether people know and practice the Dharma by whether it works as a remedy for their negative emotions and ego-clinging.[20]

The Commitments of Mind Training

W e strengthen our resolve by making a serious commitment to persevere. A certain amount of commitment (Skt. *samaya;* Tib. *dam tshig*) is an essential element in anything that requires time and effort. It's one thing to dabble casually, but an entirely different matter to become involved in something after giving it serious consideration. There are many kinds of commitments within the various Buddhist traditions, each with their own unique vows. Damshig is a very important concept in tantric Buddhism, symbolizing the bond between you and the deity, or between you and the guru. In the context of mind training, commitment relates directly to the determination to resist the seductions of our samsaric tendencies. The word *damshig* is actually made up of two words: *dam bca,'* which means "something that binds," and *tshig,* which literally means "honorary word." The English equivalent would be a pledge or oath. The idea behind being "bound by words" is essentially about honoring the commitments we have made to ourselves. If we have taken a vow that commits us to doing something, there is more likelihood we'll see it through to the end, because it carries more weight than some vague promissory intention.

We have to abide by a commitment once we've formally declared it to others. We can't underestimate the importance of actually saying, "I will practice lojong without allowing external circumstances to interfere or to cause my practice to degenerate." We make this commitment within our capacity, to the best of our ability, and with the help of mindfulness and awareness—nobody expects more of us than that.

23 • *Always practice the three general principles*

This commitment relates to our motivation to practice mind training. If we recognize from the beginning that lojong is a powerful and beneficial practice, we'll commit ourselves in a genuine and continuous way by retaining a sense of impartiality and guarding against distortion. This slogan, which comprises three separate principles, is considered one of the sixteen precepts in this chapter.

1. Remember to Value Your Commitment

From time to time, we should deliberately think about our commitment to lojong and reaffirm our determination to do something beneficial, meaningful, and purposeful with our lives. If we become more aware and attentive to our daily situation, we'll notice just how many opportunities we squander by becoming ensnared in personal dramas. When we capitalize on situations as they arise, we'll see that most of them are capable of bearing fruit. We shouldn't assume that our life has to be running smoothly in order for us to be successful; we can make equally good use of situations that aren't working out. We do this by skillfully extracting the most from the least. Instead of waiting for propitious circumstances, we need to take the initiative and utilize the opportunities that actually present themselves. Our commitment to lojong must become a lifelong habit, rather than something that we do whenever time permits or when nothing else has taken precedence. We must put all our energy behind this practice and vow, "Whatever happens in my daily life, I'll use every opportunity to practice lojong."

2. Refrain from Distorted Forms of Thinking

We need continually to approach our mind training practice with sincerity and honesty. Relinquishing our self-obsession and refusing to indulge in our personal dramas doesn't mean we should practice a level of austerity that makes us neglect our physical or mental well-being. Some people stop washing and grooming themselves, completely disregarding their health and pushing their body and mind to extremes of endurance, perhaps in the form of hermitic or ascetic practices, and refusing to seek medical assistance when they become unwell. This approach actually relies on the logic of egoism and represents a completely distorted view of lojong practice. As Se Chilbu Chokyi Gyaltsen comments:

> Do not act contrary to the Kadampas way of life, a great tradition that has been established by Geshe Dromtonpa at Radreng. Practice the teaching instead as if [lifting all] four corners of a square [cloth]. Shawopa states: "Examine where you might go wrong. You have erred when your spiritual practice becomes offensive."[1]

Trying to demonstrate success in lojong practice through acts of self-sacrifice is anathema to the lojong spirit. In fact, going to extremes to prove a lack of egoism is regarded as scandalous behavior. We need to remind ourselves of our commitments and eliminate any such lapses. The Tibetan phrase for this error means something like "a form of misinterpretation or distortion." Listed as one of the five wrong views in the *abhidharma-pitaka*—"the wrong view of moral discipline" (Tib. *tshul khrims dang brtul shugs mchog 'dzin*)— is defined in the *Treasury of Precious Qualities* by Jigme Lingpa (1730–1798), the promulgator of the Longchen Nyingthik in the Nyingma school of Tibetan Buddhism, as:

> the belief in the superiority of invalid systems of discipline or ethics that do not in fact produce the effects hoped for (liberation). This includes the practice of extreme and useless asceticism, the sacrificing of animals, and even a proud attachment to Buddhist disciplines, which effectively obstructs spiritual progress.[2]

3. Refrain from Falling into Partiality

Even though we can't maintain the same attitude toward everyone in our daily lives, it's possible to generate impartiality to everyone in the more contrived environment of meditation practice. The amazing discovery about mind training meditations is that we can train ourselves to do something we wouldn't think we could do in our everyday lives. That's why it is so important to cultivate impartiality when we practice tonglen and to generate positive feelings for people we normally find difficult to manage. It's true that we may find it much easier to generate love and compassion for certain individuals, but it's still very important to develop a more inclusive approach to tonglen practice and to gradually include more people and situations into our meditations. Sangye Gompa underscores the importance of this:

> Since no training can be achieved through a biased approach, if you train without partiality, your practice will develop and progress.[3]

Tibetans often say that "when their stomach is full and the sun is warm, everyone seems capable of heroic deeds." However, this doesn't mean that we should allow our moods or personal conditions to affect our lojong practice. That we don't feel the same every day is a natural part of life and can't be helped, but it is still possible to keep these fluctuations from interfering with our mind training. Nothing is preventing us from performing tonglen with an equal degree of intensity and sincerity at all times, regardless of the diverse mental conditions we may be experiencing at any given moment.

24 • *Change your attitude, but remain natural*

Lojong practice is about transforming the way we view the world, not changing the way we present ourselves to it. Changes in the way we perceive ourselves and in how we relate to our disturbing thoughts and emotions and our attitudes to other people are far more important than changes in our appearance, mannerisms, or personal attire. To believe otherwise would be like thinking we've become more spiritual simply as a result of donning some kind of religious habit. We are trying to transform the unwholesome, self-destructive attitudes of our self-obsession. Whether others perceive us as different or not is irrelevant; our transformation needs to be an internal one. Drukpa Kunley is scornful of all forms of self-aggrandizement:

> I, an ever-roaming Naljorpa, visited the Religious Centre
>   of Lhasa,
> Where the hostesses were hoping for their guests' gifts
>   and favors—
> So fearing to become a flatterer, I kept to myself.
> I, an ever-roaming Naljorpa, wandering throughout
>   the land,
> Found self-seeking sufferers wherever I looked—
> So fearful of thinking only of myself, I kept to myself.[4]

"Remaining natural" refers to the importance of blending in with others, rather than acting as if we were special or an outsider. We shouldn't act in ways that give ourselves airs or deliberately try to impress anyone. Our behavior should be seemly, courteous, and in keeping with the social conventions of the community. If the majority of people are saying one thing, we shouldn't contradict or dispute them by making inappropriate, irrelevant, or non-contextual comments. In Tibet, we call this "talking high Dharma talk," because it sounds very highfalutin but nobody knows what you're talking about. This lojong commitment is simply about getting along with people outwardly while trying to transform ourselves inwardly. Godrakpa notes:

> Talking about high Dharma is easy;
> applying the meaning to the mindstream is hard.[5]

25 • *Don't talk about others'*
weak points

Whenever we discuss other people, we usually mention their weak points rather than their good qualities. We say all kinds of derisive things, out of habit, without really meaning any harm. It's easy to criticize somebody's physical attributes or point out their dull-wittedness or other defects. We assume that careless speech is harmless, because it's said in jest. Tibetans are notorious for this kind of name-calling. Most Tibetan nicknames are based on the person's physical appearance; we often don't even know their real name. We say something like "Fat Sonam," and everybody knows who we mean. The lojong teachings say that even if we're only joking, it matters and can be harmful, even if we meant no offense. This kind of verbal impropriety is a symptom of our inability to maintain mindfulness and awareness.

This slogan is about committing ourselves to an attitude of noninterference and nonharm in regard to others. There may be a rare circumstance when we feel compelled to say something unpleasant to someone, in which case we must only do so with a constructive attitude and the intention to help rather than harm. If you really believe someone is behaving despicably, it's still inadvisable to say anything derogatory about them behind their back. Being the subject of other people's negative comments can be hurtful, and what is painful for us will also be injurious to others. It's more helpful to reflect on their actions from other perspectives, for just because we believe somebody is behaving improperly doesn't necessarily mean they are doing anything wrong. Shantideva reminds us:

Thus, when enemies or friends
Are seen to act improperly,
Be calm and call to mind
That everything arises from conditions.[6]

If we can't shake our conviction about their behavior, we should say so to their face rather than talking about them behind their back. Picking on someone's faults won't make them a better person; it only exposes our own deficiencies and causes problems for everyone. Our intention should always be to help people rather than cause injury. We should also approach them as equals, rather than assuming any superiority or condescension. The best course of action is to unreservedly be encouraging and comforting to others whenever we get the opportunity, leaving their character weaknesses, moral flaws, and questionable behaviors alone. If we restrain the urge to make derogatory comments, we will keep the precept of this slogan. Atisha's *The Jewel Rosary of Bodhisattvas* advises:

Avoid belittling others and
Remain respectful in your manners.
When giving advice to others,
Have compassion and thoughts for their benefit.[7]

26 • *Don't think about the affairs of others*

This precept is about minding our own business. It's similar to the previous slogan, but relates to the twisted logic we apply to others, rather than what we say about them. When we think about others, we usually concentrate on their problems and defects. Our habit is to obsess over other people's actions or situations, speculating about their romantic lives, whether they're happy or unhappy or going through a traumatic period. If somebody fails to gain a job promotion, or their marriage falls apart, we may catch ourselves taking delight in their misfortune. The lojong commentaries remind us that our criticisms and interpretations about others' lives are simply our own projections and perceptions, so instead of categorically condemning people's actions, we should learn to give them the benefit of the doubt. It's important to remember we also have faults and are not beyond reproach, even though we're very skilled at finding reasons to explain away our own shortcomings. Jamgön Kongtrül explains:

> Seeing this fault is due to the impurity in my own outlook. Such a fault is not in this person. I am like those people who saw faults in Buddha, the enlightened one.[8]

Every time our minds become preoccupied with the behavior of others, we use mindfulness and awareness to redirect our attention to something else. It doesn't make us any more successful to see somebody else's failures, nor will we be any happier if their lives are more full of misery. We must make the commitment to attend to our own business, without involving ourselves in what other people are doing. Wasting time speculating about other people's affairs can be toxic and self-destructive. On the other hand, if we make a positive impact on others, we will evolve as human beings, and our minds will be more at ease.

27 • *Work on the stronger disturbing emotions first*

In order to understand where our distorted ways of speaking and thinking originate, we have to probe still more deeply than we did with the previous two slogans. Where they come from is our conflicting emotions. Our commitment here is the reverse of what it was with the previous two slogans, for instead of admonishing ourselves and trying to transform our attitudes, we are simply advised to examine the emotions that disturb us the most. This may seem to contradict the usual lojong instructions, but the logic here is to acknowledge our limitations and work toward our goals in a gradual manner. There are many aspects of ourselves that require transformation, but the lojong teachings instruct us to simplify our approach by working with the most obvious problems first.

For instance, it's easier to recognize and gradually tame a strong disturbing emotion than it is to eliminate that emotion completely. Working with disturbing emotions as they arise is more effective than trying to eliminate our more entrenched dispositions, such as greed, lust, anger, jealousy, and so forth. Even if our disposition toward aggression and aversion remains ingrained, we can still learn to release ourselves from the physical or verbal abuses of fuming rage.

This instruction is in keeping with the Mahayana principle of acting within our capacities, instead of frustrating ourselves by having unrealistic expectations about what we can achieve. While it's important to retain our high ideals, we need to be practical in the short term. That's why this commitment isn't about eradicating the problem straight away, but about having the willingness to work at reducing it. If we do nothing to ameliorate our disturbing emotions, they will only worsen and may eventually get completely out of control. But if we commit ourselves to containing each one now, we can gradually lessen their virulence until they become quite manageable. This is why Jamgön Kongtrül advises:

> Examine your personality to determine which disturbing emotions are the strongest. Concentrate all dharma practice on them in the beginning, and subdue and clear them away.[9]

While human beings are alike in many ways, we have quite disparate personalities, predilections, character traits, and modes of expression. This is particularly evident when it comes to how we express our emotions. Because we've established our emotional dispositions over our vast and varied karmic histories, we're predisposed toward certain emotions rather than others. We all suffer from the five main poisons, but we're not equally aggressive, greedy, lustful, and so on. Some people have a predominant issue with anger, while others are troubled by jealously or one of the other emotions. As Konchok Gyaltsen explains:

> Then, taking this as the basis, [recognize that] for some attachment is stronger, for others anger, and for others envy. In your own mind each of the afflictions generally arises like bees washing themselves. Even though all the afflictions arise, examine which specific affliction is the strongest and subdue that one first.[10]

We shouldn't assume that our more subtle emotions are easier to deal with just because they have a less noticeable impact. The more disturbing the emotion, the easier it is to recognize and work with. Subtler emotions are more difficult and elusive to overcome, which is why so many methods have been provided to help us. One method is to adapt the emotion to whatever practice we're currently doing. As we feel less disturbed by that emotion, we can deal with it on deeper levels, because we'll gradually learn to recognize its subtle and insidious nature. Phadampa Sangye highlights the importance of eventually overcoming our emotional poisons:

If you don't hold on to the three or five poisons, the
     path is near;
People of Tingri, generate powerful antidotes against
     them.[11]

We make the lojong commitment to work gradually and thoroughly with our conflicting emotions because they are such disruptive forces in our everyday and spiritual lives. Our motivation shouldn't be to modify our responses so that we become more popular with others, it should be for the more exacting goal of transforming ourselves into a person with integrity, dignity, depth, and weight, rather than someone who is dominated by shallow and superficial emotions that prevent inner growth.

28 • Give up all hope for results

This slogan may sound foreign to Western ears, but it has a long history in Buddhist thinking. The lojong teachings say that whenever we become obsessed with results, we spend our time trying to manipulate the outcome of our endeavor, instead of paying attention to the activity itself. Even though we have no real idea what the result will be, we project a picture-perfect vision of our expectations into the future. This distracts us from doing the task at hand and usually ends in frustration and disappointment because the imagined result is never the same as the eventual outcome. Thus, we shouldn't concern ourselves with what benefits we're achieving from our mind training, but should simply focus on our practice with sincerity, for how we engage in the practice is what will determine the end result.

It's important to have a general notion of what we want to attain, but we shouldn't get too caught up in specifics or we'll waste our time and energy in fantasies. If we want to become great in the future, we need to do great things now, for thinking about the future only robs us of the future. Whether we're pursuing a worldly goal or a spiritual one, such as keeping our lojong commitments, its important to give up hopes for any imagined result. *The Thirty-seven Practices of Bodhisattvas* identifies this absence of expectation as one of the key aspects of the bodhisattva path:

> When those who want enlightenment must give even
>   their body,
> There's no need to mention external things.
> Therefore without hope of return or any fruition
> Give generously—
> This is the practice of Bodhisattvas.[12]

The lojong teachings use the analogy of an archer to illustrate this point. People often think focusing on the target is the most important thing for hitting it with precision, but any accomplished archer knows it's actually our posture, the way we hold the bow, and how we position the arrow that will determine the accuracy of our shot. We'll never hit the mark if we focus solely on the target and ignore our posture and technique. Similarly, getting caught up in the result of our actions rather than how we are going to obtain that result will guarantee failure in our endeavors. Konchok Gyaltsen apprises us of this aspect of our practice:

> If you fail to train unconditionally, free of expectation of rewards pertaining to this life or the hereafter, then one aspect of your spiritual practice becomes blind. It is critical, therefore, to train without any hope of reward.[13]

The slogan implies that we can't expect results to be immediately forthcoming or to find constant reassurances that things are unfolding as planned. By anticipating the kinds of signs we expect to find, we ensure our continual disappointment because we will think we've failed when those signs don't materialize. All that is really happening is that we can't see the real signs of progress because our preconceived ideas have blinded us to any genuine developments that are taking place. Because our lojong commitment is not about some grand, elaborate fantasy of the future, we should constantly remind ourselves of the futility of hopes and expectations.

29 • *Give up poisonous food*

Nutritious food is nourishing because it keeps us healthy. Poisonous food, on the other hand, is extremely dangerous to our health. Similarly, while virtuous thoughts and actions are highly valued, if we engage in them for the wrong reasons, they become poisoned. If we have hidden agendas involving ego gratification, our actions may appear laudable and admirable, but we'll spoil whatever we do with our selfishness. Even if we succeed in doing something constructive and worthwhile, we won't gain the full benefit if we have unclear motivations. We can only harm others and ourselves when we poison our actions with selfishness. It's important to note that there's a huge difference between personal gratification and ego gratification, for the latter compromises our virtuous qualities by infusing them with conflicting emotions. Our desire for other people's love and admiration will taint what would otherwise have been a powerful and beneficial act. We must constantly guard against the tendency to infuse our good intentions with desires for personal gain, as the following story by Patrul Rinpoche illustrates:

One day Geshe Ben was expecting a visit from a large number of his benefactors. That morning he arranged the offerings on his shrine in front of the images of the Three Jewels particularly neatly. Examining his intentions, he realized that they were not pure and that he was only trying to impress his patrons; so he picked up a handful of dust and threw it all over the offerings, saying, "Monk, just stay where you are and don't put on airs!"

When Phadampa Sangye heard this story, he exclaimed: "That handful of dust that Ben Kungyal threw was the best offering in all Tibet!"[14]

Without mental clarity, what we do to help others can be corrupted by the subtle manipulations of ego, massaging our self-esteem. That's why part of the lojong commitment is an exercise in alertness. We have to remain focused on our motivation to prevent any deviousness mingling with our good intentions. Drukpa Kunley satirizes that kind of hypocrisy in these lines:

Happily I am no common ritualist Lama
Gathering followers, power and wealth,
Without time to experience the fullness of life.
Happily I am no scholarly monk
Lusting for novice lovers,
Without time to study the Sutras and Tantras.
Happily I do not stay in a Mountain Hermitage
Entranced by the smiles of the nuns,
Without time to ponder the Three Vows.[15]

The best way to prevent self-obsession from corrupting our practice is to contemplate emptiness. The real poison is fixation, which comes through thinking of people and things as discrete, self-sufficient entities. When our principal focus is love, compassion, and overcoming defilement, it's easy to lapse into the misapprehension that everything is substantial and real. When the wisdom that perceives things as they are is taken from us, fixation becomes poisonous food. We should meditate on impermanence to counteract this tendency and pursue beneficial acts for their own sake rather than as methods for gaining the praise and admiration of others.

Our actions should be their own rewards. The moment we perform a meaningful act, we've already been rewarded. Expecting a more personal reward is an example of the self-obsessive thinking that keeps us trapped in conditioned existence. Just as selfishness has an adverse effect on everyone, beneficial acts create a general wholesomeness. Whatever is beneficial to others is beneficial to us, so if worthwhile acts become corrupted or compromised, they will produce negative results for everyone. Another very important aspect of our lojong commitment is to ensure we stay true and authentic to ourselves, with no room for doubt or questioning our motives.

30 • *Don't rely on your good nature*

The contradictions implicit in this difficult and enigmatic slogan are reflected in the varying interpretations found in different lojong commentaries. The Tibetan phrase literally means "don't rely on a dependable object," but the Tibetan word for "dependable object" implies a friend more than a nondescript thing. The contradiction comes from the fact that it would normally be considered good to rely on a friend. A more accurate English rendition of this term would be "good nature," and some lojong commentators have understood this slogan to mean that we should not always be constantly shifting our focus to something new. Once we have made up our mind to do something, we must stick to that course of action until we've reached our goal. Sangye Gompa explains:

> You will not succeed if you act sometimes one way and sometimes another. Some people act overenthusiastically and then, as if frustrated, give up [easily]. When relating to others, do not act as if you never tire of forging intimacy and engaging in conflict; rather, like a perfectly strung bow, engage in your [mind training] practice with finesse and firmness, free of fatigue or vexation.[16]

Another traditional interpretation of this slogan advises us not to be too accepting of our own shortcomings, or too tolerant of what is harmful. Normally we don't know what to tolerate and what to condemn, enduring all kinds of unpleasant experiences without complaint. This slogan points out that relying on and becoming too comfortable with such unwholesome mental states will have an insidious and corroding effect on our character and that we must do everything in our power to avoid being duped in this way.

Another interpretation of this slogan refers to the many forms of ill will we are prone toward. Because we often mistake our own selfish thoughts and motivations for our allies, we need to be clear that just because someone has a friendly appearance does not necessarily mean that they're trustworthy. We have to exercise caution with our emotional responses, learning not only to recognize destructive and insidious responses, such as resentment, vengeance, and anger, but allowing ourselves to be repelled by the seductions that they invite. Even if they seem at first to provide us with protective armor, they will only lead to our downfall, making us more vulnerable than ever. That's why Aryadeva can say:

Desire is no friend, but seems like one,
Which is why you do not fear it.
But shouldn't people particularly
Rid themselves of a harmful friend?[17]

Mind training practice is not about simply learning how to be accommodating. Sometimes people get the idea that only our samsaric mind rejects things, and that our problems would be solved if we could learn to be more open and responsive. The emphasis here is on skillful means, not simply on working with every situation in an accepting way. Whether we tolerate a situation or not isn't the problem, it's whether we can recognize what is beneficial for us and what is only going to be harmful. If we examine ourselves more closely, we may find that blindly showing good-naturedness is one of our most problematic impulses.

31 • *Don't react on impulse to critical remarks*

This slogan relates to our anger and the impulsive responses we make when we are completely filled with aggression. Its immediate concern is the ways we lash out at others over derogatory remarks made about us. Words carry enormous power. We must be sensitive to how we express ourselves and resist the temptation to follow our impulses and jump to conclusions about what others say. We should not think our ears are neutral receptors, whose sole purpose is to receive information in an unadulterated fashion. We often hear what we want to hear, or even what we are afraid of hearing, because our receptivity is so intermingled with our fears, desires, and expectations. The very idea that someone said something disagreeable is enough to make us angry. These days we are constantly confronted with phenomena such as road rage, where every little aggression, imagined or not, compels us to become physically or verbally abusive.

If we take the time to reflect on what others have said, we'll often find it was not as bad as it initially appeared, or that we may have interpreted something as critical when it was never intended that way. There is often a tremendous gap between what a speaker intends and what we actually hear, especially if there is a hint of criticism in their words. If somebody says something slightly sardonic to us, we retort with something even more sarcastic, without stopping to think about the exchange. *The Thirty-seven Practices of Bodhisattvas* counsels us to renounce this kind of behavior:

Harsh words disturb the minds of others
And cause deterioration in a Bodhisattva's conduct.
Therefore give up harsh words
Which are unpleasant to others—
This is the practice of Bodhisattvas.[18]

We must make the lojong commitment to refrain from negative conclusions about other people's remarks. This is another habit-forming behavior, because constant eruptions of this kind will gradually become part of our psychological makeup. If we refrain from jumping to conclusions, we might respond to critical remarks in a more constructive way. That's why it's so important to make a sustained effort to work with our strong emotions and restrain our impulsive and aggressive tendencies. Padma Karpo puts this in context in the following verse:

When you hear flattery from others, your mood lifts;
You spend days and nights engaging in or listening
    to meaningless gossip.
There is an appropriate cause and effect of every action.
Shouldn't you become more conscious about what
    you do?
Please turn your mind within and reflect on this.[19]

32 • Don't wait in ambush

This slogan literally means "don't wait in a narrow passage," and derives from old Tibet, where robbers would lie in wait for travelers in the narrow gorges between mountains, just as we often wait for the opportune moment to attack our enemies when they least expect it. If our enemy is more powerful than we are, we can't take them on openly and instead use cunning and strategy to gain the upper hand. We can relate this mentality to the anger of the previous slogan, only instead of reacting impulsively, we fixate on what has been said or done to us, without forgetting or forgiving, until such time as we can safely retaliate. This is a very devious way to behave and quite contrary to the lojong spirit. Konchok Gyaltsen discusses this point in the context of tonglen:

> If you are cultivating the awakening mind and practicing mind training, there is simply no room for such thoughts. As long as you harbor such vengeful thoughts (including acting out a grudge against others to repay previous harms), it is impossible for the two [giving and taking] to arise.[20]

Our lojong practice involves always focusing on behavior that is beneficial for everyone. The most valuable thing we can do is to make the most of every day. Each day is a new day and promises new and more positive beginnings, so we have to learn to live in the present and exploit that to its full potential. When our thoughts are constantly straying to themes of revenge, we waste inordinate amounts of precious time and energy simmering with rage, wallowing in bitterness, and scheming about ways to undermine someone. That time would be put to better use thinking about how to improve our lives in both a worldly and a spiritual sense. Allowing somebody to dominate our thoughts gives them the upper hand. While we intended to undermine the other person, we've distorted the situation so much that we fail to recognize we have given them more power over us than ever.

To counteract this tendency to harbor feelings of resentment and revenge, we make the lojong commitment not to be opportunistic and wait for someone we dislike to suffer some misfortune or attack them when they are most vulnerable. Instead, we undertake to spend our days, weeks, and months trying to do things that will make us better human beings and lead a life that is spiritually richer and fuller. Shantideva sees this as a guarantee of greater happiness:

> All these ills are brought about by wrath,
> Our sorrow-bearing enemy.
> But those who seize and crush their anger down
> Will find their joy in this and future lives.[21]

33 • Don't make insincere comments

Although the lojong commentaries vary, this slogan can basically be understood in two different ways. The first way of understanding it is based on the observation that human beings have a tendency to take pleasure in identifying other people's weak points and exploiting them for their own benefit. If someone is the jealous type, we try to arouse their jealousy; if they're prone to anger, we enrage them; if they're consumed by greed, we might try to exploit their weakness by convincing them to invest in a nonexistent business venture. This slogan is therefore saying that we should refrain from pinpointing other people's defects when we argue or any time we want to gain some kind of advantage over them.

The second way of understanding this slogan is based on the recognition that since we have the impulse to say hurtful things to others, we often attempt to do it in an underhanded way that doesn't immediately appear hurtful. Such sugarcoated comments may initially sound pleasant, but they have a cutting and malicious intention that's designed to deliver emotional pain. This isn't the same as sarcasm, which is usually quite transparent in its intent. Rather, it often takes time for the meaning of remarks such as these to register. Eastern Tibetans like to think that central and Western Tibetans are very good at these kinds of insincere comments. They say something so beautifully and nicely, but mean to put you down and make you feel like a real nomad. There is an old Tibetan proverb that captures this:

> Words have no arrows nor swords, yet they tear men's minds to pieces.[22]

We have various kinds of strategies for dealing with other people, but they are almost always involved with gaining a stronger position or in some way dominating others. The things we say are often designed to manipulate and exploit situations by making others feel inferior, deficient, or unattractive. In this slogan, we make the lojong commitment not to elevate ourselves by paying false complements, making sarcastic comments, or blatantly pointing out someone else's weakness. Although we may derive some temporal pleasure from these demeaning and superficial strategies, our actions are counterproductive to a cultivation of the true lojong spirit and only bring tremendous harm to us in the long run. His Holiness the Dalai Lama has said:

> We are all here on this planet, as it were, as tourists. None of us can live here forever. The longest we might live is a hundred years. So while we are here we should try to have a good heart and to make something positive and useful of our lives.[23]

34 • Don't shift a 'zo's burden to an ox

Tibetans value their 'zo (female yak) far more than their oxen, so even though a 'zo is stronger than an ox, a Tibetan would typically think, "If the ox dies, I can easily replace it, but a new 'zo would cost me dearly, so I'll make the ox carry this load, even though it isn't really strong enough." We often employ the same logic in our relationships with others. We can understand this slogan by placing ourselves in the position of the 'zo and another person as the ox, for we often transfer our responsibilities onto someone less experienced than ourselves and place them under enormous pressure simply because we are disinclined to do something ourselves. We may also undertake a project in collaboration with someone and then shift the blame onto that person when things go wrong, even if the project is a disaster because of our own errors of judgment. Sometimes we may even put the responsibility for something onto someone less competent than ourselves in order to humiliate or embarrass them. Wanting to pass the buck in this way is another very common trait in human beings. Padma Karpo puts this very succinctly:

> When you work with others and do the job well you
>> want to take the credit;
> When the work is not well done and people complain,
>> you blame others.
> You get completely lost in secretive tactics.
> Isn't your approach underhanded?
> Please turn your mind within and reflect on this.[24]

Another way to interpret this slogan applies to the way we evaluate and judge others. There may be two people at your workplace, one of whom is a dear friend and the other who is barely an acquaintance. There's a quite difficult task that needs completing and your friend is qualified and competent to do it, but you think, "This job will be time-consuming for my friend, so I'll give it to this other person instead, even though they have no experience in this area." You place that person under considerable stress without giving him any consideration, because you don't want to inconvenience your friend. We must make the lojong commitment to refrain from abusing or disregarding others and to complete all our projects thoroughly and to the best of our ability. *The Wheel-Weapon Mind Training* of Dharmaraksita is unequivocal about this kind of dishonest behavior:

> Having no precognition, I eagerly resort to lying and
>   depreciation.
> Having no compassion, I snatch away the confidence
>   from others'
> hearts. Roar and thunder on the head of the destroyer,
>   false construction! Mortally strike at the heat of the
>   butcher, the enemy, ego![25]

35 • Don't aim to win

Human beings are by nature competitive and constantly want to outperform other people. It really doesn't matter what we are doing, we always act as if we were in some kind of a race, which must have a winner and a loser. This slogan is a reminder that this fixation on winning, outperforming, and outsmarting everyone else is a very harmful distraction. It only engenders pride and arrogance when we do a little better than someone else, and gives rise to resentment, envy, and jealousy when we perform a little worse.

This slogan is not saying that we shouldn't try to excel at the things we do, for that would be contrary to the Mahayana vision; it's only suggesting that we can excel without having to compete with others. We can attain excellence by ourselves, simply by doing something to the best of our ability. Even when we're performing in an actual race, we can run that race without thinking we have to be the fastest. If you do manage to be the fastest, that's all very well and good, but you shouldn't enter the race with that expectation. Jamgön Kongtrül advises:

> In a horse race, the aim is to be the fastest. Among dharma people there are often hopes of receiving more attention or being more highly regarded than others, and little schemes are made up to find ways to acquire possessions. Give these up.[26]

Many people actually describe their lives as some kind of race, with some people getting farther ahead and others getting left behind. From the lojong perspective, the samsaric idea that we have to compete with others to gain ground is completely erroneous. We only obsess over winning because of the elation we experience when we have gained superiority over others and see someone else losing. This is only an illusory victory, fabricated by the samsaric mind, and we'll experience many obstacles if we continue to see things this way. There will always be people who are richer, more attractive, and more intelligent than we are, with many other qualities besides, and we'll always feel like a failure in relation to them no matter what kind of victories we have. In any case, today's winner is yesterday's loser.

Life isn't a race, and there don't have to be any winners and losers. Nor do we need to see somebody else lagging behind in order to feel good about ourselves. This preoccupation with competition is a form of self-deception. We need to think more about what we're doing in relation to ourselves if we want to excel. The Mahayana teachings advise us "to compete with our previous selves," using our past successes and failures as the measure of our progress in overcoming old constraints, fears, suspicions, and self-doubts. Reinventing ourselves in this way is in complete accord with the Mahayana teachings on self-transformation. If we're too competitive, our lives will become a never-ending battle where we squander our energies trying to outperform others. There can be no real victory in this approach. If we think in terms of excellence, on the other hand, we can achieve constant victory.

This lojong commitment to noncompetitiveness is about doing our best for our own sake, rather than as a way of competing with others. We vow to renounce our need to compare ourselves with others or achieve any kind of worldly victories and simply concentrate on performing our everyday activities and lojong practice to the best of our ability.

36 • *Don't put exchange value on things*

This slogan is about the need for sincerity and honesty in our spiritual pursuits. We should never use spiritual activities to further our own dubious and self-centered motivations and goals. We may be doing all the right things in our lojong practice externally, helping somebody in need, showing kindness to others, or lending an ear to the tormented, but our actions lack real sincerity because we are trying to manipulate a situation to our own advantage so that we don't have to relinquish our egoistic domain. Some notion of trickery is involved here, because we are trying to shortchange something or someone.

The basis of this slogan relates to quasi-shamanistic practices, or making offerings to spirits in order to procure some kind of favor. The Tibetan for this is *ru bzlog rkyen ja,* where *bzlog* means "reversal" and *rkyen ja* means "quasi-shamanistic ritual practices." The combination of *ru bzlog* means "wanting to buy things" and infers the performance of some sort of trickery to gain what we want. Se Chilbu Chokyi Gyaltsen explains:

> Therefore avoid [behavior] such as this that fails to root out the jaundice of self-centeredness from its depth. Some [practitioners] seem to think that mind training [practice] is beneficial from such a result or purpose. If this is true, there is no real difference between [practicing mind training] and engaging in shamanistic rites. To be called Dharma practice, [mind training] must become an antidote to afflictions and false conceptualization.[27]

Trying to coerce spiritual results from a halfhearted demonstration of our practice is like adopting a trader's mentality to spirituality. We'll never obtain results if we covet other people's praise or admiration and let that motivate our actions. Behaving in this way is very protective and defensive as far as our ego is concerned. We shouldn't expect other people to acknowledge what we do or to feel gratitude or indebtedness toward us if we do something beneficial. Other people's recognition is no concern of ours. This lojong commitment is simply about doing everything we undertake as thoroughly as possible, without sloppiness or expectations of receiving anything in return. The Kadampa tradition is constantly reiterating that sloppiness is a sign of ignorance and should be countered with mindfulness and awareness at all times. Padma Karpo warns:

Even when you spend time listening, contemplating and
    meditating on the teachings
You only do it to prop yourself up in the eyes of others.
When you behave with morality it is only to obtain
    other people's respect.
Don't you think it would be better to do something that
    will benefit yourself?
Please turn your mind within and reflect on this.[28]

37 • *Don't turn gods into demons*

This slogan has a similar theme to the previous one, except that here gods and demons are mentioned. Tibetan people often seek help from quasi-shamanistic rituals, where gods and demons are evoked and supplicated to curry favor or request an intervention over the prevailing negative visitations. Tibetan culture acknowledges gods that are very benign and protective and demons that are very malicious and injurious to the living, and this slogan extends this popular idea to the symbolic level of lojong practice, where the benevolence of gods and the malevolence of demons represent aspects of our own minds. We are angelic in certain respects and totally demonic in others, but these two aspects are never totally separate sides of ourselves, and they are capable of influencing, interacting with, and diluting one another. Therefore, if we're not vigilant with our practice, the angelic aspect of ourselves can degenerate into the demonic one. Se Chilbu Chokyi Gyaltsen explains this in the following terms:

It becomes the act of allowing a thief to escape into the forest while looking for his footprints on a rocky mountain.

Avoid all such conduct and, by disgracing to self-grasping, ensure that the medicine is applied right where the illness is. Comport yourself as the lowest of the low among the servants of all sentient beings.[29]

Some people start to become extremely conceited and arrogant about their lojong practices, feeling and acting quite superior to everyone else. They may have started out with sincerity and enthusiasm, but this gradually became corrupted when they began to turn something beneficial and worthwhile into something egoistical and self-congratulatory. Even if we are extremely well versed and learned in spiritual matters, we'll compromise all our good qualities with this one defect if we don't guard against our egoism, for an inflated sense of self-esteem is completely anathema to the lojong spirit. This lojong commitment is about being aware of our demonic tendencies and resolving to avoid their temptations at all costs. As Shantideva points out:

All the harm with which this world is rife,
All fear and suffering that there is,
Clinging to the "I" has caused it!
What am I to do with this great demon?[30]

38 • Don't seek others' pain as a means to happiness

Seeking happiness at someone else's expense is another common human trait, according to the lojong commentaries. We all want happiness, but we tend to look for it in all the wrong places, and as a result, the pleasures and joys we experience can quickly degenerate into suffering and sorrow. His Holiness the Dalai Lama says:

From one life to another we have always sought happiness, and yet, because we have always been dominated by negative emotions, we have only met with difficulties. Reborn as humans, birds, deer, insects, and so forth, we have never had lasting happiness.[31]

This slogan focuses on the error of looking for happiness in the wrong places, by thinking that someone else's misfortunes could bring us joy. Someone we know may have lost a loved one, filed for divorce, squandered the family fortune, fallen seriously ill, failed to gain a promotion, or had their home repossessed by the bank, but instead of feeling sympathy for their plight, we derive a certain amount of pleasure at their predicament and cheerfully gossip about it to others. Some people think that life is terrible, and when anyone experiences something worse than what they go through, they feel a sense of gratification rather than concern. We often wish harm on people we dislike, hoping that they might be struck down by an incurable illness, lose their business, or have some misfortune befall their children. Privileged people with money, resources, and education also tend to look down with scorn and disdain on those who have less. Human beings have a tendency to savor malicious gossip about other people's misfortunes and take delight in them, which is why Buddhism defines gossip in the following terms:

Pieces of gossip that seem to have come up quite naturally and spontaneously are for the most part, when you look more closely, motivated by desire or hatred, and the gravity of the fault will be in proportion to the amount of attachment or hatred created in your own and others' minds.[32]

A lojong practitioner should never search for happiness in the privations of others or stand to gain something from someone else's loss. Drawing pleasure from the suffering of others is completely reprehensible and anathema to the lojong spirit. We may think we gain enjoyment from it, but it only increases our own misery in the long run. This attitude comes from our deluded thinking, and for as long as these delusions persist, we'll experience intense dissatisfaction, frustration, and disappointment in our lives. We must seek happiness for its own sake and make a concerted effort to overcome the spite, vindictiveness, and ill will that compel us to seek others' pain as an adornment of our happiness. Happiness does not come from someone else or from obtaining something else as a reward for our labor; it comes from a happiness-bestowing act and the wholehearted commitment to realizing the awakened heart. This lojong commitment is therefore about checking our own responses whenever we hear of someone else's misfortune, and instead cultivating a self-generating form of happiness. We should only seek happiness in the happiness and joy of others, as Sangye Gompa says:

> Rejoice when sentient beings are happy. He who is joyous when happy is called warm-hearted; you should behave in that manner.[33]

Conclusion

The commitments of this sixth lojong point are about arresting common human traits that are in fact quite unhelpful to us in both our spiritual practices and our everyday lives. If we fail to pay attention to them, our mind training practices will be corrupted or curtailed and we'll fail to derive any real benefit from them. We often neglect to pay sufficient attention to these traits because their familiarity and frequency seduce us into thinking they are of little real consequence, so the full virulence of their harmful effects manages to slip under our radar.

From our deluded samsaric standpoint, it may seem that many of these traits are necessary for our well-being, self-esteem, and self-worth. Talking about others' defects may make us appear more desirable, or gossiping about others' misfortunes may make our own misery seem less, but we have to examine these tendencies much more closely to see that this is a completely mistaken aspect of our lives.

This lojong point is emphasizing the fact that despite having a good motivation and the best intentions, our mind training will have little success if we can't commit ourselves strongly enough to undermining these traits. These tendencies don't bring us any self-confidence or happiness. In fact, they undermine our personal autonomy and well-being and obstruct our spiritual progress. It's important to put an end to these negative and paranoid tendencies and replace them with love, compassion, and the development of a kind heart. Kindheartedness is one of the central premises of the Kadampa tradition, as the following anecdotal story by Patrul Rinpoche illustrates:

> Atisha always placed a unique emphasis on the importance of a kind heart, and rather than ask people, "How are you?," he would say, "Has your heart been kind?"[34]

Guidelines for Mind Training

The seventh and final point concerns our approach to mind training in everyday life. Unlike the prescriptive slogans of the previous point, which were binding definitions of what we should and shouldn't do, these depict the overall lojong spirit we require in order to progress with our practices. Each slogan is meant to act as a triggering mechanism that will help us recall our attention to the present moment whenever we become distracted. If we treat each slogan as a mindfulness practice and memorize them properly, they will automatically spring to mind when the appropriate situations arise and make us more aware of what we're doing.

39 • All spiritual practices should be done with one intention

If we examine our minds closely, we'll see that our thoughts, speech, and actions are almost entirely motivated by egoistic obsessions. We need to develop the same single-mindedness in our spiritual practice (Skt. *yoga;* Tib. *naljor*) by taking bodhichitta as the object of our attention.[1] It's quite counterproductive to the lojong spirit to approach mind training with a heavy-handed, aggressive, and uptight attitude, waging war on our egoism or trying to force our negative tendencies into submission. If we deliberately bring kindness, sensitivity, and gentleness into our thoughts, speech, and actions, we'll start to experience a natural diminution of our self-obsessive tendencies. Sangye Gompa explains:

> The purpose of all the scriptures and treatises is to attain liberation, and for this it is necessary to subdue self-grasping. Therefore all activities of study, reflection, and meditation are for the sake of subduing self-grasping.[2]

The Kadampa teachings say that if we use our activities to open ourselves to the world with loving-kindness, patience, and understanding, we'll bring the lojong spirit into everything we do. While our practices may be diverse, if our bodhichitta attitude is natural and self-correcting, we'll be doing everything with one intention. Patrul Rinpoche relates the following story to illustrate this:

> When Trungpa Sinachen asked him for a complete instruction in a single sentence, Phadampa Sangye replied, "Whatever you want, others all want as much; so act accordingly!"[3]

40 • *All corrections are made in one way*

Maintaining the lojong spirit of bodhichitta in the face of adversity is integral to the practice of mind training. While spiritual practice eases our weariness and brings relief from the drudgery of samsaric existence, it isn't a cure for all our ills. People will still be unkind to us, and we'll still experience ill health or personal and financial difficulties. We may be the subject of gossip, litigation, harmful intentions, or abandonment and suffer from the temporary upsurge of conflicting emotions. From time to time, we may also succumb to laziness, lose all joy in our practice, or be afflicted by bouts of depression, anxiety, and despair. These experiences are characteristic of conditioned existence. The lojong teachings acknowledge very clearly that we can't stop the vagaries of life and that we have no choice but to experience them when they arise. Instead of giving in to hostility or despair, however, when we cultivate the lojong spirit, we learn to utilize difficult situations to help us generate compassion, and this in turn gives everything a positive spin. In this way we use our pain to develop compassion for all beings, and we dedicate this compassion directly to their happiness. Sangye Gompa says that the Kadampa way of correcting adversity is to welcome pain as part of our practice and use it to transform our minds:

> Therefore, when the desire for not encountering undesirable events or the fear of these occurring arises in your heart, take upon yourself the similar feelings of all sentient beings. When this is understood, the understanding of emptiness, too, arises naturally.[4]

There are obvious psychological advantages to this approach, because thinking about others lessens our own psychological distress. Wallowing in pain and self-pity only generates more negativity, while using it to reflect on the suffering of others will gradually transform the whole texture of our suffering until we can experience the world as Serlingpa does in *Leveling Out All Conceptions:*

Adverse conditions are your spiritual teacher;
Demons and possessor spirits, the Buddha's emanations;
Sickness is a broom for negative karma and defilements;
Sufferings are displays of ultimate reality's expanse—[5]

41 • *At the beginning and at the end, two things to be done*

Another helpful way to maintain the lojong spirit is to practice bodhichitta meditation at the beginning and end of each day. The Kadampa teachings continually emphasize that no two days are ever the same. We aren't caught in some kind of eternal recurrence that makes it impossible to take charge of our lives. If we wake up in a bad mood or start the day with the wrong attitude, we'll only capitulate to our habitual ways of responding to the world. Regular morning practice clears our mental cobwebs and helps us to face the day in a calm and positive frame of mind. We shouldn't feel as if we were surviving each day with a sense of relief, then drift complacently into the evening without thinking about anything. The lojong spirit discourages the ennui associated with coming home, having a few drinks, and falling asleep on the sofa. Remaining alert and practicing lojong will help relieve our minds of stress as well as give us the opportunity to review the day and reflect on our bodhichitta activities. Jamgön Kongtrül explains:

> During the day, maintain [bodhichitta] with continuous mindfulness. At the end, when you go to sleep in the evening, examine your thoughts and actions of the day. If there were infringements of bodhichitta, enumerate the instances and

acknowledge them, and make a commitment that they will not occur in the future.[6]

A joyous and positive attitude motivates us to be productive and good, while the last thing we feel like doing when we're feeling down is assisting somebody else. If we generate the loving-kindness of bodhichitta, we will gradually increase our positive outlook on life and fill our lives with richness and purpose. We need to understand that it isn't so difficult to lift ourselves up or to change our mood—we just need to be willing to educate ourselves to think positively. Then the insidious negative thoughts that lurk in our unconscious won't get the opportunity to swamp our minds. It's almost as simple as that. Our future is in our own hands. We can either lift ourselves out of our negative states or sink into despondency. That's why meditating both morning and evening is so important; it will remove our doubts, lift our spirits, and prepare us to greet each day in a happy and uplifted frame of mind.

42 • *Whichever of two occurs, be patient*

Even if we diligently practice mind training, our fortunes will continue to wax and wane. We're constantly dealing with beings who have differing karmic patterns and interconnections, so situations won't always go in our favor. Contrary to what we might sometimes think, things never remain the same. We're either feeling as if we're making progress or we're backsliding and losing any gains we might have made. Mind training is the only thing that can center our lives. Without it, we'll be swept by the winds of change as if we had no control over our existence. Despite this fact, we rarely do anything that has a galvanizing force in our lives, and as a result, our ups and downs are often quite extreme. As the following traditional verse makes clear, an intelligent form of patience is required if we're to avoid being hurt and destabilized by the vicissitudes of life:

Even if you are prosperous like the gods,
Pray do not be conceited.
Even if you become as destitute as a hungry ghost,
Pray do not be disheartened.[7]

Life's trials often reduce us to damaged, bruised, and battered emotional wrecks. If we can bring a modicum of intelligence to our patience, we won't become so exhilarated by our highs or self-defeated by our lows, as if we were suffering from bipolar disorder. Whichever of the two occurs, we'll be able to maintain a sense of stability and groundedness. Patience is not a form of passivity, where we have no power over what life might throw at us. The lojong teachings are not advocating that kind of acquiescence. Even when life's trials are unpleasant or upsetting, patience allows us to face them in a creative and beneficial way, with courage and dignity.

Lojong practice is not just about trying to survive the rough patches in life; we're trying to transform ourselves into better people as a direct result of our experiences. If things always went our way, we wouldn't be able to develop high ideals and live a meaningful life. Instead of responding to difficulty the way we normally do, with frustration or impotent rage, we learn to approach life's contingencies with patience and intelligence. The skillful exercise of patience will make us less flaky and predictable, and we'll be able to utilize situations to our advantage. Sangye Gompa illustrates this point with the following story:

If you possess this [instruction], even though you might appear ordinary to others' eyes, whatever you do can become nothing but a cause for attaining omniscience; everything turns into a great act. [Chekawa] embraced this as his sole heart practice such that even at the threshold of death he would say, "There is no more melodious sound in this world than the sound of mind training. Pray make this sound in my ears."[8]

43 • Observe these two, even at the risk of your life

According to the Kadampa masters, the Buddha's teachings are summarized in the following passage from the Dhammapada: "By engaging in everything that's wholesome and refraining from everything that's unwholesome, you will tame your mind. That is the essence of my teachings." Interacting with others with a sense of wholesomeness in our bearing, demeanor, and activities is adhering to the essence of the Buddhist teachings, because that is how we tame our minds. We should never approach life in terms of expedience but should rather think about our actions in the context of the benefit they might bring. We should always be thinking about the long-term benefits rather than pursuing dubious actions for short-term gains. We should always abstain from anything that is unsavory, even at the risk of our lives. Someone may threaten us by saying, "I will kill you unless you shoot this person" or "I will spare your life if you kill this goat," but we should never sacrifice our lojong commitment and allow ourselves to be contaminated by evil and pernicious behavior. Dharmarakshita's The Poison-Destroying Peacock Mind Training reinforces this point:

Even at the risk of your own life, keep the practice of austerities and endure suffering for others' sake.[9]

44 • *Learn the three difficult points*

I. Recognizing Conflicting Emotions

Much of our suffering is caused by our own delusory states and conflicting emotions rather than by other people. Strong emotions such as intense jealousy, covetousness, greed, unbridled lust, anger, and pride make it quite difficult for us to control our responses to others. The sheer force of our negative emotions make it difficult to even identify our emotions, so we just get swept along by their energy without recognizing what has taken place. The first thing we need to do therefore is to practice self-reflection and learn to recognize strong emotions when they arise. We all have the five poisons of excessive desire, anger, jealousy, pride, and ignorance, but they aren't evenly distributed in our psyche. Some people may have an overwhelming problem with aggression, while others struggle with jealousy, and still others with lust. For example, an attractive member of the opposite sex may walk past and we're instantly overcome by lust, only to recognize after the fact how much we have embarrassed ourselves. We may have even caused a car accident as we are driving along. That has never happened to me, of course, but only because I don't drive. It's quite difficult to identify a particular conflicting emotion and then recognize it when it arises in the mind, because our conflicting emotions generate so much confusion. As Aryadeva points out:

> Desire is painful because of not getting,
> Anger is painful through lack of might,

And confusion through not understanding.
Because of this, these are not recognized.[10]

2. Managing Conflicting Emotions

Even when we accurately identify our conflicting emotions, they remain quite a challenge to moderate or control, because recognition alone is not enough to lessen their impact. We can only learn to overcome these emotions through shamatha meditation, and practicing the four immeasurables of love, compassion, joy, and equanimity, for only these can sufficiently calm our minds enough to enable us to process our emotions as they arise. Unless we learn to overcome our strong emotions, we'll never find a gentle and constructive way to respond to other people and situations. Serlingpa alludes to the destructiveness of our emotions in this verse from *Stages of the Heroic Mind:*

When disturbances occur within,
Alas, even medicinal wine may turn to poison.
Without slaying the life force of the five poisons . . .
Alas, you will feel remorse from the depths of your
      heart.[11]

3. Eliminating Conflicting Emotions

Despite gaining some control over our conflicting emotions, it's still not possible to overcome them completely unless we learn to transform them. Transformation comes from understanding the nature of our emotions through vipashyana meditation. Our emotions seem so overpowering when we can't see them properly, but we find they have no real substance when we learn to analyze them in meditation. Emotions are fleeting, rising and falling beyond our reach, and it's only when we try to really grasp them in meditation that we realize how impossible they are to pin down. As we deepen this understanding, the effects of our emotions will gradually diminish, until they eventually cease to cause us any real discomfort.

45 • *Acquire the three root causes*

We won't learn to deal with difficulties if we're left to our own devices, because our samsaric minds don't know how to overcome their own shortcomings. We need the assistance of others to receive the guidance, learn the methods, and gain the support we require to traverse the spiritual path. The three root causes of enlightenment show us how to tackle our difficulties and make real progress with our mind training.

1. The Spiritual Friend

The first root cause is the spiritual friend (Skt. *kalyanamitra;* Tib. *dge gshes*), who can impart the requisite knowledge to us. The lojong teachings don't mention gurus, they talk only about the spiritual friend who can act as our mentor or guide. Togme Sangpo expresses the Kadampa view of the kalyanamitra in this verse:

When you rely on them your faults come to an end
And your good qualities grow like the waxing moon.

Cherish spiritual teachers
Even more than your own body—
This is the practice of Bodhisattvas.[12]

The wisdom and advice of a good kalyanamitra can guide us through the stages of spiritual development with consummate ease. Without their help we will just be stumbling around in the dark without knowing what to do. An experienced kalyanamitra is there to teach the proper methods and attitudes to our spiritual practice. Contact with someone who has this prior knowledge and experience circumvents the need to reinvent the whole process and assures our steady progress. As Patrul Rinpoche explains:

As the sick man relies on his doctor,
The traveler on his escort,
The frightened man on his companion,
Merchants on their captain,
And passengers on their ferryman—
If birth, death and negative emotions are the enemies
    you fear,
Entrust yourself to a teacher.[13]

The topic of gurus and Eastern teachers has become a contentious issue in the West, and I admit to having my own opinions on this matter. The guru is often the scapegoat for everything that's gone wrong in modern spirituality. We'd be well advised to remember that many cult leaders in the West belong to Christian rather than Tibetan or Zen lineages. I don't know any Buddhist communities that barricade themselves in the remote desert and refuse to pay taxes, nor do I know any Tibetan Buddhist teachers who encourage their students to take up arms. Nonetheless, there seems to be this notion that a guru is all-powerful and will dominate one's personal life.

It could easily be argued that psychotherapists have a greater degree of control over their patients than Eastern teachers have over their students. The sole purpose of having a therapist is to tell them all your secrets. Anyone who knows our secrets has a hold over us, as we all know. Yet people routinely go to see psychotherapists, handing over their money and revealing their deepest fears, sexual inadequacies, and murderous impulses toward their father, or whatever the case may be. They willingly hand over a degree of power to their therapists for a fee in exchange for the hour or so once a week that the therapist might spare in return. Spiritual teachers don't have any such power, but are expected to be available at all times, receiving no financial remuneration for their advice. Nonetheless, despite working very hard, they are often accused of leading a privileged life.

Psychotherapists question the ability of Buddhism and Buddhist meditation to solve our existential dilemmas, yet they themselves offer no real advice for working with our problems. For example, if you had an issue with jealousy, the prevailing counsel you would receive would be that your jealousy is the result of childhood rivalry, where your siblings were favored over you, and your memory of having a favorite toy snatched away from you is the root of your problems. Now, even if that were true, how could that knowledge help you solve your problems? It would only create further problems for you, because it would intensify your resentment toward your parents and siblings. This kind of analysis is quite shallow and gratuitous. We compete with our siblings because we're already competitively oriented by nature. Particular incidents of jealousy or anger are never the actual origin of our troubles.

In recent years many therapists have been quite vocal in their criticism of Buddhist teachers. Their comments seem unjustified, and it isn't hard to turn their arguments around to reveal their own shortcomings. It's also not uncommon to find a marriage counselor who has been divorced six or more times, yet tells their clients nothing about it. I personally find that very disturbing. While the media like to make a big deal of scandals involving teachers and cult leaders, they ignore the fact that many therapists and psychiatrists have been deregistered or sent to prison as a direct result of abusing or defrauding their patients. I'm not saying all therapists behave in this way or that therapy is a bad thing per se. I have many friends who are therapists. However, claims that Western psychology is superior to Buddhism, that it has a greater capacity to help, or that it's a more complete approach to personal health than meditation are completely misleading and unfounded. Unless we genuinely examine our own minds and expose our self-obsessive tendencies, we might fit the description in the following verse by Godrakpa:

> Not having relied on a master and solitude,
> for those who are attached to their yaks at home,
> familiarity with confused afflicting emotion is easy
> while clothed in evil habitual propensities.[14]

2. The Spiritual Instructions

The spiritual instructions we receive from the kalyanamitra are also an indispensable source of guidance, especially if we receive them in a way that is appropriate to our personalities, predilections, and propensities. If there's a good fit between the practice and the practitioner, we can apply the teachings and practices that are most beneficial. This is done by hearing the teachings, contemplating their meaning, and finally assimilating their content into our being through meditation. We should never be cavalier or half-hearted in our approach to understanding the teachings, for it's only by embracing them fully that we can attain results of any profundity. As Patrul Rinpoche says:

> Just as the trunk of an ordinary tree
> Lying in the forests of the Malayan mountains
> Absorbs the perfume of sandal from the moist leaves
>   and branches,
> So you come to resemble whomever you follow.[15]

3. A Supportive Environment

According to the lojong teachings, a supportive environment includes both people and their physical surroundings. If we're going to benefit from the practice, we need to place ourselves in an environment that supports our spiritual goals. This means not associating with people who have negative habits or unwholesome influences, such as those who indulge in unsavory acts of violence, overindulge in sense pleasures, or while away their time in frivolous activities. A proper environment means fewer obstacles and disruptive events, while an improper environment just about guarantees the disruption of our efforts. It is especially critical for a beginner to have an appropriate physical and mental space in which to practice, otherwise the constant bombardment of negativities will be too disruptive. That's why it is advisable to go into retreat and do lojong intensives from time to time. As Nagarjuna says in his *Instructions from a Spiritual Friend:*

To dwell in a favorable place, to associate
With worthy people, to practice true devotion, and
To possess good merits of previous lives—
These four great opportune interactions enable you to
    attain your purpose in life.[16]

46 • Don't allow three things to diminish

When we've found a spiritual friend, received their teachings, and found a supportive environment, there are three things we need to maintain for the duration of our lives.

1. Interested Humility toward the Kalyanamitra

Having made a real connection with the kalyanamitra, we must ensure that we don't become too familiar with him or her, or we may fail to benefit from the instructions. It's like the old adage "Familiarity breeds contempt," which happens sooner or later in every relationship. While we don't necessarily go so far as to experience contempt, our appreciation and respect for our spiritual friend may begin to deteriorate. You may feel very enthusiastic, respectful, and humble toward your teacher initially, but as you become more familiar with him or her, you start to lose those qualities and may even begin to belittle him or her in the process.

We need to have both intimacy and space in our relationship with the kalyanamitra. We can't be completely intimate, because that might blur the boundaries and become confusing for both parties, but our intimacy should be based on a general sense of trust and respect. There must be enough space to provide room for movement so that you don't stifle each other emotionally. It isn't enough to make a connection to our kalyanamitra and leave it at that; we need to work on all of these elements and continually ensure that our connection is genuine and strong. That's why it's so vital to maintain the interested humility we spoke about in the first chapter. Shantideva advises:

> Never, at the cost of life or limb,
> Forsake your virtuous friend, your teacher,
> Learned in the meaning of the Mahayana,
> Supreme in practice of the bodhisattva path.[17]

2. Joy in Our Practice

An ongoing and respectful relationship with the kalyanamitra isn't in itself sufficient; we need to make sure that our relationship does not diminish. At the beginning, we may be very enthusiastic and excited about practicing lojong, but after a while it can start to become routine and we no longer see it as special. If our practice ceases to bring us joy, we have to find a way to regenerate our enthusiasm and lift our spirits, because a failure to take delight in what we're doing will gradually reduce the benefit we derive from it, and we won't develop the qualities that are necessary for traversing the bodhisattva path. As Godrakpa states, "Relying on a master is easy; adopting good qualities is hard."[18]

3. Commitment to the Path

The Kadampa teachings place enormous emphasis on commitment because we're more likely to succeed at something if we're resolute about it. There are commitments such as the five precepts,[19] the novice vows, and the vows of a fully ordained monk or nun. The most important aspect of whatever commitment we choose to make, however, is to keep it strong. The lojong teachings may seem simple and straightforward, but they're also a vast and profound repository of the practices, methods, transmissions, and teachings of Mahayana Buddhism, and we should never waver in our dedication to that.

47 • Make the three inseparable

This guideline is about creating virtue through our body, speech, and mind. These are often called "the three gates," because they are the three faculties through which we interact with others. The things that leave or enter through these three faculties determine everything about us, including our self-perception. In our ordinary deluded state, our body, speech, and mind tend to work at cross-purposes. Our body might be busy doing one thing, while our mind is engaged in something else, and our words seem to have little conscious awareness of either. The lojong teachings emphasize that our three gates should work together with a common purpose rather than operating separately. We need to feel that we're occupying our body as a single unit, rather than experiencing some kind of enforced residency. If we can employ body, speech, and mind equally and coherently in our lojong practices, we'll gradually overcome the habitual patterns that compel us to behave in a disembodied way. Konchok Gyaltsen states:

> Thus through striving in virtue with your three doors [of body, speech, and mind], your practice of mind training will become greatly enhanced, like adding fresh logs to a fire.[20]

48 • *Train in all areas without partiality*

From the lojong point of view, any circumstances or situations can be employed to our advantage, so we shouldn't allow external or internal conditions to dictate how we practice. Maintaining an attitude of evenness toward whatever occurs in our lives will help us maintain a sense of impartiality (Skt. *samanartha;* Tib. *nyam pa nyid*), so that we approach all our experiences in a non-biased and non-preferential way. While things do manifest in varying ways on the relative level, there is no difference between them at the absolute level, because everything has the nature of emptiness. The lojong spirit comes from integrating equanimity and loving-kindness, so that we ground our compassion in impartiality. This will help us to keep our practice real and ensure that it retains a sense of lightness and movement, for lack of movement will cause our energy to stagnate, while too much movement will create a restless energy that disperses in all directions.

We maintain a sense of impartiality in tonglen meditation by remembering that everyone in samsara is suffering in one way or another. It's not just the poor, the sick, or the disadvantaged who suffer; everyone who lives is suffering in his or her own unique way. Samsaric existence is suffering. The people who complain the loudest are not always suffering the most. In my limited experience, people who have very difficult lives often don't complain that much, while those who have relatively little to contend with never stop complaining. While it may not be possible to consistently maintain this impartiality in everyday life, meditation practice affords us the luxury of imagining whatever we wish without restrictions. Viewing everybody in the same way during meditation will help us to develop a semblance of impartiality in everyday life, even if we don't yet have the wisdom of equanimity. Jamgön Kongtrül explains:

> Without partiality for certain areas, mind training by it-self should pervade everything, good or bad, which arises as an object of experience: other sentient beings, the four elements, or nonhuman beings. Deeply trained proficiency, not just lip service, is important.[21]

49 • *Always meditate on difficult points*

It's important to have joy and enthusiasm for our practice, but we should still find it challenging enough to test our capabilities for growth. Difficulties must be welcomed because it's only by overcoming challenges that we develop. We should gradually introduce into our meditation those areas that we normally find upsetting or difficult, instead of choosing meditations that always ease our minds or make us feel good without requiring much effort on our part. If our practice becomes tedious, unproductive, or painful, we need to correct that instead of blaming the practice or succumbing to a defeatist attitude. The distinctive feature of lojong is the importance it places on topics that challenge our understanding, test our endurance, and stretch our mental capabilities.

Lojong practice provides the opportunity to exercise our minds in ways we might find difficult to implement in real life. However, the benefit of doing things as an imaginative exercise is almost the same as actually doing them in the real world, because these imaginative exercises still have a transformative effect on our attitudes and karmic dispositions. If we just stay within our comfort zone and never challenge ourselves, our progress will be slow. Very often we think, "I can't do that, it's just too much," but that timidity only comes from our self-obsession. We must realistically assess what we can and can't do and then make a concerted effort to keep extending ourselves. Otherwise, we'll stay trapped within the samsaric condition and continue to wander aimlessly, like the people in the following verse by Godrakpa:

In samsara, which is like a dream and illusion,
sentient beings roam like blind lunatics.
Not realizing the truth that confused appearances have
    no essence,
those who cling to the false as true get so exhausted.[22]

If we face challenges properly, instead of grimly enduring them, we'll find them much easier to deal with in the future. The Mahayana teachings say that there is nothing that doesn't get easier once we become familiar with it. A sign of success in mind training is feeling more at ease with something that we once found difficult. When we're new to lojong, we may prefer to start with the easy things and practice tonglen only in regard to the people we care about. The lojong teachings actually do recommend that we begin this way, in fact. However, we need to gradually stretch and expand our scope as we become more proficient with the practice. It's only an imaginative exercise, after all. This is the only way to develop the qualities that are necessary to become a bodhisattva.

50 • *Don't depend on external conditions*

As lojong practitioners we should practice whenever and wherever possible, not just when the right conditions are present. If we believe we can only practice well under certain conditions, we'll make a habit of only practicing when these conditions arise. There will always be conditions that are detrimental to our lives, because external situations are beyond our control. Konchok Gyaltsen illustrates this point in the following story:

[Chekawa once said:] "At Chenga Monastery there were limited offerings and resources. Thinking, 'I shall go to the countryside to obtain these,' I went to Yarlung, but failed to find them there either. Because of my ignorance I had failed to understand that 'cyclic existence' is a name for deficiency."[23]

Nobody is ever consistently happy, and for as long as we live, we'll meet with favorable and unfavorable conditions. We can view all situations as favorable to our lojong practice because every situation can serve the development of bodhichitta. If we continue to practice loving-kindness and bodhichitta, we'll develop a general sense of cheerfulness and happiness, irrespective of the circumstances we meet. The true lojong spirit has no limit, and we'll find that we can persevere in all situations if our guiding principle becomes "Because everything that I experience is only my own perception, where I am or what I'm doing becomes part of lojong practice."

51 • *This time, practice the important points*

The lojong spirit is about investing our time and energy into whatever advances our spiritual development. This slogan also has three points.

1. Other People Are More Important Than We Are

Training ourselves to think constantly that others are more important than we are and to perform all actions with other people's welfare in mind is far more important than expecting our practice to improve our own circumstances. The lojong teachings are essentially saying that while we may be practicing mind training, if we're worrying more about our own progress than the welfare of others, we're not practicing it properly.

2. Practice Is More Important Than Understanding

While Buddhism emphasizes learning, we still have to put what we've learned into practice. Instead of thinking, "Do I really understand this?" or "Am I on the right track?" we should be asking, "Did I practice today?" or "Did my thoughts go anywhere near wishing somebody happiness?" In other words, instead of worrying about our own ongoing problems, we should concentrate on applying what we've learned to our everyday lives.

3. Bodhichitta Is Most Important of All

We shouldn't practice with cold detachment or extreme efficiency, but with true feeling and a warm heart. Lojong isn't something we should approach with the disciplined precision of a military exercise. Trungpa Rinpoche used to speak a great deal about precision and discipline, but at the same time he emphasized gentleness and the need to have a "soft spot" in our hearts. The most important aspect of any spiritual practice is that we do it with the loving-kindness of bodhichitta—there is nothing more profound than this. If bodhichitta isn't present in our practices, they'll never be of any real consequence, but if bodhichitta is there, whatever we do will be instantly transformed into a genuinely spiritual exercise. Se Chilbu Chokyi Gyaltsen reinforces this point:

> Of the two aspects of Dharma, exposition and practice, the latter is more important. Compared to all other meditative practices, the practice of training in the awakening mind is more important.[24]

52 • Avoid misunderstandings

Despite our best intentions, it's easy to misunderstand things or apply them incorrectly in our lives. This confusion is the result of not being able to distinguish what we need to cultivate and what we need to eliminate from our lives. There are six fundamental errors we should assiduously try to avoid in our lojong practices.

1. Misunderstanding Patience

We know the general difference between wholesome and unwholesome pursuits, but there are always gray areas, especially when something can be virtuous in one situation and non-virtuous in the next. As we've already observed, patience is a very good example of this, for while patience is lauded as one of the most important virtues, practicing it wrongly can have catastrophic results. We often lack fortitude in the face of spiritual hardship, but are quite willing to accept difficult or unpleasant circumstances in our everyday lives. As Sangye Gompa says:

> Misplaced forbearance refers to being able to bear the various hardships involved in farming, subduing [outer] enemies, and protecting loved ones instead of the forbearance involved in being able to endure hardships for the sake of Dharma practice.[25]

We show enormous patience in our search for mundane entertainments and willingly sacrifice all kinds of things without complaint. We also put ourselves through enormous stress in our jobs and may even be prepared to risk our lives in search of adventure. People who climb Mount Everest often lose life and limb, but no one ever complains. However, when it comes to spiritual practice, we don't even have the patience to sit on the cushion for half an hour, preferring to complain about all our insurmountable aches and pains, pins and needles, and so forth. Shantideva asks us to put our spiritual trials in perspective with this verse:

> The doctor and those skilled in healing arts,
> Use bitter remedies to cure our ills.
> Likewise we, to uproot dreadful sorrow,
> Should bear what are indeed but little pains.[26]

This lack of patience doesn't just relate to our spiritual endeavors. We find it difficult to do anything that's beneficial, such as sticking to a nutritious and well-balanced diet, yet we quite happily endure the obesity and high blood pressure that come from eating the wrong foods. We have to recognize that not being patient when something is beneficial for us, while still enduring hardship in pursuit of fleeting pleasures, is the work of a deluded mind.

2. Misunderstanding Interest

Maintaining our interest in a particular act indicates that a sense of curiosity is compelling us to explore and learn new things. However, we often show no interest in what might benefit us and instead have an enormous curiosity for what is pointless or harmful. Our interest in drugs or wasting hours in Internet chat rooms is often so resilient that the activity becomes addictive. If we wish to develop as human beings, we need to let go of our interest in trivial, counterfeit, or distracting pursuits and turn our attention to spiritual matters instead. As Shantideva comments:

> Indeed, O foolish and afflicted mind,
> You want, you crave for everything,
> This "everything" will grow and turn
> To suffering increased a thousandfold.[27]

It's only our delusions that blind us and drag us deeper into darkness and despair. Instead of pursuing preoccupations that lead to a totally meaningless endgame, we should pursue those interests that bring us spiritual nourishment and enrich our lives.

3. Misunderstanding How to Savor Things

Just as a moth is drawn to a flame, our samsaric conditioning leads us to experiment with harmful or dangerous pursuits that never allow us to learn from our experiences. The Mahayana teachings say that like elephants, which are drawn to mud baths only to drown in the swamp; or butterflies, which are drawn to flowers only to be entrapped by their petals; we are led by our taste for sensual pleasures to "lick honey from a razor blade." Shantideva eloquently turns this metaphor around:

> And since I never have enough of pleasure,
> Honey on the razor's edge,
> How could I have enough of merit,
> Fruits of which are happiness and peace?[28]

If we don't follow Shantideva's advice, the myriad tastes of samsaric life will eventually jade us so that nothing will excite us anymore and our ability to feel moved will be permanently blunted. If we learn to appreciate nutritious sustenance instead of junk food, we'll enjoy what is good for us rather than what is degrading. Savoring the taste of spiritual bliss instead of the fake and simulated pleasures of the samsaric world will bring us genuine excitement and joy.

4. Misunderstanding Compassion

This misunderstanding relates to what Trungpa Rinpoche used to call "idiot compassion": misunderstanding compassion by not skillfully using our intelligence to distinguish between worthy and unworthy objects. While our compassion must be impartial and we should never discriminate between people on an individual basis, it's important to direct our compassion to people who are genuinely in need of it. Allowing our heart to override our intelligence by being fooled, blackmailed, or coerced into helping someone is not an expression of genuine compassion. Often we mistakenly feel sorry for someone who is following the spiritual path, instead of directing our compassion toward the multitudes of suffering sentient creatures wandering aimlessly in samsaric existence. Whatever difficulties spiritual people may undergo, these hardships are not worthless. The real objects of our compassion should be people who have no sense of direction and not enough insight into their existential condition to realize they have gone astray. Se Chilbu Chokyi Gyaltsen states:

> If, instead of cultivating compassion for those caught in suffering and its conditions, you have compassion for those who undergo sufferings as part of their ascetic life and meditative pursuits—this is misplaced compassion.[29]

5. Misunderstanding How to Give Help to Others

While the desire to help others is obviously a laudable and noble intention, giving someone what they want is not necessarily a helpful act, just as supplying drugs to an addict is not going to help overcome their addiction. When somebody is unhappy and confused, placing a psychic Band-Aid on their emotional wound is not especially constructive. Saying, "You should be angry with that bastard, how could he do that to you?" or "You should be jealous of that woman, that princess!" may seem to make someone feel better, but it only really exacerbates the situation by encouraging further entanglement in delusory states. Extending ourselves to someone by helping them to see through the fog of their self-recrimination and anger is how we offer them genuine assistance. It's important to be really clear and discerning about this point—our aim should be to help others reduce their deluded states of mind.

This point also refers to misunderstandings that may occur in relation to our own needs. We shouldn't reject help from others just because we're practicing lojong, or refuse material aid from someone who has a genuine interest in supporting the Dharma. However, while it's permissible to receive someone's assistance to pursue the Dharma, it's completely reprehensible to rely on their help to raise our own profile or to give or receive help as a way of impressing others.

6. Misunderstanding What It Means to Rejoice

Even though we should cultivate joy to lift our mood and cheer us in our practice, it's also possible to rejoice at inappropriate occasions. Before we rejoice in someone else's actions, we should learn whether they are motivated by any of the five poisons. The lojong teachings advise us to rejoice in other people's joy, but that obviously doesn't apply when people are taking pleasure in the wrong things. We don't rejoice when someone we know is experiencing a state of ecstasy as a result of consuming narcotics or if he or she has harmed another being, nor do we rejoice if somebody we dislike experiences misfortune. As Shantideva admonishes:

If unhappiness befalls your enemy,
Why should this be a cause for your rejoicing?
The wishes of your mind alone,
Will not in fact contrive his injury.[30]

Our ability to rejoice in someone else's joy doesn't have to be restricted to spiritual activities; we can also rejoice when someone gets married, receives a promotion, buys a new car, and so forth. For example, if we walk past a restaurant and see a couple we know laughing and having a good time, it's better to rejoice at their happiness than think, "Why isn't that me in there?"

53 • Don't fluctuate

We should work at being consistent with our practice, rather than cultivating an all-or-nothing approach. There is little benefit in being upbeat, enthusiastic, and big-hearted about lojong one day and then completely apathetic about it the next. Cramming all our practice into intensive periods and then falling back into worldly life will bear far less fruit than doing small amounts of practice consistently over the long haul. Jamgön Kongtrül says:

> A person who sometimes practices and sometimes doesn't has not developed a definite understanding of dharma. Don't have a lot of projects on your mind, but do mind training single-mindedly.[31]

This slogan also points out that we need to be open to change and learning while remaining reliable and trustworthy so that we don't make promises to people only to let them down. A stable approach that gradually immerses us in something is far more productive than acting in sporadic bursts. According to the Kadampa masters, that kind of fluctuation consumes our energy very quickly and discourages us from making further attempts for long periods of time. This slogan is not saying we can't find new and innovative ways to approach things, just that we need to look at our spiritual practice as having a cumulative effect. We need to work out very honestly and realistically what we can do given our current circumstances, and model our practice around that. Regular practice becomes part of us, while fluctuating practice has very little benefit at all, which is why Patrul Rinpoche counsels us:

> Until you attain perfect Buddhahood, you will still have past actions and tendencies to remove, and will still need to attain more and more spiritual qualities. So do not fall into indolent and sporadic practice. Practice Dharma with diligence from the depth of your heart, without ever feeling that you have done enough.[32]

54 • Train wholeheartedly

A wholehearted commitment is about seeing something through to the end. It's not about making a big splash to see what happens, thinking that all is well and good if things work out and then moving on to something else if they don't. A total, wholehearted commitment doesn't involve sporadic outbursts but rather a judicious expenditure of energy over the long term. Courage is also an essential element in our practice, and it's far better to overestimate what we want to achieve than to underestimate it. We should never think, "I'll just aim small because I only have the capacity to become a slightly better person." Our expectations must be realistic and we have to fulfill them in a graduated manner, but we should always set our goals high and do what we can without "hope" or "fear." We shouldn't run away or hide from things, but learn to deal with them in an upfront way, without any deviousness or manipulation. Se Chilbu Chokyi Gyaltsen echoes the true Kadampa spirit in these words:

> When a minor nerve is damaged, you treat it by cutting it clean. In the same way, when you engage in the training of mind, do not remain hesitant but direct your entire mind. You should remain resolute in your decision and train with no hesitation.[33]

55 • *Find freedom through investigation and examination*

It's important to complement the practice of compassion with analytical skills if we're to gain understanding and insight, because we'll never be free of confusion without the investigation (Tib. *tok*) and examination (Tib. *chod*) of our mental processes. From time to time we need to ask penetrating questions such as the following: What is the self? What is the mind? What is ultimate reality? What is samsara and ignorance? Investigation is about analyzing things in general terms, while examination is about analyzing them in detail. In other words, we have to look at our overall situation and then break that down into specific elements. A detective will investigate a particular case and then examine the evidence, analyzing the crime in both general and specific terms. If we approach our mental processes in this manner, we'll solve many of our problems and clarify much of our confusion. Learning to know our own minds honestly and fearlessly through these methods will liberate us from self-obsessive thoughts and overcome our mental dullness, giving a tremendous boost to our lojong commitments. As Chandrakirti states in his *Madhyamakavatara:*

Common folk are fettered by their thoughts;
Without such concepts, yogis are set free.
The very halting of discursiveness is fruit
Of true analysis, the wise have said.[34]

56 • *Don't expect gratitude*

Generally speaking, when we are too desirous of something in life, we're less likely to attain it. Success seems to increase in direct proportion to the diminution of our desires. The same logic applies to our need for recognition. We might want to be appreciated and respected, but we have only a limited ability to influence how other people respond and we can't make somebody show us gratitude any more than we can force someone to love us. If we show love without expecting it to be reciprocated, we will have more chance of finding love than if we simply yearn for it. Likewise, doing something without expecting gratitude is more likely to elicit appreciation for what we do. Whether someone can acknowledge our actions or not should be no concern of ours. We simply commit ourselves to doing things to the best of our ability and in as thorough a manner as possible without sloppiness. We should never think that other people are indebted to us or obligated to help us in return. We should simply do things because we love doing them, not because we want other people to feel indebted to us. Shantideva says:

The work of bringing benefit to beings
Will not, then, make me proud and self-admiring.
The happiness of others is itself my satisfaction;
I do not expect another recompense.[35]

We shouldn't think the Buddhas and bodhisattvas owe us anything or that our teachers or fellow practitioners owe us. They owe us nothing. We have to see the world this way and not expect anyone's acknowledgment. Whether we're seeking success in daily life, personal relationships, or our spiritual aspirations, we always get the best results when we are naturally more at ease with ourselves. If we want to show kindness, we should just leave it at that. Jamgön Kongtrül clearly states the lojong perspective:

> Don't make a big fuss even when you are kind to another person, because you are, in fact, just working at regarding others as more important than yourself.[36]

57 • Don't react impulsively with anger or irritation

It's not necessary to always react impulsively, allowing our instinctual responses to get the better of us. We tend to think anger is empowering, but recurrent anger only has a toxic effect on our mind and body and gradually reduces our self-esteem so that we feel more vulnerable, threatened, and prone to pervasive feelings of insecurity. We turn on the television, and everything we see makes us angry or anxious. Our children are running around creating havoc, and we become even more disturbed and angry, imagining that everyone is conspiring against us, interpreting everything as a personal attack that must be countered by vindictiveness or spite. Outbursts such as these may cause us to try to make amends later, but the damage will have been done. The main point is that we are less likely to react with anger or irritation if we feel good about ourselves. We can lift our spirits by learning to express our emotions in a healthy and fruitful way. Lojong practice won't lead to conflict or friction with others, but instead will enable us gradually to acquire the ability to temper our emotional reactions and eradicate our impulsiveness. A traditional Kadampa saying captures this point:

The mind that is full of defects
Has nonetheless a multitude of qualities:
Whatever is cultivated, that comes to be.[37]

58 • *Don't be like an open book*

We don't need to display every passing emotion, as if some kind of drama were going on every minute of the day. That approach is often confusing for other people. This Tibetan phrase literally means "letting everybody know whatever emotion we are feeling." We don't have to make every emotion blatantly obvious, like actors on a daytime soap opera. Most of the thoughts and emotions that take place in our minds are temporary anyway and don't endure for very long. If we express these to others, it's easy for them to draw the conclusion that we're a certain type of person when that's far from the truth. We need to show integrity and dignity and refrain from acting out like narcissists or drama-queens. That kind of behavior is anathema to the lojong spirit and makes it extremely difficult for us to train our minds. Whether we feel happy or sad, we should be as even-tempered as possible, not suppressing our emotions but presenting a consistent demeanor so that others will welcome any help we have to offer.

59 • *Don't expect people to make a fuss over what you are doing*

It's very easy to transfer our mundane habitual patterns and delusions onto our spiritual practices when in reality nothing has changed. Many people put on a theatrical display, expecting others to be impressed enough to make a big fuss over them and write them up in the newspaper or commemorate them on television. You shouldn't expect to gain credentials from your spiritual attainments. Even if you've made advances with your practice, you shouldn't expect the trees to bend toward you or celestial firecrackers to light up the sky, for such displays demonstrate nothing. Shantideva says:

> Thus when I work for others' sake,
> No reason can there be for boasting or amazement.
> For it is just as when I feed myself—
> I don't expect to be rewarded.[38]

We just do our practice with sincerity and regard the practice as its own reward. The reward is not like a pot of gold at the end of the rainbow—the practice itself is the goal. That goal lasts until the day we attain enlightenment. If we let go of the expectation that some big reward is awaiting us, we'll realize we're rewarded every time we embody the lojong spirit. Every time we generate bodhichitta, every time we think about someone else, every time we sit down on the meditation cushion, every time we help an old person to cross the street or engage in other acts of kindness, we are benefiting ourselves. That is the whole point.

What further reward is there beyond finding that our actions are gratifying, meaningful, and purposeful in themselves? We should constantly contemplate the following sentiments of Shantideva:

> The goal of every act is happiness itself,
> Though, even with great wealth, it's rarely found,
> So take your pleasure in the qualities of others.
> Let them be a heartfelt joy to you.[39]

Conclusion

L ojong is a very powerful practice that I hope you will continue whenever and wherever you can. It's important to
maintain the friendly spirit of the practice as well as its inherent
sense of politeness and decorum. We don't just practice mind
training on the meditation cushion, we do it in every facet of our
lives, so the way that we act and speak becomes extremely important. These days people often dismiss the importance of manners, giving themselves permission to say and do whatever they
want. This kind of liberalism usually only applies to their own
actions, however, as they become very upset when they're at the
receiving end of someone else's thoughtlessness. We're not talking about having a stiff upper lip or anything of that nature. I
hope our upper lips remain loose and relaxed, for being kind to
each other is the way to maintain the spirit of lojong. If we practice lojong sincerely, we cannot fail to gain some benefit, for as
this text constantly reiterates, the practice begins with us.

Throughout this book I have tried to faithfully follow the traditional presentation of the lojong teachings. The language might
be more contemporary, but the format is otherwise unchanged,
because I dispute the contemporary notion that Buddhism requires

modernization to be accessible to the Western mind. The traditional Buddhist teachings are already very accessible and do not require modification or adaptation. I don't believe there's any such thing as a Western mind that is different from an Eastern mind. There may be a modern mind and a traditional mind, but that's a completely separate issue. The Buddhist teachings are speaking to our personal experiences, and these experiences haven't changed much from the dawn of history to the present time. I truly believe that Westerners will benefit tremendously from the traditional teachings. Trying to change them too much only dilutes their power. Translating Buddhism into the languages of secular cultures also diminishes its impact. The Western vocabulary often makes Buddhism indistinguishable from other disciplines because it dilutes the spiritual elements. Someone who takes an interest in traditional Buddhism will therefore engage a richer and more profound world than someone who only chooses to follow a diluted version of the teachings. In my humble opinion, drawing inspiration from the profound wisdom of the traditional Buddhist teachings is not in conflict with leading a spiritually fulfilling and meaningful life in the present time. In fact, it is sorely needed.

Jamgön Kongtrül's Lojong Prayer

Translated by Traleg Kyabgon

To the supremely elevated Avalokiteshvara
and all the Buddhas and bodhisattvas.
May the veracity of your perfect compassion
for myself and all migrating beings equal to the expanse
    of space
give birth to supreme bodhichitta in all sentient creatures.

Under the influence of aggression,
sentient creatures experience the hot and cold hells.
May the karmic cause and fruit of their suffering dissi-
    pate within me.
I offer my intention of loving-kindness
and the virtuous root of nonaggression
to all migrating beings equal to the expanse of space.
May the dwelling place of the hell of aggression be
    emptied.
May they realize Avalokiteshvara of the Vajra-family
and attain mirrorlike wisdom.

Under the influence of miserliness and passion,
hungry ghosts experience hunger and thirst.
May the karmic cause and fruit of their suffering
    dissipate within me.
I offer my thought of renunciation
and the virtuous root of dispassion
to all migrating beings equal to the expanse of space.
May the dwelling place of miserly hungry ghosts be
    emptied.
May they realize Avalokiteshvara of the Padma-family
and attain the wisdom of discrimination.

Under the influence of ignorance,
sentient creatures are born as animals.
May the karmic cause and fruit of their suffering
    dissipate within me.
I offer my innately born or cultivated intellect
and the virtuous root of non-ignorance
to all migrating beings equal to the expanse of space.
May the dwelling place of ignorant animals be emptied.
May they realize Avalokiteshvara of the Buddha-family
and attain the wisdom of *dharmadhatu*.

Under the influence of the internal conflicts produced
    by jealousy,
the demigods engage in constant warfare and struggle.
May the karmic cause and fruit of their suffering
    dissipate within me.
I offer the patience I have practiced through the three gates
and the virtuous root of non-jealousy
to all migrating beings equal to the expanse of space.

May the dwelling place of the fighting demigods be
    emptied.
May they realize Avalokiteshvara of the Karma-family
and attain the wisdom of all-accomplishments.

Under the influence of egoism,
gods experience various highs and lows.
May the karmic cause and fruit of their suffering
    dissipate within me.
I offer whatever wholesome endeavors I have engaged in
and the virtuous root of nonegoism
to all migrating beings equal to the expanse of space.
May the dwelling place of the gods of fluctuating
    fortunes be emptied.
May they realize Avalokiteshvara of the Ratna-family
and attain the wisdom of equanimity.

Due to karmic obscurations accumulated from
    beginningless time,
sentient beings experience birth, old age, sickness, and
    death.
May the karmic cause and fruit of their suffering
    dissipate within me.
I offer whatever virtue I have accumulated from
    beginningless time
through my body, speech, and mind
to all migrating beings equal to the expanse of space.
May the dwelling place of hurried human beings be
    emptied.
May they realize Avalokiteshvara of unsullied dharmakaya
and attain the spontaneously arisen supreme wisdom.

Due to breaking the *pratimoksha*, bodhisattva, and tantric vows,
the lives of migrating sentient beings are cut short.
May the harm incurred from these transgressions dissipate
    within me.
I offer whatever virtue I have accumulated
through observing the triple vows
to all migrating beings equal to the expanse of space.
May the three vows be purified so that not even a hint of
    harm is experienced.
May they realize Vajrasattva
and attain the embodiment of all families.

Due to the acts of taking life and destroying the three
    objective dependencies,[1]
the lives of migrating sentient beings are cut short.
May their karmic delusions dissipate within me.
I offer whatever virtue I have accumulated
by constructing the three objective dependencies and
    protecting lives
to all migrating beings equal to the expanse of space.
May they not even have to hear of untimely death.
May they realize Vajra Amitayus
and attain long life.

Due to the afflictions caused by the confluence of
    phlegm, bile, and wind,
the lives of migrating sentient beings are cut short.
May all the sickness of sentient beings dissipate within me.
I offer whatever virtue I have accumulated through
    renouncing threatening behavior
and giving my health and enjoyment to others

to all migrating beings equal to the expanse of space.
May their three poisons be transformed
into the medicine Buddha.
May they realize the Bendruya body of light.

Due to stealing statues and other forms of theft,
the lives of migrating beings are cut short.
May hunger, thirst, and poverty resulting from these
    transgressions dissipate within me.
I offer whatever virtue I have accumulated
through giving away the Dharma and my possessions
to all migrating beings equal to the expanse of space.
May all their wishes be fulfilled
spontaneously and without effort.
May they indulge in the luxuries of the Treasure of Space.

Due to engaging solely in unwholesome deeds,
migrating beings take rebirth in impure realms.
May whatever karmic delusions they have incurred
    dissipate within me.
I offer whatever virtue I have accumulated
through practicing the ten transformative bodhisattva
    attitudes[2]
to all migrating beings equal to the expanse of space.
May they take rebirth in Manifest Joy
and the Endowment of Bliss.[3]
May all beings take rebirth in only pure realms.

Due to having meditated only on distorted views,
migrating beings cause displeasure to the precious
    protectors.

May whatever karmic delusions they have dissipate
     within me.
I offer whatever virtue I have accumulated
through cultivating the three faiths[4] and implanting the
     root virtues
to all migrating beings equal to the expanse of space.
May they develop a conviction from the depths of their
     being
in the unfailing veracity of karmic cause and effect.
May they cultivate virtue and abandon non-virtue.

Due to the habit of being singularly self-centered,
migrating beings perceive whatever arises in themselves
     to be the enemy.
May their experience of attraction and aversion dissipate
     within me.
I offer whatever virtue I have accumulated
through cultivating the four infinities
to all migrating beings equal to the expanse of space.
May they cultivate merit
by engaging in love and compassion.
May their mind be filled with joy and equanimity.

Due to a mind that sees illusion to be true,
migrating beings are led deeper into samsara.
May the suffering induced by this fixation dissipate
     within me.
I offer whatever virtue I have accumulated
through realizing emptiness and selflessness
to all migrating beings equal to the expanse of space.
May the realization of profound emptiness

be born in their mental continuum.
May they be transported to the state of Buddhahood.

In brief, we may try to be free from the sixteen forms of
    fear,[5]
from contact with people we dislike,
or separation from desirable objects such as food, clothing,
    and shelter.
We may try to defeat enemies
or protect friends, property, and secrets
as well as wealth, power, and reputation.
But these are things we can never attain.
Even if we look everywhere for this freedom
we will never find it.

Therefore, may I appropriate
the sudden eruption of obstacles and other sufferings
    of change
on my egoistic fixation from this day forward.
I offer the virtue, power, and influence I have accumulated
throughout the three times and even life itself
to migrating beings equal to the expanse of space.
May all sentient beings
be happy and well.
May they embark on the path of awakening.

Virtuous teachings, meat consumed, yogurt drunk,
    transport taken, and respect received
as well as the disrespect, ill will, derision, and being
    robbed and beaten
all connect me with migrating beings.

As a result of whatever beneficial or harmful karmic
    relationships I may have had
with anyone who has seen my qualities
or simply smelled my waft on the wind—
may all their karmic delusions be exhausted.
May they be delivered into Sukhavati
through the power of Avalokiteshvara's great compassion.

May whatever actions I engage in through body, speech,
    and mind
and even my bodily odor
have only beneficial effects on migrating beings.
May anyone who wants to cause harm to my life or body,
whether they be human or nonhuman,
that carry ill intent
be the first to attain Buddhahood.
May I never be the basis or the slightest cause
of bringing the negative karma of others to fruition.

If we examine dreams, the reflection of the moon in
    water, a mirage,
we will see they have no true nature in themselves
it is only because of egoistic fixation that we have been
    utterly deceived by them.
I and all migrating beings equal to the expanse of space,
including evil spirits and nonhumans,
are equal in emptiness, the ultimate truth.
May we understand this without fixation.
May we never become attached
to the truth of emptiness.[6]

There is not one migrating being
who has not been my mother or father in this world of
    sentient beings.
Where can I find anyone, anywhere, who has shown me
    more kindness?
To wish harm to one's mother or her offspring
is clearly delusional.
Far better to appreciate their kindness.
May I hand over gain and victory to others
and take loss and defeat upon myself
in order to remember the kindness of all migrating
    beings without partiality.

Through the power of the exceedingly noble intention
generated by me, as a result of this prayer,
may the obscurations and defilements of others be purified.
May all migrating beings accomplish the two accumulations.
The essence of this precious bodhichitta is emptiness
    and compassion,
the incontrovertible path of all the Buddhas.
May bodhichitta arise suddenly and with ease.
Having given birth to this precious bodhichitta,
may I speedily attain omniscient Buddhahood.

Sarva Mangalam
May everything be well

Thus, Jamgön Kongtrül Lodrö Thaye, who has the inclination as well as the application to practice lojong, has put down this lojong prayer. This was composed in a secluded mountainside retreat and was written from the bottom of his heart.

Notes

Introduction

1. There are many different versions of the Tripitaka—Pali, Sanskrit, Chinese, Tibetan, and Japanese—all of which are fairly consistent with one another. Collectively these constitute the complete Buddhist canon.

2. A version of this text, with commentary, can be found in *The Complete Works of Atisa*, trans. and annot. Richard Sherburne (Delhi: Aditya Prakashan, 1967). You can find a good translation of Shantideva's classic titled *The Way of the Bodhisattva*, trans. the Padmakara Translation Group (Boston: Shambhala, 1997).

Point One

1. Patrul Rinpoche, *The Words of My Perfect Teacher: A Complete Translation of a Classic Introduction to Tibetan Buddhism*, trans. the Padmakara Translation Group (Boston: Shambhala Publications, 1998), p. 10.

2. Aryadeva, *Yogic Deeds of Bodhisattvas: Gyel-tsap on Aryadeva's Four Hundred: Textual Studies and Translations in Indo-Tibetan Buddhism*,

trans. Ruth Sonam, with commentary by Geshe Sonam Rinchen (Ithaca, N.Y.: Snow Lion, 1994), p. 239.

3. Jamgön Kongtrül, *The Torch of Certainty*, trans. Judith Hanson (Boston: Shambhala Publications, 1977), p. 48.

4. Garma C. C. Chang, *The Hundred Thousand Songs of Milarepa* (Boston: Shambhala Publications, 1962), p. 194.

5. Shantideva, *Way of the Bodhisattva*, p. 57.

6. The six realms of existence comprise the long-lived gods, the jealous gods, the humans, the animals, the hungry ghosts, and the hells. These realms constitute samsara, and beings are thought to be cycling through them since beginningless time, taking rebirth in one realm or another in no particular order, depending on their karma. The only way to break this round of birth and death is to attain the liberation of enlightenment.

7. Dilgo Khyentse and Phadampa Sangye, *The Hundred Verses of Advice: Tibetan Buddhist Teachings on What Matters Most*, trans. the Padmakara Translation Group (Boston: Shambhala Publications, 2002), p. 137.

8. There are eight states that characterize a lack of freedom to pursue a spiritual path. As Patrul Rinpoche explains, "Being born in the hells, the preta realm, as an animal, a long-lived god or a barbarian, having wrong views, being born when there is no Buddha or being born deaf and mute; these are the eight states without freedom." *Words of My Perfect Teacher*, p. 20.

9. Jamgön Kongtrül, *The Autobiography of Jamgön Kongtrul: A Gem of Many Colors*, trans. and ed. Richard Barron (Ithaca, N.Y.: Snow Lion Publications, 2003), pp. 55–56.

10. Dilgo Khyentse and Padampa Sangye, *Hundred Verses of Advice*, p. 137.

11. Chögyam Trungpa and Nalanda Translation Committee, *The Rain of Wisdom* (Boston: Shambhala Publications, 1980), p. 175.

12. Aryadeva, *Yogic Deeds of Bodhisattvas*, p. 86.
13. Chögyam Trungpa, *The Rain of Wisdom*, p. 64.
14. Jamgön Kongtrül, *Torch of Certainty*, p. 42.

Point Two

1. B. Alan Wallace, *The Seven-Point Mind Training* (Ithaca, N.Y.: Snow Lion Publications, 2004), p. 30. B. Alan Wallace's lojong instructions include a slogan that relates directly to this emphasis on emptiness: "Having attained stability, let the mystery be revealed."

2. Thupten Jinpa, trans., *Mind Training: The Great Collection* (Somerville, Mass.: Wisdom Publications, 2006), pp. 486–87. Thupten Jinpa's recent translation of *Mind Training*, a fourteenth-century compilation of lojong literature by the Kadampa master Shonu Gyalchok and the Sakya master Konchok Gyaltsen (1388–1469), includes forty-three short texts on mind training. In Konchok Gyaltsen's own commentary, "Supplement to the 'Oral Tradition,'" he discloses that there were three different instruction lineages on lojong, those of Dharmaraksita, Maitriyogi, and Serlingpa. He then states, "Of these, the method of training according to the first two is to engage first in the practice of the ultimate awakening mind, and then with respect to the conventional mind, practice equalizing self and others and then exchanging self and others. This is difficult for a beginner, the master said. According to the tradition of Serlingpa, however, you undertake the practice of conventional awakening mind while remaining in your present state—with self-grasping still manifest—and do not first practice the ultimate awakening mind. Here, too, you engage in the practice of exchanging self and others right from the start. This method is far superior, it is taught, because it is easier to foster in the heart

of a beginner and since it yields great benefit." Indeed, most of the texts included in the *Great Collection* exclude the slogans associated with absolute bodhichitta.

3. There are numerous *shamatha* and *vipashyana* meditation manuals, beginning with the Buddha's own discourse in the Satipatthana Sutra.

4. To clarify any possible confusion for readers regarding the practice of tranquillity meditation, what follows is a more traditional approach to the technique of shamatha, whereas my instructions on how to practice lojong shamatha proper are a blend of this traditional approach with the more unusual Mahamudra emphasis on resting in the natural state. These two approaches are discussed at length in my books *Essence of Buddhism* and *Mind at Ease*, respectively.

5. Quoted in Herbert V. Guenther and Leslie S. Kawamura, trans., *Mind in Buddhist Psychology* (Berkeley, Calif.: Dharma Publishing, 1975), p. 32.

6. Ibid, 54.

7. Geshe Lhundub Sopa, with Michael Sweet and Leonard Zwilling, *Peacock in the Poison Grove: Two Buddhist Texts on Training the Mind* (Somerville, Mass.: Wisdom Publications, 2001), p. 111.

8. Paul Williams, *The Unexpected Way: On Converting from Buddhism to Catholicism* (Edinbugh and New York: T. & T. Clark Publishers, 2002), p. 51.

9. David Kalupahana, *Causality: The Central Philosophy of Buddhism* (Honolulu: Hawaii University Press, 1975), p. 10.

10. Jay L. Garfield, *The Fundamental Wisdom of the Middle Way: Nagarjuna's* Mulamadhyamakakarika (London: Oxford University Press, 1995), p. 69.

11. His Holiness the Dalai Lama, *The Universe in a Single Atom:*

The Convergence of Science and Spirituality (New York: Morgan Road Books, 2005), p. 47.

12. Aryadeva, *Yogic Deeds of Bodhisattvas,* p. 234.

13. Dalai Lama, *Universe in a Single Atom,* pp. 47–48.

14. Christopher deCharms, *Two Views of Mind: Abhidharma and Brain Science* (Ithaca, N.Y.: Snow Lion, 1998), p. 49.

15. Heinrich Dumoulin, *Understanding Buddhism: Key Themes* (Boston: Weatherhill, 1994), p. 73.

16. Shantideva, *Way of the Bodhisattva,* p. 70.

17. Francis H. Cook, *Hua-yen Buddhism: The Jewel Net of Indra* (University Park: The Pennsylvania State University Press, 1977), p. 109.

18. Jamgön Kongtrül, *The Great Path of Awakening,* trans. Ken McLeod (Boston: Shambhala Publications, 1987), pp. 10–11.

19. Ibid., p. 11.

20. Lobsang P. Lhalungpa, *The Life of Milarepa* (New York: Penguin, 1992), p. 127.

21. Jamgön Kongtrül, *Great Path of Awakening,* p. 11.

22. Western Buddhists sometimes talk about a karmic cosmic law as if it meant that we were somehow preprogrammed. That is not the Buddhist view, for even though Buddhism teaches that our past karma affects our present state, this does not necessarily mean that our karma will invariably bring about a result. We can preempt our karma by processing our thought patterns during meditation. If we can let go of our experiences, we can ameliorate their impact, which is the whole point of spiritual practice.

23. Jamgön Kongtrül, *Great Path of Awakening,* p. 67.

24. Chandrakirti, *Entry to the Middle Way* (*Madhyamakavatara*) (Boston: Shambhala Publications, 2005), p. 59.

25. Shantideva, *Way of the Bodhisattva,* p. 35.

26. Ibid., p. 51.

27. Jinpa, *Mind Training*, p. 420.

28. Shantideva, *Way of the Bodhisattva*, p. 165.

29. Jampa Tegchok, *Transforming Adversity into Joy and Courage: An Explanation on the Thirty-Seven Practices of Bodhisattvas*, ed. Thubten Chodron (Ithaca, N.Y.: Snow Lion, 1995), p. 165.

30. Shantideva, *Way of the Bodhisattva*, p. 100.

31. Ibid., p. 135.

32. See the first of the five powers in chapter 4 for a fuller discussion of aspiration.

33. Shantideva, *Way of the Bodhisattva*, p. 82.

34. Jamgön Kongtrül, *Great Path of Awakening*, p. 16.

35. Geshe Lhundub Sopa, *Peacock in the Poison Grove*, p. 63.

36. Shantideva, *Way of the Bodhisattva*, p. 127.

37. Ibid., p. 75.

Point Three

1. Shantideva, *Way of the Bodhisattva*, p. 81.

2. From Padma Karpo, "Precious Sun," trans. Traleg Kyabgon, in *Mind at Ease: Self-Liberation through Mahamudra Meditation* (Boston: Shambhala Publications, 2005), p. 288.

3. Shantideva, *Way of the Bodhisattva*, p. 79.

4. Geshe Lhundub Sopa, *Peacock in the Poison Grove*, p. 81.

5. Ibid., p. 191.

6. John W. Schroeder, *Skillful Means: The Heart of Buddhist Compassion* (Delhi: Motilal Banarsidass, 2004), p. 3.

7. Chandrakirti, *Entry to the Middle Way*, pp. 84–85.

8. Shantideva, *Way of the Bodhisattva*, p. 132.

9. Geshe Lhundub Sopa, *Peacock in the Poison Grove*, p. 83.

10. Shantideva, *Way of the Bodhisattva*, p. 64.

11. Jampa Tegchok, *Transforming Adversity into Joy and Courage*, p. 85.

12. Shantideva, *Way of the Bodhisattva*, p. 129.

13. The four demons (Tib. *bdud bzhi*) are as follows: (1) the demon of the aggregates (Tib. *phung po bdud*), the demon of the conflicting emotions (Tib. *nyon mongs pa'i bdud*), the demon of the Lord of Death (Tib. *'chi bdag gi bdud*), and the demon of the sons of gods (Tib. *lha'i bu'i bdud*). The demon of the aggregates is so-called because without the five aggregates, there would be no basis for the sufferings of samsara. The demon of the conflicting emotions arises from a belief in a self and gives rise to negative actions. The demon of the Lord of Death refers to impermanence and the fact of the inevitability of death. The demon of the sons of the gods prevents us from proceeding to nirvana (Tib. *mya ngan las 'das pa*) through distraction, attachment, and fixation.

14. Aryadeva, *Yogic Deeds of Bodhisattvas*, p. 138.

15. For example, we often don't learn much more about Buddhism than the personal anecdotal stories of the authors when we read popular books by Westerners. "I went down to Manhattan and saw this dress and I wanted it. Suddenly I knew what the Buddha meant by desire." We need real Dharma in our lives, or we'll reduce the Buddhist teachings to the kind of stuff we read in pop-culture magazines.

16. Shantideva, *Way of the Bodhisattva*, p. 93.

17. Geshe Lhundub Sopa, *Peacock in the Poison Grove*, p. 81.

18. Chandrakirti, *Entry to the Middle Way*, p. 64.

19. Atisha, *Atisha's Lamp for the Path to Enlightenment*, trans. Ruth Sonam with commentary by Geshe Sonam Rinchen (Ithaca, N.Y.: Snow Lion, 1997), p. 104.

20. Mark Tatz, *The Skill in Means* (Upayakausalya) *Sutra* (Delhi: Motilal Banarsidass, 1994), p. 46.

21. Quoted in C. W. Huntington Jr., *The Emptiness of Emptiness: An Introduction to the Early Indian Madhyamika* (Honolulu: University of Hawaii Press, 1989), 37.

22. Shantideva, *Way of the Bodhisattva*, p. 121.

23. From Atisha's "Advice to Namdak Tsuknor," in Thupten Jinpa, trans., *Mind Training*, p. 264.

24. Dilgo Khyentse and Phadampa Sangye, *Hundred Verses of Advice*, p. 131.

25. From "The song of Ngotrup Gyaltsen," in Chögyam Trungpa, *Rain of Wisdom*, p. 265.

26. Shantideva, *Way of the Bodhisattva*, p. 158.

27. Padma Karpo, in *Mind at Ease*, p. 290.

28. Ibid.

29. Aryadeva, *Yogic Deeds of Bodhisattvas*, p. 144.

30. Patrul Rinpoche, *Words of My Perfect Teacher*, p. 265.

31. Geshe Lhundub Sopa, *Peacock in the Poison Grove*, p. 207.

32. From the "Songs of Jetsun Milarepa," in Chögyam Trungpa, *Rain of Wisdom*, p. 204.

33. There is a kind of folk Buddhism in the Himalayas, where people do practice such things, but the lojong teachings are not advocating that; rather, they are simply talking about making peace with these bothersome evil spirits.

34. Cyrus Stearns, trans., *Hermit of Go Cliffs: Timeless Instructions from a Tibetan Mystic* (Somerville, Mass.: Wisdom Publications, 2000), p. 73.

35. Machik Lapdron and Sarah Harding, trans. and ed., *Machik's Complete Explanation: Clarifying the Meaning of Chöd* (Ithaca, N.Y.: Snow Lion, 2003), p. 117.

36. Cyrus Stearns, *Hermit of Go Cliffs*, p. 55.

Point Four

1. Patrul Rinpoche, *Words of My Perfect Teacher*, p. 326.

2. Shantideva, *Way of the Bodhisattva*, p. 103.

3. Patrul Rinpoche, *Words of My Perfect Teacher*, p. 130.

4. Thupten Jinpa, trans., *Mind Training*, p. 113.

5. Shantideva, *Way of the Bodhisattva*, p. 80.

6. Chandrakirti, *Entry to the Middle Way*, p. 106.

7. Jamgön Kongtrül, *Great Path of Awakening*, p. 24.

8. Quoted in Patrul Rinpoche, *Words of My Perfect Teacher*, p. 119.

9. Atisha, *Atisha's Lamp for the Path to Enlightenment*, p. 82.

10. Chandrakirti, *Entry to the Middle Way*, p. 60.

11. Garma C. C. Chang, *Hundred Thousand Songs of Milarepa*, p. 564.

12. Patrul Rinpoche, *Words of My Perfect Teacher*, p. 239.

13. The Mahamudra method of self-liberation, as discussed in my book *Mind at Ease*, advocates regarding whatever arises in the mind as just thoughts, but this belongs to the special method of Mahamudra meditation and is not helpful in the context of mind training.

14. Quoted in Patrul Rinpoche, *Words of My Perfect Teacher*, p. 123.

15. Shantideva, *Way of the Bodhisattva*, p. 134.

16. Dilgo Khyentse and Phadampa Sangye, *Hundred Verses of Advice*, p. 152.

17. Patrul Rinpoche, *Words of My Perfect Teacher*, p. 126.

18. Geshe Rabten and Gehse Dhargyey, *Advice from a Spiritual Friend*, p. 6.

19. Shantideva, *Way of the Bodhisattva*, p. 35.

20. Patrul Rinpoche, *Words of My Perfect Teacher*, pp. 325–26.

21. "The Great Commentary" in *Treasury of Precious Qualities* tells us, "An essential point concerning the dedication is that it

should be expressed in the words of someone who has attained the sublime grounds so that the formula is thus composed of words of truth. It should be noted also that there is a difference between dedication prayers and prayers of aspiration. The former is focused on merit while the latter expresses a wish of some kind. Dedication necessarily includes aspiration, but the reverse is not always the case." In Kangyur Rinpoche, *Treasury of Precious Qualities,* trans. the Padmakara Translation Group (Boston: Shambhala Publications, 2001), p. 373.

22. Ibid., pp. 173–74.

23. Dilgo Khyentse and Padampa Sangye, *Hundred Verses of Advice,* p. 34.

24. Shantideva, *Way of the Bodhisattva,* p. 88.

25. From "The Bodhisattva's Jewel Garland," in Thupten Jinpa, trans., *Mind Training,* p. 25.

26. Patrul Rinpoche, *Words of My Perfect Teacher,* p. 265.

27. Shantideva, *Way of the Bodhisattva,* p. 170.

28. Keith Dowman, *The Divine Madman: The Sublime Life and Songs of Drukpa Kunley* (Middletown, Calif.: Dawn Horse Press, 1980), p. 109.

29. Cyrus Stearns, trans., *Hermit of Go Cliffs,* p. 83.

Point Five

1. Geshe Lhundub Sopa, *Peacock in the Poison Grove,* p. 229.

2. Cyrus Stearns, trans., *Hermit of Go Cliffs,* p. 83.

3. Chandrakirti, *Entry to the Middle Way,* p. 89.

4. Rupert Gethin, *The Foundations of Buddhism* (Oxford and New York: Oxford University Press, 1998), p. 141.

5. Patrul Rinpoche, *Words of My Perfect Teacher,* p. 255.

6. Konchok Gyaltsen, "Supplement to the 'Oral Tradition,'" in Thupten Jinpa, trans., *Mind Training*, p. 496.

7. Nagarjuna and Lama Mipham, *Golden Zephyr: Instructions from a Spiritual Friend*, trans. Leslie Kawamura (Berkeley, Calif.: Dharma Publishing, 1975), p. 22.

8. Patrul Rinpoche, *Words of My Perfect Teacher*, p. 52.

9. Shantideva, *Way of the Bodhisattva*, p. 69.

10. Se Chilbu Chokyi Gyaltsen, "A Commentary on the 'Seven-Point Mind Training,'" in Thupten Jinpa, trans., *Mind Training*, p. 116.

11. Konchok Gyaltsen, "Supplement to the 'Oral Tradition,'" in Thupten Jinpa, trans., *Mind Training*, p. 497.

12. Thupten Jinpa, trans., *Mind Training*, pp. 387–88.

13. Shantideva, *Way of the Bodhisattva*, p. 79.

14. Quoted in Patrul Rinpoche, *Words of My Perfect Teacher*, p. 121.

15. Shantideva, *Way of the Bodhisattva*, p. 102.

16. Garma C. C. Chang, *Hundred Thousand Songs of Milarepa Songs*, p. 111.

17. Jamgön Kongtrül, *Great Path of Awakening*, p. 28.

18. Konchok Gyaltsen, "Supplement to the 'Oral Tradition,'" in Thupten Jinpa, trans., *Mind Training*, p. 497.

19. Sangye Gompa, "Public Explanation of Mind Training," in Thupten Jinpa, trans., *Mind Training*, p. 383.

20. Patrul Rinpoche, *Words of My Perfect Teacher*, p. 259.

Point Six

1. Chilbu Chokyi Gyaltsen, "A Commentary on the 'Seven-Point Mind Training,'" in Thupten Jinpa, trans., *Mind Training*, p. 118.

2. The other four wrong views are as follows: (1) the view of the transitory composite (Tib. *'jig tshogs la ta ba*), where the five aggregates are regarded as a permanent entity; (2) the view of extremes (Tib. *mthar 'dzin pa'i lta ba*) of eternalism and nihilism; (3) the view of doctrinal superiority (Tib. *lta ba mchog 'dzin*), which is the belief that our false opinions are universally valid; and (4) wrong views (Tib. *log lta*), where we hold opinions that are contrary to the facts. In Kangyur Rinpoche, *The Treasury of Precious Qualities*, p. 291.

3. Sangye Gompa, "Public Explanation of Mind Training," in Thupten Jinpa, trans., *Mind Training*, p. 394.

4. Keith Dowman, *Divine Madman*, p. 108.

5. Cyrus Stearns, trans., *Hermit of Go Cliffs*, p. 65.

6. Shantideva, *Way of the Bodhisattva*, p. 82.

7. In Rabten and Dhargyey, *Advice from a Spiritual Friend*, p. 6.

8. Jamgön Kongtrül, *Great Path of Awakening*, p. 30.

9. Ibid.

10. Thupten Jinpa, trans., *Mind Training*, p. 500.

11. Dilgo Khyentse and Phadampa Sangye, *Hundred Verses of Advice*, p. 164.

12. Jampa Tegchok, *Transforming Adversity into Joy and Courage*, p. 277.

13. Thupten Jinpa, trans., *Mind Training*, p. 503.

14. Patrul Rinpoche, *Words of My Perfect Teacher*, p. 127.

15. Keith Dowman, *Divine Madman*, p. 111.

16. Thupten Jinpa, trans., *Mind Training*, p. 406.

17. Aryadeva, *Yogic Deeds of Bodhisattvas*, p. 154.

18. Jampa Tegchok, *Transforming Adversity into Joy and Courage*, p. 288.

19. Padma Karpo, "Precious Sun," trans. Traleg Kyabgon, in *Mind at Ease*, p. 232.

20. Thupten Jinpa, trans., *Mind Training*, p. 504.

21. Shantideva, *Way of the Bodhisattva*, p. 79.

22. Patrul Rinpoche, *Words of My Perfect Teacher*, p. 115.

23. His Holiness the Dalai Lama, *A Flash of Lightning in the Dark of Night: A Guide to the Bodhisattva's Way of Life* (Boston: Shambhala Publications, 1994), p. 125.

24. Traleg Kyabgon, *Mind at Ease*, p. 233.

25. Geshe Lhundub Sopa, *Peacock in the Poison Grove*, p. 101.

26. Jamgön Kongtrül, *Great Path of Awakening*, p. 32.

27. Thupten Jinpa, trans., *Mind Training*, p. 121.

28. Traleg Kyabgon, *Mind at Ease*, p. 233.

29. Thupten Jinpa, trans., *Mind Training*, p. 122.

30. Shantideva, *Way of the Bodhisattva*, p. 129.

31. Dalai Lama, *Flash of Lightning in the Dark of Night*, p. 85.

32. Patrul Rinpoche, *Words of My Perfect Teacher*, p. 109.

33. Thupten Jinpa, trans., *Mind Training*, p. 413.

34. Patrul Rinpoche, *Words of My Perfect Teacher*, p. 215.

Point Seven

1. *Naljor* means "the attainment of the authentic state," which is a truer translation of the word *yoga* than "spiritual practice."

2. Thupten Jinpa, trans., *Mind Training*, p. 402.

3. Patrul Rinpoche, *Words of My Perfect Teacher*, p. 223.

4. Thupten Jinpa, trans., *Mind Training*, p. 403.

5. Ibid., p. 194.

6. Jamgön Kongtrül, *Great Path of Awakening*, p. 35.

7. Thupten Jinpa, trans., *Mind Training*, p. 124.

8. Ibid., p. 319.

9. Geshe Lhundub Sopa, *Peacock in the Poison Grove*, p. 205.

10. Aryadeva, *Yogic Deeds of Bodhisattvas*, p. 153.

11. Thupten Jinpa, trans., *Mind Training*, p. 179.

12. Jampa Tegchok, *Transforming Adversity into Joy and Courage*, p. 88.

13. Patrul Rinpoche, *Words of My Perfect Teacher*, p. 144.

14. Cyrus Stearns, trans., *Hermit of Go Cliffs*, p. 89.

15. Patrul Rinpoche, *Words of My Perfect Teacher*, p. 138.

16. Nagarjuna and Lama Mipham, *Golden Zephyr*, p. 55.

17. Shantideva, *Way of the Bodhisattva*, p. 76.

18. Cyrus Stearns, trans., *Hermit of Go Cliffs*, p. 65.

19. The five precepts are as follows: not lying, not killing, not stealing, not engaging in sexual misconduct, and not imbibing intoxicants. These precepts can be taken by any level of practitioner.

20. Thupten Jinpa, trans., *Mind Training*, p. 508.

21. Jamgön Kongtrül, *Great Path of Awakening*, pp. 37–38.

22. Cyrus Stearns, trans., *Hermit of Go Cliffs*, p. 107.

23. Thupten Jinpa, trans., *Mind Training*, p. 511.

24. Ibid., p. 127.

25. Ibid., p. 409.

26. Shantideva, *Way of the Bodhisattva*, p. 101.

27. Ibid., p. 122.

28. Ibid., p. 107.

29. Thupten Jinpa, trans., *Mind Training*, p. 127.

30. Shantideva, *Way of the Bodhisattva*, p. 90.

31. Jamgön Kongtrül, *Great Path of Awakening*, pp. 39–40.

32. Patrul Rinpoche, *Words of My Perfect Teacher*, p. 247.

33. Thupten Jinpa, trans., *Mind Training*, p. 128.

34. Chandrakirti, *Entry to the Middle Way*, p. 84.

35. Shantideva, *Way of the Bodhisattva*, p. 125.

36. Jamgön Kongtrül, *Great Path of Awakening*, p. 40.

37. Thupten Jinpa, trans., *Mind Training*, p. 512.

38. Shantideva, *Way of the Bodhisattva*, p. 126.

39. Ibid., p. 73.

Lojong Prayer

1. The three objective dependencies are the various symbolic representations of body, speech, and mind. Buddha statues represent the body, texts represent speech, and stupas and monasteries represent mind. As Buddhists, we are encouraged to rely on these three dependencies.

2. The ten transformative acts are the ten paramitas: generosity, ethical conduct, patience, vigor, meditative concentration, wisdom, skillful means, aspiration, spiritual power, and wisdom consciousness.

3. Manifest Joy and Endowment of Bliss are the names of specific pure lands.

4. The three faiths are unsullied faith, the faith of conviction, and inconvertible faith.

5. The sixteen forms of fear are as follows: fear of persecution by authorities, fear of the wrath of God, fear of disease caused by disturbances in the environment, fear of plague and disease without cause, fear of starvation, fear of becoming a victim of war, fear of incantations, fear of ghosts and spirits, fear of being struck by lightning, fear of being killed by storms or hail, fear of being buried alive during earthquakes, fear of dying by fire, fear of drowning, fear of being struck by meteorites, fear of space, and fear of disturbing dreams and nightmares.

6. This refers to the importance of not reifying emptiness.

Glossary

ARYADEVA (third century). A scholar of the Madhyamaka school in southern India, he is best known for the text *Catusataka* (*Four Hundred Verses*).

ASPIRATION (Skt. *pranidhana;* Tib. *smon lam*). The act of directing our positive intentions into the future. We utilize the extremely powerful and affirmative energy that accumulates from our positive intentions and practices and direct it into the future so that whatever we want to realize is drawn nearer to us.

ATISHA DIPAMKARA SHRIJNANA (982–1054): A disciple of Dharmarakshita, he went to Tibet, where he helped revive Buddhism after its destruction by Langdarma's regime. His most famous work is *Lamp for the Path to Enlightenment* (*Bodhipathapradipa*).

AWARENESS (Skt. *jneya;* Tib. *shes bzhin*). The process of being alert and perspicacious. This type of awareness is deliberately generated in meditation practice as the principle means of accessing the innate wisdom consciousness.

BASIC CONSCIOUSNESS (Skt. *alaya-vijnana;* Tib. *kun gzhi rnam shes*). The neutral, unconscious, and impartial ground that serves as the repository of all our karmic traces and dispositions. The transformation of this basic consciousness into wisdom consciousness is the psychological equivalent of the attainment of enlightenment.

BODHICHITTA (Tib. *byang chub sems dpa'*). There are two aspects to enlightened heart: an ultimate and a relative one. Ultimate enlightened heart refers to the nature of the mind and relative enlightened heart refers to the cultivation and generation of compassion. The cultivation of wisdom and compassion are the components of relative bodhichitta until the innate wisdom consciousness is realized and absolute bodhichitta is attained. Wisdom and compassion are encapsulated in the six transcendental actions. (*See also* paramitas)

BODHISATTVA (Tib. *byang chub sems depa'*). Literally "wakening being," this is the Mahayana ideal of someone who is traversing the spiritual path by cultivating relative bodhichitta through the six transcendental actions of wisdom and compassion. (*See also* paramitas)

BUDDHA-NATURE (Skt. *tathagatagarbha*). Our innate, primordial nature, which is defined as the middle ground between a merely empirical self and any kind of psychic substance. This is not something we have as part of our psychological makeup, but something we are in our very being.

CHANDRAKIRTI (600–650). Abbot of Nalanda University, a disciple of Nagarjuna, and a commentator on his works. He was the most famous member of what the Tibetans came to call the Prasangika school of Madhyamaka and author of the *Madhyamakavatara*.

CHEKAWA YESHE DORJE (1101–1175). An accomplished Kadampa master, he was the author of the *Seven Points of Mind Training*.

When Chekawa read Langri Thangpa's *Eight Verses,* he was so moved that he sought out Geshe Sharawa, a disciple of the author, to find out how to practice these teachings. The secret oral teachings Chekawa received from Geshe Sharawa are the foundation of the *Seven Points of Mind Training.*

COMPASSION (Skt. *karuna;* Tib. *snying rje*).One of the principle antidotes to self-obsession in Mahayana Buddhism, compassion is the wish that other beings may be free of suffering and the cause of suffering. This is an active form of responding to the suffering of others without becoming immersed in their despair.

CONDITIONED EXISTENCE (Skt. *samsara;* Tib. *'khor ba*). The endless round of transmigration that arises out of ignorance and is characterized by suffering.

CONFESSION (Tib. *bshags pa*). A method for acknowledging to ourselves the things we feel ashamed about or that gnaw away in the back of our minds without ever being fully processed. If we generate a real sense of regret when we confess, we can bring these things back into consciousness and discharge the latent karmic tendencies they have created.

CONFLICTING EMOTIONS (Skt. *klesha;* Tib. *nyon mongs*). The emotional properties that dull the mind and cause us to misapprehend the true nature of existence.

DELUDED MIND (Tib. *namshey*). Our ordinary samsaric state of mind, from moment to moment, which is driven to a state of confusion by conflicting emotions.

DEPENDENT ARISING (Skt. *pratityasamutpada;* Tib. *rten 'brel*). The fact that things have no inherently existing, self-sufficient existence of their own and simply come into existence due to causes and conditions.

DHARMARAKSHITA (tenth century). A renowned Sumatran Buddhist teacher who composed an important Mahayana text called the *Wheel of Sharp Weapons*.

DISCURSIVE THOUGHTS (Skt. *vikalpa;* Tib. *rnam rtog*). The tendency to dwell on the past, anticipate the future, and discriminate between thoughts and emotions as either good or bad. This tendency is based upon the fixation of binary concepts at a fundamental level of thought.

DROMTONPA (1005–1064). The chief disciple and successor of Atisha, he is remembered as initiator of the Tibetan Kadampa lineage. Together with Atisha, he translated the *Wheel of Sharp Weapons* by Dharmarakshita from Sanskrit into Tibetan.

EMPTINESS (Skt. *shunyata;* Tib. *stong pa nyid*). The understanding that both the person and phenomena are devoid of any independent, lasting substance and therefore nothing more than mere appearances. This concept should not be taken to mean that nothing exists at all, just that everything exists as in a dream, because it has no inherent existence.

EQUANIMITY (Skt. *upeksha;* Tib. *mnyam bzhag*). A spacious state of mind that is free from attraction, aversion, and indifference.

FIXATION (Tib. *'dzin pa*). A state that comes about through thinking of people and things as discrete, self-sufficient entities. When we convince ourselves that self and other are real in this way, we cannot relax our hold on certain ideas, and our fixation grows stronger until it causes distortions in our habits of thought, making us biased and prejudicial. These fixations have a way of reaching very deeply into our psyche and spoiling everything.

FOUR INFINITIES (Skt. *brahmaviharas*). A meditation practice that arouses positive states of love, compassion, joy, and equanimity in order to generate compassion and wisdom and radiate them in all directions.

FOUR KAYAS (Tib. *sku*). The "aspects of Buddha's being" that help us to maintain some kind of enlightened perspective on our world. The nirmanakaya is the physical appearance of a Buddha's being, the sambhogakaya is the embodiment of the wisdom qualities of a Buddha's being, and the dharmakaya is the transcendental aspect of a Buddha's being. The svabhavivakaya is not a fourth body so much as a unifying concept, which signifies the physical, mental, and transcendental aspects of Buddha's being are an inseparable whole.

GYALSAY TOGME SANGPO (1295–1369). Renowned as a bodhisattva in Tibet and revered for living according to the bodhisattva ideals and practices that he taught, he inspired his direct disciples as well as generations of practitioners up to the present day. He wrote the *Thirty-seven Practices of Bodhisattvas*, which is studied by followers of all schools of Tibetan Buddhism.

IMPERMANENCE (Skt. *anitya;* Tib. *mi rtag pa*). The idea that the transient nature of everything is the fundamental property of every conditioned thing. This fact is the basis of life because without it existence would not be possible.

INNATE AWARENESS (Skt. *vidya;* Tib. *rigpa*). A state that manifests spontaneously because it is a natural quality of mind.

INNATE WAKEFULNESS (Skt. *jnana;* Tib. *ye shes*). Something that is present in the mind even when the delusions and obscurations of the mind are at work. This is synonymous with absolute bodhichitta or our authentic and original state of being.

INSIGHT MEDITATION (Skt. *vipashyana;* Tib. *lhag mthong*). The cultivation of wisdom consciousness by gaining insight into our mind through the use of analytical methods.

INTERESTED HUMILITY (Tib. *mögu*). A state that comes from recognizing the impoverishment of a life without spiritual practice and an eagerness to continue learning without becoming complacent or self-important.

JAMGÖN KONGTRÜL LODRO THAYE (1813–1900). A polymath, scholar, and yogi from Tibet, he was one of the most prominent Tibetan Buddhist masters in the nineteenth century and championed the non-sectarian (Tib. *rime*) movement of Tibetan Buddhism. He compiled a compendium called *Five Treasuries of Knowledge,* which incorporated a great number of teachings from both the old and new traditions. His best-known works in English are *The Torch of Certainty* and *The Great Path of Awakening.*

KADAMPA (Tib. *bKa' gdams pa*). A Tibetan Buddhist school founded by Dromtonpa and mainly emphasizing the sutric Mahayana teachings. The Kadampas were quite famous and respected for their proper and earnest Dharma practice. The most evident teachings of that tradition were the teachings on bodhichitta and the stages of the path.

KADAMPA BROTHERS, THREE. The main disciples of Dromtonpa and the secret recipients of Atisha's legacy of teachings. The three disciples were Chengawa Tsultrim Bar (1038–1103), Potawa Rinchen Sel (1031–1105), and Puchungwa Shonu Gyaltsen (1031–1106).

KANGYUR. The Tibetan version of the Buddhist canon containing both sutra and tantra teachings.

KARMA (Tib. *las*). The universal law of cause and effect whereby our actions determine our predispositions, personal tendencies, habitual patterns, and the kind of experiences we have in our lives. Unwholesome karma will plunge us into demeaning states of existence, and wholesome karma will transport us to elevated states of existence.

KARMIC IMPRINTS (Skt. *vasana;* Tib. *bag chag*). The predispositions and tendencies that reside in our basic consciousness.

LANGRI THANGPA (1054–1123). One of the forefathers of the lojong lineage and author of the *Eight Verses on Mind Training.*

MEDITATIVE CONCENTRATION (Skt. *dhyana;* Tib. *bsam gtan*). This term encompasses a variety of concentration methods, all of which are designed to bring consciousness to the state of enlightenment. A mind that is stable and not easily distracted is generally said to be a mind in meditation. In Buddhism, there are two principle types of meditation: tranquillity (Skt. *shamatha*) and insight (Skt. *vipashyana*).

MERIT (Skt. *punya;* Tib. *bsod nams*). The psycho-spiritual dispositional properties that we need to cultivate if we want to enrich our lives and cease feeling so empty and vacuous. The accumulation of merit is what determines the kind of human beings we will become for it enables us to avert obstacles and prevent adversity, while a lack of merit only attracts adversity into our lives.

MIND (Skt. *chitta;* Tib. *sems*). An overarching term for the operations of consciousness, which give rise to mental events.

MINDFULNESS (Skt. *smrti;* Tib. *dran pa*). Something we apply more or less deliberately, it is the opposite of forgetfulness. The Tibetan term *dran pa* means "remembrance" in the sense of remembering to focus on a familiar object and to maintain that remembrance in an unwavering fashion.

NAGARJUNA (150–250). An Indian philosopher who founded the Madhyamaka (Middle Path) school of Mahayana Buddhism and arguably the most influential Indian Buddhist thinker after the Gautama Buddha himself. He systematized and deepened the teachings presented in the Perfection of Wisdom (*Prajna-paramita*) sutras and gave the most comprehensive and methodological presentation of the concept of emptiness.

NIRVANA (Tib. *mya ngan las 'das pa*). Characterized as the cessation of suffering, nirvana is the goal of spiritual practice in Buddhism and signifies the departure from cyclic existence and freedom from karma.

PARAMITAS (SIX TRANSCENDENTAL ACTIONS). Generosity (Skt. *dana;* Tib. *sbyin pa*), patience (Skt. *ksanti;* Tib. *bzod pa*), vigor (Skt. *virya;* Tib. *brston 'grus*), moral precepts (Skt. *shila;* Tib. *tshul khrims*), meditative concentration (Skt. *dhyana;* Tib. *bsam gtan*), and wisdom (Skt. *prajna;* Tib. *shes rab*).

PHADAMPA SANGYE (d. 1117). From southern India, he traveled widely in India, Tibet, and China until his death. It is widely believed that Phadampa Sangye was an incarnation of the eighth-century monk Kamalashila, one of the early teachers of the Dharma in Tibet. When he arrived in Tibet, he found the people in the area of Tingri, which is on the Tibetan side of Mount Everest, to be especially amenable to his instruction, so he settled and established a monastery there.

PITH INSTRUCTIONS (Skt. *upadesha;* Tib. *man ngag sde*). The distillations of the teachings that can be clearly distinguished from the strictly logical or metaphysical approaches of Buddhist doctrine because they get to the heart of what we need to cultivate in our everyday lives.

PSYCHO-PHYSICAL CONSTITUENTS (Skt. *skandhas;* Tib. *phung po*). The early Buddhist teachings enumerated five psycho-physical constituents that constitute a person. These are physical form, psychic propensities, feeling, cognition, and consciousness. When all of these parts come together we have the concept of a self, but no self can be found independent of its constituent parts.

SANGYE GOMPA (1179–1250). Author of *A Public Explanation*, composed after Langri Tangpa wrote *Eight Verses for Training the Mind* and before Geshe Chekawa wrote *Seven Points of Mind Training*.

SELFLESSNESS (Skt. *anatman;* Tib. *bdag med pa*). Absence of any kind of immutable, psychic substance that is unchanging and permanent. This term does not refute an individual self-identity of some kind, but maintains that it is only an empirical self that is contingent on ever-changing psycho-physical conditions.

SENDING AND TAKING MEDITATION (Tib. *tong len*). A meditative practice for adopting a radically new attitude or new way of looking at things. Sometimes called "exchanging self for others," it involves visualizing giving away everything that is good in our lives and taking on everything that is bad in the lives of others as a way of training ourselves in courage. All forms of self-obsession lead to negative emotions, and tonglen is the antidote to that.

SHANTIDEVA (695–743). An Indian Buddhist scholar at Nalanda University and an adherent of the Madhyamaka philosophy. He is particularly renowned as the author of the *Bodhicharya-vatara*, a long poem describing the process of enlightenment from the first thought to full Buddhahood, which is distinguished by its poetic sensitivity and fervor.

SKILLFUL MEANS (Skt. *upaya;* Tib. *thabs*). An expression of compassion that relates directly to the first five transcendental actions of Mahayana Buddhism. This term generally conveys the sense that enlightened beings teach the Dharma skillfully depending on the needs and capacities of sentient beings.

SOLIPSISM. Not recognizing any reality other than, or independent from, our own experience.

TENGYUR. Complied as a supplement to the teachings contained in the Kangyur, the translations in this collection consist of commentarial material from mostly Sanskrit sources. There are also treatises on logic, metaphysics, epistemology, composition, grammar, and literature.

TRANQUILLITY MEDITATION (Skt. *shamatha;* Tib. *zhi gnas*). A basic meditation practice common to most schools of Buddhism, the aim of which is to tame and stabilize the mind in order to practice insight meditation.

TRANSCENDENTAL ACTION (Skt. *paramita;* Tib. *pha rol tu phyin pa*). Mahayana practices that actualize wisdom and compassion and symbolize going beyond our conventional notion of the self so that our actions and attitudes are performed in a nonegocentric manner.

ULTIMATE REALITY (Skt. *dharmata;* Tib. *chos nyid*). Synonymous with emptiness; can only be known through direct experience.

WISDOM (Skt. *prajna;* Tib. *shes rab*). The immediate experience of genuine, penetrating, intuitive insight that cannot be conveyed in intellectual terms. This is still a conceptual form of understanding but it is the precondition for the spontaneous manifestation of wisdom consciousness.

WISDOM CONSCIOUSNESS (Skt. *alaya-jnana;* Tib. *kun gzhi ye shes*). An innate capacity of the mind that gives rise to the generation of genuine, penetrating insight and realized upon the eradication of deluded consciousness.

Bibliography

Alaka Chattopadhyaya. *Atisha and Tibet.* Dehli: Motilal Banarsidass, 1967.

Arya Maitreya. *Buddha Nature: The Mahayana Uttaratantra Shastra with Commentary.* Ithaca, N.Y.: Snow Lion Publications, 2000.

Aryadeva. *Yogic Deeds of Bodhisattvas: Gyel-tsap on Aryadeva's Four Hundred: Textual Studies and Translations in Indo-Tibetan Buddhism.* Translated and edited by Ruth Sonam with commentary by Geshe Sonam Rinchen. Ithaca, N.Y.: Snow Lion Publications, 1994.

Atisha. *Atisha's Lamp for the Path to Enlightenment.* Translated and edited by Ruth Sonam with commentary by Geshe Sonam Rinchen. Ithaca, N.Y.: Snow Lion Publications, 1997.

Chandrakirti. *Entry to the Middle Way (Madhyamakavatara).* Boston: Shambhala Publications, 2005.

Chang, Garma C. C. *The Hundred Thousand Songs of Milarepa.* Vols. 1–2. Boston: Shambhala Publications, 1962.

Chödrön, Pema. *No Time to Lose: A Timely Guide to the Way of the Bodhistattva.* Boston: Shambhala Publications, 2005.

————. *Start Where You Are: A Guide to Compassionate Living.* Boston: Shambhala Publications, 2004.

Cook, Francis H. *Hua-yen Buddhism: The Jewel Net of Indra.* University Park: Pennsylvania State University Press, 1977.

Dalai Lama. *A Flash of Lightning in the Dark of Night: A Guide to the Bodhisattva's Way of Life.* Boston: Shambhala Publications, 1994.

————. *The Universe in a Single Atom: The Convergence of Science and Spirituality.* New York: Morgan Road Books, 2005.

deCharms, Christopher. *Two Views of Mind: Abhidharma and Brain Science.* Ithaca, N.Y.: Snow Lion, 1998.

Dowman, Keith. *The Divine Madman: The Sublime Life and Songs of Drukpa Kunley.* Middletown, Calif.: Dawn Horse Press, 1980.

Druppa, Gyalwa Gendun. *Training the Mind in the Great Way.* Translated by Glenn H. Mullin. Ithaca, N.Y.: Snow Lion Publications, 1993.

Dumoulin, Heinrich. *Understanding Buddhism: Key Themes.* Boston: Weatherhill, 1994.

Garfield, Jay L. *The Fundamental Wisdom of the Middle Way: Nagarjuna's* Mulamadhyamakakarika. London: Oxford University Press, 1995.

Gethin, Rupert. *The Foundations of Buddhism.* Oxford and New York: Oxford University Press, 1998.

Griffiths, Paul J. *On Being Buddha: The Classical Doctrine of Buddhahood.* Albany, N.Y.: SUNY Press, 1994.

Guenther, Herbert V., and Leslie S. Kawamura, trans. *Mind in Buddhist Psychology.* Berkeley: Dharma Publishing, 1975.

Huntington, C. W., Jr. *The Emptiness of Emptiness: An Introduction to the Early Indian Madhyamika.* Honolulu: University of Hawaii Press, 1989.

Jinpa, Thupten, trans. *Mind Training: The Great Collection.* Somerville, Mass.: Wisdom Publications, 2006.

Kalupahana, David. *Causality: The Central Philosophy of Buddhism.* Honolulu: University of Hawaii Press, 1975.

Kangyur Rinpoche. *Treasury of Precious Qualities.* Translated by the Padmakara Translation Group. Boston: Shambhala Publications, 2001.

Khenpo Karthar Rinpoche. *Karma Chakme's Mountain Dharma.* Vols. 1–2. Woodstock, N.Y.: KTD Publications, 2006.

Khyentse, Dilgo, and Phadampa Sangye. *The Hundred Verses of Advice: Tibetan Buddhist Teachings on What Matters Most.* Translated by the Padmakara Translation Group. Boston: Shambhala Publications, 2002.

Kongtrül, Jamgön. *The Autobiography of Jamgön Kongtrul: A Gem of Many Colors.* Translated and edited by Richard Barron. Ithaca, N.Y.: Snow Lion Publications, 2003.

———. *The Great Path of Awakening.* Translated by Ken McLeod. Boston: Shambhala Publications, 1987.

———. *The Torch of Certainty.* Translated by Judith Hanson. Boston: Shambhala Publications, 1977.

Kyabgon, Traleg. *The Benevolent Mind: A Manual in Mind Training.* Auckland: Zhyisil Chokyi Ghatsal Publications, 2003.

———. *The Essence of Buddhism: An Introduction to Its Philosophy and Practice.* Boston: Shambhala Publications, 2001.

———. *Mind at Ease: Self-Liberation through Mahamudra Meditation.* Boston: Shambhala Publications, 2005.

Lapdron, Machik. *Machik's Complete Explanation: Clarifying the Meaning of Chod.* Translated and edited by Sarah Harding. Ithaca, N.Y.: Snow Lion, 2003.

Lhalungpa, Lobsang P. *The Life of Milarepa.* New York: Penguin, 1992.

Nagarjuna, and Lama Mipham. *Golden Zephyr: Instructions from a Spiritual Friend.* Translated by Leslie Kawamura. Berkeley: Dharma Publishing, 1975.

Patrul Rinpoche. *The Words of My Perfect Teacher: A Complete Translation of a Classic Introduction to Tibetan Buddhism.* Translated by the Padmakara Translation Group. Boston: Shambhala Publications, 1998.

Rabten, Geshe, and Geshe Dhargyey. *Advice from a Spiritual Friend.* Somerville, Mass.: Wisdom Publications, 1977.

Schroeder, John W. *Skillful Means: The Heart of Buddhist Compassion.* Delhi: Motilal Banarsidass, 2004.

Scott, Jim. *Maitreya's Distinguishing Phenomena and Pure Being.* With commentary by Mipham. Ithaca, N.Y.: Snow Lion Publications, 2004.

Shantideva. *The Way of the Bodhisattva.* Translated by the Padmakara Translation Group. Boston: Shambhala Publications, 1997.

Sopa, Geshe Lhundub, Michael Sweet, and Leonard Zwilling. *Peacock in the Poison Grove: Two Buddhist Texts on Training the Mind.* Somerville, Mass.: Wisdom Publications, 2001.

Stearns, Cyrus, trans. *Hermit of Go Cliffs: Timeless Instructions from a Tibetan Mystic.* Somerville, Mass.: Wisdom Publications, 2000.

Tatz, Mark. *The Skill in Means* (Upayakausalya) *Sutra.* Dehli: Motilal Banarsidass, 1994.

Tegchok, Jampa. *Transforming Adversity into Joy and Courage: An Explanation on the Thirty-seven Practices of Bodhisattvas.* Edited by Thubten Chodron. Ithaca, N.Y.: Snow Lion Publications, 1995.

Tharcin, Sermey Khensur Lobsang. *The Essence of Mahayana Lojong Practice: A Commentary to Geshe Langri Tangpa's Mind Training in Eight Verses.* Howell, N.J.: Mahayana Sutra and Tantra Press, 1998.

Thinley Norbu. *A Cascading Waterfall of Nectar.* Boston: Shambhala, 2006.

—————. *Magic Dance: The Display of the Self-Nature of the Five Wisdom Dakinis.* Boston: Shambhala Publications, 1999.

—————. *The Small Golden Key.* Boston: Shambhala Publications, 2001.

—————. *White Sail: Crossing the Waves of Ocean Mind to the Serene Continent of the Triple Gems.* Boston: Shambhala Publications, 2001.

Thrangu Rinpoche. *The Middle Way Meditation Instructions of Mipham Rinpoche.* Translated by Ken Holmes. Kathmandu: Namo Buddha Seminar, 2000.

—————. *The Ornament of Clear Realization.* Auckland: Zhyisil Chokyi Ghatsal Publications, 2005.

—————. *Transcending Ego: Distinguishing Consciousness from Wisdom.* Kathmandu: Namo Buddha Publications, 2001.

—————. *The Uttara Tantra: A Treatise on Buddha Nature (Bibliotecha Indo-Buddhica Series, No. 131).* Delhi: Sri Satguru, 1994.

Trungpa, Chögyam. *Training the Mind and Cultivating Loving-Kindness.* Boston: Shambhala Publications, 1993.

—————, and Nalanda Translation Committee. *The Rain of Wisdom.* Boston: Shambhala Publications, 1980.

Wallace, B. Alan. *The Seven-Point Mind Training.* Ithaca, N.Y.: Snow Lion Publications, 1992, 2004.

Williams, Paul. *The Unexpected Way: On Converting from Buddhism to Catholicism.* Edinbugh and New York: T. & T. Clark Publishers, 2002.

Index